GANDHI'S DILEMMA

GANDHI'S DILEMMA

ॐ

Nonviolent Principles and Nationalist Power

Manfred B. Steger

St. Martin's Press
New York

GANDHI'S DILEMMA
Copyright © Manfred B. Steger, 2000. All rights reserved. Printed in the United States of America. No part of this book may be used or reproduced in any manner whatsoever without written permission except in the case of brief quotations embodied in critical articles or reviews. For information, address St. Martin's Press, 175 Fifth Avenue, New York, N.Y. 10010.

ISBN 0-312-22177-0

Library of Congress Cataloging-in-Publication Data
Steger, Manfred B., 1961–
    Gandhi's dilemma : nonviolent principles and nationalist power / Manfred B. Steger.
        p.   cm.
    Includes bibliographical references and index.
    SBN 0-312-22177-0
    1. Nonviolence.   2. Passive resistance.   3. Gandhi, Mahatma, 1869–1948.   4. Nationalism—India.   I. Title.
HM1281.S74   2000
303.6'1—dc21   00–038239
            CIP

Design by Letra Libre, Inc.

First edition: September 2000
10   9   8   7   6   5   4   3   2   1

*To my first academic mentors
at the University of Hawai'i-Manoa:*

ॐ

*Robert Bobilin, Professor of Religion
Manfred Henningsen, Professor of Political Science
Peter T. Manicas, Professor of Sociology and Philosophy*

CONTENTS

PREFACE

My fascination with Mahatma Gandhi's political and moral thought goes far back to my undergraduate student years at the University of Hawai'i-Manoa, where I wrote a seminar paper exploring his views on ethical socialism. Later, I published several journal articles dealing with the influence of Western thinkers on Gandhi. Teaching political theory at Whitman College and Illinois State University, I developed an undergraduate course and a graduate seminar on political theories of nonviolence. I knew from the beginning that my eventual attempt to engage in a book-length examination of Gandhi's political thought would present a number of formidable challenges. For one, Gandhi was a prolific writer and correspondent, and anyone doing research on this topic is faced with the unenviable task of poring over one hundred volumes of his *Collected Works* as well as other related sources. Fortunately, Gandhi wrote many of his letters, pamphlets, and books in English, and virtually all of his original Gujarati writings are available in translation.

In addition to the difficulties of working out a comprehensive cross-cultural framework linking European and Asian traditions, any encounter with Gandhi's political ideas requires a broad knowledge of Indian religions and history. As a comparative political theorist working in both European and Asian traditions, I have sought to enrich my own interpretation by consulting representative studies of area specialists working in the fields of Indian history, religion, politics, and economics. However, I have deliberately kept my focus on Gandhi's attempt to reconcile his quest for nationalist power with his nonviolent principles, always with an eye toward incorporating relevant arguments from works on nationalism, language, and identity by contemporary social scientists and cultural theorists.

Finally, there exists a veritable mountain of secondary literature on Gandhi, scrutinizing almost every conceivable aspect of his long and distinguished career as a political activist, social thinker, journalist, lawyer, nationalist, dietitian, *karma yogi,* and modern Hindu saint. Indeed, Gandhi may well be one of the most studied political figures of the twentieth century. For this reason, no scholar can honestly claim to have digested all, or even most, of the numerous books, monographs, essays, and articles on Gandhi that have appeared in many different languages around the globe. To be sure, in the course of my research I surveyed a sizable portion of the pertinent secondary literature, particularly studies dealing with Gandhi's views on nonviolence, religion, and nationalism. The insights contained in some of these books have greatly aided my own understanding of Gandhi's nonviolent nationalism. For example, the interpretations of his life and thought offered in the seminal works of Joan Bondurant, Judith M. Brown, Yogesh Chadha, Margaret Chatterjee, Partha Chatterjee, Dennis Dalton, Richard G. Fox, Martin Green, Raghavan Iyer, Mark Juergensmeyer, Ved Mehta, B. R. Nanda, Ashis Nandy, Thomas Pantham, Bhikhu Parekh, and Ronald J. Terchek—to name but a few—are indispensable readings for anyone engaged in making sense of Gandhi's political thought and practice.

At the same time, however, another significant portion of the existing literature on Gandhi amounts to little more than a collection of rather shallow and apologetic exercises in hagiography. In these uncritical studies, Gandhi is often portrayed as a largely misunderstood thinker far ahead of his time or a nearly infallible saint and miracle worker who bequeathed his pure political and spiritual vision to an admiring, but woefully inadequate, world of ordinary mortals. The authors of these works often make very little reference to the shifting intellectual currents and historical contexts that simultaneously enabled and constrained Gandhi's conceptual universe. In their apparent attempts to distract the reader's attention from his theoretical inconsistencies and political blunders, some commentators even go so far as to augment their idol's moral purity and political ingenuity with blanket condemnations of a political stage populated by myopic figures who failed to live up to the Mahatma's vision.

It is because I greatly admire both Gandhi's fundamental decency and the innovative quality of his political and moral thought that I believe he deserves more than uncritical acclaim. As a man who pledged himself to the nonviolent search for truth, Gandhi would probably not want to be read as someone to whom the standards of immanent criticism do not apply. Hence, the present study approaches him with a mix of imaginative sympathy and scholarly care, and with a critical gaze at his intellectual and practical dilemmas. I do realize, however, that scratching the paint at the surface of an icon may be interpreted as a sacrilegious act by the faithful, who, for too long, have closed their eyes to Gandhi, the fallible human being who struggled throughout his life to infuse political power with moral principles.

In the wake of recent outbursts of nationalist violence and narrow parochialisms around the world, it has become especially important to assess Gandhi's embeddedness within the ambiguous discourse of nationalism in a way that eschews his canonization for a more balanced exploration of his theoretical vision and political maneuvers. Such a critical-appreciative approach to Gandhi's political thought is imperative for a deeper understanding of nationalism as an influential tradition forged from a given complex of ideas and goals, material interests, and institutional strategies, as well as divergent styles and constituencies. It is my hope that this critical analysis of the existing tension between Gandhi's nationalist thought and his philosophy of nonviolence will contribute to a better understanding of central issues in the history of political ideas, normative political theory, and the interdisciplinary study of nationalism.

It is a pleasant duty to record my debts of gratitude. The research and writing of this book would not have been possible without the help of a large number of institutions and individuals. I am deeply grateful to the librarians of Illinois State University (particularly to Joan M. Winters and Alan Nourie), University of Illinois-Champaign-Urbana, The University of Chicago, University of Wisconsin-Madison, Columbia University, and Princeton University for extending to me the privilege of borrowing books. I want to thank especially the administrators at the University of Hawai'i-Manoa and the adjacent East-West Center for allowing me to consult their large South Asia collections. In addition, I have used the collections of the New York Public Library, Harvard University, University of Washington-Seattle, Washington University-St. Louis, University of Vienna, and Rutgers University.

I wish to thank Illinois State University for supporting my work and professional travels related to this book with three university research grants during the summers of 1997, 1998, and 1999. I am particularly grateful to the National Endowment for the Humanities for graciously funding this project with a grant for a Summer Institute in 1997 and a Summer Stipend in 1999. It was during the first of these extended periods of funded research that I met M. Crawford Young at the University of Wisconsin-Madison. His generosity and scholarly expertise have been invaluable to this project. As the director of the 1997 Summer Institute, Crawford read several early drafts and outlines of this book, and his insightful comments have helped me to refine my thesis. My thanks also go out to the members and staff of the Department of Sociology at the University of Hawai'i-Manoa, especially Kiyoshi Ikeda, Peter T. Manicas, and Georgia Niimoto, for providing me both ample office space and gracious hospitality during the summer of 1999.

My dear friends and colleagues at Illinois State University, particularly Jamal R. Nassar, Chair of the Department of Political Science, and Lane Crothers, have been extremely supportive of my work. Indeed, without Jamal's kind words of encouragement and Lane's erudite criticism, this study might have never seen the light of day. I also would like to thank the following friends and colleagues who read portions of this study or related papers and/or offered important comments: Nikhil Hemmady Aziz, Ursula Baatz, Lawrence L. Besserman, Steven Eric Bronner, Jorge Canizares-Esquerra, Terrell Carver, Fred Dallmayr, Michael Forman, Ellen Glassman, Robert Hunt, Manfred Henningsen, Rashida Hussain, Fumio Iida, Jeffrey Isaac, Timothy Kaufman-Osborn, Elizabeth Kelly, Ramdas Lamb, Janie Leatherman, Nancy Lind, Bradley MacDonald, Peter Manicas, Scott McLean, Carlos Parodi, Glenn Paige, Richard Payne, Michael J. Shapiro, Deepak Shenoy, R. Claire Snyder, Selma Sonntag, Mohamad Tavakoli-Targhi, and Cassandra Veney. Moreover, I greatly appreciate the help of James von Bockmann, Jason Hahn, and Amentahru Wahlrab, who served as my graduate assistants over a period of three years. Amentahru also provided me with valuable comments on the completed manuscript.

Karen Wolny, my editor at St. Martin's Press, deserves special recognition. Karen's catching enthusiasm, mixed with her patience and attention to detail, as well as her professional competence, have been instrumental in guiding this book toward completion. Finally, I would like to express my deepest gratitude to my wife, Perle Besserman, whose keen editorial eye and unwavering support for this project helped me to persevere through some difficult moments.

INTRODUCTION

෴

*Always there has been the inner conflict within him, and in our national poli-
tics, between Gandhi as a national leader and Gandhi as a man with a
prophetic message which was not confined to India, but was for humanity and
the world. It is never easy to reconcile a strict adherence to truth as one sees it
with exigencies and expediencies of life, especially of political life.*

—Jawaharlal Nehru[1]

*His [Gandhi's] doctrine was contradictory: he was a nationalist who believed in
democracy yet at the same time hated Western technology and industry. . . . His
teachings had a double and contradictory objective: to free the Indian people from
British domination and to return to a peaceful society, outside of time, dedicated
to agriculture, opposed to material gain, and believing in traditional religion.*

—Octavio Paz[2]

GANDHI'S THEORY OF NONVIOLENCE:
A BRIEF OVERVIEW

In their pursuit of political goals, adherents of a philosophy of nonviolence face significant constraints on their choice of means to
turn their ideals into reality. As illustrated throughout this book,
this problem is particularly relevant for advocates of nonviolence
such as Mohandas K. Gandhi (1869–1948), for whom the notion of
ahimsa (not harming, nonviolence) represents not merely a political
tactic or a prudent means toward an end, but a moral way of life
grounded in a metaphysical-religious view about the nature of reality. Reading Indian traditions of nonviolence through a lens colored
by his Western education, Gandhi considered *ahimsa* a mode of being
and action consistent with a deeper ontological "truth" that points
to the unity of all beings. Adding a Christian-Tolstoyan notion of

"active love" to his understanding of nonviolence, Gandhi departed significantly from orthodox Hindu interpretations: "Belief in non-violence is based on the assumption that human nature in its essence is one and therefore unfailingly responds to the advance of love."[3] Consequently, he identified two basic expressions of nonviolence: "In its negative form, it [nonviolence] means not injuring any living being, whether by body or mind. I may not therefore hurt the person of a wrong-doer, or bear any ill will to him and so cause him mental suffering. . . . In its positive form, *ahimsa* means the largest love, the greatest charity."[4]

This citation encapsulates not only Gandhi's lifelong conviction that love and *ahimsa* are interchangeable concepts, but also captures his willingness to extend the scope of nonviolence beyond the phys-ical dimension. In his view, the phenomenon of violence was not limited to the use of force to cause bodily injury or death; it also re-ferred to more subtle psychological forms of harm embedded in words, images, and thoughts that usually underpin oppressive and exclusionary political practices: "Not to hurt any living thing is no doubt a part of *ahimsa*. But it is not its least expression. The princi-ple of *ahimsa* is hurt by every evil thought, by undue haste, by lying, by hatred, by wishing ill of anybody."[5] In fact, Gandhi went so far as to suggest that physical violence represents merely a reflection of a deeper layer of conceptual violence: "Our violence in word and deed is but a feeble echo of the surging violence of thought in us."[6]

Although he sometimes recognized limitations on the human capacity to live up to the ideal of perfect *ahimsa,* he nonetheless em-phasized time and again that "there was no remedy for the many ills of life save that of nonviolence."[7] As Joan Bondurant observes with great clarity, his writings and speeches are pervaded by an almost dogmatic elevation of nonviolence as the supreme value and the only cognizable standard by which truthful action can be deter-mined: "And that meaning of *ahimsa* took him into a realm much higher than simply non-killing."[8]

Gandhi's broad understanding of nonviolence had important ramifications for his ambitious nationalist project in that the national liberation of India had to be pursued in words and deeds that were unencumbered by both physical and conceptual forms of violence. This does not mean that he should have been expected to remain politically passive and abstain from challenging the unjust structures of colonial domination. Yet, in order to live up to his own high standards of nonviolence, Gandhi's nationalism would have to employ both a language and a method of political resistance that did not involve the infliction of physical and psychological violence on friends and enemies alike: "Ahimsa really means that you may not offend anybody, you may not harbor an uncharitable thought even in connection with one who may consider himself to be your enemy. . . ."[9]

Emphasizing that nonviolence contained the universal ethico-political imperative to treat human beings in all respects as ends in themselves—and that nonviolent action was therefore morally right *in general*—Gandhi proceeded on the fundamental premise that his political opponents, too, were worthy of the same love and goodwill as his allies: "If I am a follower of *ahimsa*, I must love my enemy. I must apply the same rule to the wrong-doer who is my enemy or a stranger to me, as I would to my wrong-doing father or son."[10]

THE DILEMMA: MORAL PRINCIPLES
VERSUS POLITICAL POWER

It is this very emphasis on universal love as both the means and the end of all political activity that gives Gandhi's theory of nonviolence its moral authority. At the same time, however, it also limits the range of his political weapons to those "benign" methods involving discussion, persuasion, appeals, and various other forms of nonviolent resistance. As Ronald Terchek puts it,

> Gandhi wants to make it [love] universal not only in the sense that anyone is capable of loving and worthy of love but in the sense that anyone can love everyone, including those who cause harm and suffering. With this move, Gandhi seeks to make love political as well as spiritual and moral. He believes that if love can be transported to the political terrain, new possibilities present themselves for openness and mutuality, for moving beyond particularities, and for nonviolently discovering what the participants share.[11]

While Gandhi's moral universalism does not necessarily have to be predicated upon an abstract humanism that rides roughshod over, or refuses to acknowledge, the differences that are constitutive of persons' individual and collective identities, it nonetheless commits him to endorse social justice, equality, and dignity for *all* persons solely on the basis of their shared humanity. Hence, the followers of his ahimsic tradition would be expected to eschew physical and psychological forms of violence even if it appears likely that such methods will result in the attainment of the desired political end (home rule in the case of colonial India). In their unwavering devotion to principle, rather than abandon their ethical ideals demanding the convertibility of means and ends, nonviolent activists might have to settle for the dire prospect that their efforts will never result in the seizure of political power. As Max Weber pointed out in his celebrated 1918 lecture, "The Profession and Vocation of Politics," clinging to such a morally pure posture under all circumstances contains the tragic possibility that such social movements might be doomed to continual political impotence.[12]

On the other hand, even a temporary relinquishment of nonviolent principles for the sake of advancing power interests would most likely inflict irreparable damage to the moral authority of a movement based on *ahimsa*. After all, even a qualified compromise of principles in the name of defending a "just cause" would heighten the potential for expressions of insensitivity toward the Other, in the process stoking the fires of fear, distrust, hatred, and revenge. Indeed, such a compromise might lead to the adoption of ever more conciliatory attitudes toward the exercise of violence in the future. Once taken, the road of violence and exclusivism might be hard to abandon.

Throughout his impressive career as a political thinker and activist, Gandhi encountered precisely this agonizing dilemma of either remaining faithful to his nonviolent principles and risking the failure of the Indian nationalist movement, or focusing on the seizure of political power at the expense of his moral message. Moreover, he faced the difficult task of having to construct a particularistic, nationalist discourse that would not infringe upon the conceptual purity of his universal, nonviolent principles. To my mind, Gandhi's dilemma represents a particularly intriguing example of the more general political predicament involving the reconciliation of moral principles with political power. A discussion of this thorny problem stands at the center of several excellent studies in political theory.[13] Following in the footsteps of these works, my book attempts to close a gap in the existing literature on Gandhi by examining the origins, meaning, and unfolding of this dilemma as it applies to the tension between his principles of nonviolence and his nationalist project, which aimed at wresting political power from the hands of the British colonizers.[14]

Conceived as a study in the history of political ideas, my endeavor is consciously limited to the task of supplying the reader with both a critical evaluation and a historically sensitive interpretation of how this dilemma emerged and played itself out in Gandhi's life and thought. Incorporating biographical materials only when necessary, the book is designed neither as a comprehensive biography nor as a wide-ranging survey of Gandhi's political and moral thought. Given that the last few decades have seen the publication of several excellent books in these respective genres, it is not necessary to add to these efforts.[15] Rather, this study assesses the success of Gandhi's attempts to resolve his dilemma.

THE PROPOSED SOLUTION:
GANDHI'S NONVIOLENT NATIONALISM

Cherishing the role of bridge-builder and mediator, Gandhi came to believe that it was indeed possible to reconcile his nonviolent principles with the effective pursuit of nationalist power. He spoke in glowing terms of his vision of a "nonviolent nationalism" that represented the "necessary condition of corporate or civilized life."[16] In other words, Gandhi argued that Indian self-rule could be achieved *without* sacrificing the universalist moral imperatives of his nonviolent philosophy: "The task before nationalists is clear. They have to win over by their genuine love all minorities including the Englishmen. Indian nationalism, if it is to remain non-violent, cannot be exclusive."[17]

This pivotal statement contains Gandhi's own standards for the successful resolution of his dilemma: the theoretical construction and practical realization of Indian nationhood must honor the inclusive principles of nonviolence.[18] In addition, his standards demanded the nonviolent, inclusive resolution of different conceptions of nationhood *within* the Indian nation as well as the reconciliation of India's national interests with the interests of all humanity. Harmonizing the seemingly antagonistic dynamics of boundless love and the particularistic love of country may strike the reader as a hopeless enterprise, but one must concede that Gandhi's nationalist vision is rather unique in its insistence that the struggle for national liberation ought to be rooted in a moral "soul-force" or "truth-force" (*satyagraha*). Referring to this enterprise as a "process of purifying politics," Gandhi hoped to connect political action to the religious task of becoming one with the cosmic spirit.[19] According to this view, the spiritual emancipation of the individual (*moksha*) and the liberation of the nation converged in the political and moral duty to serve and love one's fellow human beings. Gandhi's notion of the interconnectedness of nationalism, moral goodness, and spiritual purity is also reflected in his view that the spheres of morality, spirituality, and politics were inseparable.[20]

Examining both the theoretical assumptions of Gandhi's nonviolent nationalism and its translatability into practical politics, this study does not judge his views on the relationship between nonviolence and nationalism according to criteria imposed from without. Rather, I evaluate the cogency of Gandhi's claims by using his own standards. As noted by C. A. Coady, violence is a pivotal idea in political theory but there is very little agreement among scholars about how it should be understood.[21] For the purposes of this study, then, I rely on Gandhi's broad definition of violence, which accommodates not only instances of physical violence, but also more subtle forms of structural and conceptual (epistemic) violence embedded in words, images, and social structures of domination and exclusion.

The spirit behind my desire to approach Gandhi's nonviolent nationalism according to the rules of immanent critique also extends to the more general evaluation of historical phenomena, which dictates that particular events and intellectual constellations be reconstructed from within the context of their age. Yet, as the German philosopher Hans-Georg Gadamer notes in his path-breaking study on hermeneutics, every act of understanding is conditioned by the motivations and prejudices of the interpreter-in-time. In other words, an acknowledgment of Gadamer's central idea—the inescapable historicity of our being operates not merely as a restriction but constitutes the very principle of understanding itself—makes an "objective" representation of historical events an elusive enterprise.[22] Likewise, the restriction of language and meaning to theoretically explicit propositions studied in isolation from their historical contexts exchanges the richness and ambiguity of the living experience for the poverty of lifeless abstractions.

At the same time, however, one must concede that any historian of political ideas must perform the unavoidable task of somehow reducing social complexity for the sake of understanding—hence the importance of analytical precision and the value of conceptual distinctions made for heuristic purposes. In the end, one's refusal to equate knowledge simply with results yielded by the "scientific method" must be balanced against its opposite extreme—the danger of getting caught in the ruse of subjectivist obfuscation by refusing to strive for a "better" understanding of the phenomena under investigation. In my view, critical interpretations of political ideas yield far better insights if they focus on concrete problems or dilemmas that help to clarify the conceptual contributions of various thinkers, the unique development of their visions, and also how their ideas both enabled and confined them in their attempt to solve particular problems of political practice.[23] Thus, my quest to elucidate Gandhi's dilemma is anchored in the classical understanding of "hermeneutics" as referring to the process of making unfamiliar ideas or obscure meanings intelligible.[24]

In addition to focusing on Gandhi's utilization of ideas and language, my study identifies some of the constraints and obstacles he encountered and navigated, as well as the material interests he embraced. A mere analysis of his ideas divorced from an investigation of the obstacles preventing their realization would neglect the conflict-ridden nature of politics as a dynamic clash of ideals and material interests, lofty aspirations, and institutional strategies.[25] I am therefore suspicious of overdrawn dichotomies isolating "text(s)" from "context(s)," "structure" from "agency," and "politics" from "culture." To ignore the fundamental interdependence of these categories is to undermine the historicist desire to understand the particular in the context of the whole to which it belongs.

Finally, my investigation of Gandhi's dilemma is inextricably linked to important and timely issues that are critical for the study of nationalism from a moral and evaluative perspective. As Bruce Haddock observes, one of the paradoxes of the recent resurgence of interest in nationalism is that too little attention has been devoted to what nationalists actually thought.[26] In my view, many pivotal questions raised in the field of nationalism cannot be properly addressed without focusing on the role of leading nationalist theorists. Gandhi forces us to ask whether it is indeed conceivable to construct a benign type of nationalism that is rooted in neither physical nor conceptual forms of violence. This question spawns a host of new queries that help to bring into sharper focus the theoretical roots of Gandhi's dilemma. Did his nonviolent principles inevitably become tainted as a result of their association with a nationalist discourse? More generally, does the construction of national identity necessarily involve the employment of invidious comparisons and exclusivist distinctions? If so, aren't all forms of nationalism predicated on more or less flexible boundaries separating "us" from "them"—dichotomies that tend to encourage violence in the political arena?[27]

Posing such questions with reference to this century's greatest advocate of nonviolence amounts to a test of an "extreme case." If nationalism can indeed be "purified," then Gandhi's vision ought to be given much more public consideration in a world plagued by destructive nationalist conflicts. Conversely, if his nationalist vision is predicated upon constant recourse to forms of conceptual violence, then his attempts to construct a nonviolent nationalism must be judged as having already failed on the theoretical level. Moreover, if it can be shown that Gandhi's quest for nationalist power required the dilution of nonviolent principles (or vice-versa), then his vision of nonviolent nationalism would also fail the test of practice, thereby giving a strong indication that nonviolent principles cannot be preserved within a nationalist framework. In that case, Gandhi's "nonviolent nationalism" may still be a useful guidepost, but only in the more modest sense of pointing to the possibility of constructing *less violent* forms of nationalism.

CONFRONTING THE DILEMMA

Drawing his main inspiration from the writings of various European thinkers as well as his daily readings of the *Bhagavad Gita,* Gandhi's nonviolent nationalism envisioned a crucial leadership role for heroic *satyagrahis* (adherents to a nonviolent "truth-force") who were committed to the arduous task of purifying themselves and the nation. Their exemplary dedication to morality would activate the spiritual power of inspiring and energizing the masses while at the same time providing a check on the cold instrumentalism of conventional politics. Ideally, then, the political quest for nationalist power would proceed hand in hand with the moral task of achieving perfect self-control. To reach this goal, Gandhi evoked the myth of a regenerated nation, rooted in the spiritual and moral virtues of an "ancient Indian civilization." Other prominent Indian nationalists, such as B. G. Tilak, Krishnavarma, V. D. Savarkar, Aurobindo

Ghose, and M. N. Roy, pursued similar ideas of forging national unity based on a religious vision of Indian spiritual purity, but Gandhi's attachment to *ahimsa* as the only acceptable political means sets his blueprint for achieving national self-rule (*swaraj*) squarely apart from the violence-condoning program of his contemporaries.

Emphasizing Gandhi's philosophical commitment to nonviolence and moral individuation, some scholars have erroneously suggested that he was perhaps not a nationalist after all, at least not in the Western sense of the term.[28] Gandhi's own writings on this subject sometimes seem to encourage such interpretations by insisting that his nonviolent brand of nationalism was "as broad as the universe," and therefore perfectly compatible with his universalist ideals: "My nationalism includes the love of all the nations of the earth irrespective of creed."[29] However, a careful reading of his oeuvre reveals that he also assigned to Indian nationalism the special role of functioning as a catalyst for moral progress: "Let it be the privilege of India to turn a new leaf and set a lesson to the world. . . . It is because of all the nations in the world India is the one nation which has a message, however limited and crude it may be, in that direction that it must have immediate freedom to enable it to play its part."[30] Passages such as these point to the distinct possibility that Gandhi accepted a mild form of nationalistic exceptionalism that contends that India is unique and morally as well as spiritually more advanced than other nations.

Indeed, there are many more examples that disclose existing ambiguities in Gandhi's nationalist outlook. Perhaps the best known is his public exchange with the Nobel Prize–winning Indian poet Rabindranath Tagore over the meaning of Indian self rule. Strongly disagreeing with Tagore's vehement attack on nationalism as an unmitigated evil that could only thwart India's quest for *swaraj*, Gandhi cast the Indian nationalist movement as a manifestation of his own vision of nonviolent nationalism, which, in his eyes, was perfectly compatible with an ethos of inclusivity and universalism: "Indian nationalism is not exclusive, nor aggressive, nor destructive. It is health-giving, religious and therefore humanitarian."[31] On other occasions, however, his professed inclusivism would give way to statements that sounded much less tolerant: " . . . I am a Hindu first and nationalist after. I do not become on that score a less nationalist than the best of them. I simply thereby imply that the interests of my country are identical with those of my religion."[32] Even Romain Rolland, whose early biography barely fell short of a wholesale sanctification of the

Mahatma, seized upon the tension between Gandhi's ethical inclusivism and his nationalist exclusivism to venture a rare critique of his
idol: "Why does he [Gandhi] allow his universalist ideal to be shut up
within the narrow limits of an Indian theocracy? . . . With all venera-
tion to the Mahatma, I am with Tagore."[33] While there remain open
questions with regard to the contents of Gandhi's nationalism, there
should be little doubt that, both as political leader and thinker, he was
a staunch nationalist. As Ainslie Embree observes, "[O]ne dares to venture the opinion that no other leader in history in his own lifetime has
done so much to make a people into a nation."[34]

Yet, Gandhi was not the first nationalist leader to claim that the
seemingly opposing impulses of nationalism and nonviolence could
be reconciled in both theory and actual political practice. For example, the prominent Irish nationalist Daniel O'Connell (1775–1847)
demanded from his followers strict adherence to the principles of
nonviolence. Respecting the then-existing constitutional framework
of the British government, he confined his nationalist agitation to
the exertion of a nonviolent, parliamentary "moral force," expressed
in rational demands for legal-reformist measures. Condemning the
members of the radical "Young Ireland" faction, which advocated
the use of violence in the Irish struggle for self-rule, O'Connell repeatedly urged that they heed his Repeal Party's pledge of nonviolence. His liberal defense of the rule of law culminated in his attack
on the "illegal" character of radical forms of nonviolence such as
massive noncooperation campaigns and collective acts of civil disobedience. Insisting that such methods would merely contribute to
a general disregard for law and order, O'Connell argued that acts of
civil disobedience were not really "nonviolent," because they were
ultimately bound to fuel uncontrollable passions that would find
their expression in popular outbursts of violence. Hence, he reiter-
ated time and again that the only nationalism compatible with true
nonviolence was one committed to gradual methods of reformism
and carried out by moral politicians through constitutional means.[35]
In the end, O'Connell's appeal to a "moral force" failed to resolve
the dilemma of nonviolent principles and nationalist power. Faced
with the choice of either accepting violent repression and political
defeat or abandoning his philosophy of pure means, he opted for the
former, thereby indicating his willingness to pay the ultimate political price for his moral convictions.

At the outset of his political career as a defender of the civil and
economic rights of the Indian immigrant community in South

Africa, Gandhi found himself in a similar situation. At first, he adhered to the methods of British constitutionalism. However, as his reformist strategy failed to achieve tangible results, Gandhi convinced himself that the drawing up of petitions and formal notes of protest had to be complemented by more radical *satyagraha* campaigns, which, though remaining nonviolent, would nonetheless include elements of direct action such as public demonstrations, strikes, boycotts, noncooperation, and civil disobedience. Unlike O'Connell, Gandhi turned against the tenets of British liberalism and saw, therefore, no conflict between the principles of nonviolence and the breaking of "immoral" laws.

Upon his return to India in 1915, he used his considerable political experience and the religious ideals he had acquired in South Africa to create a mass-based national liberation movement. For the rest of his life, Gandhi would remain wedded to the notion that the successful involvement of the masses in nonviolent direct action was not only possible, but indispensable to his project of forging an Indian national identity consonant with his moral principles. Expressed most famously in his 1909 pamphlet *Hind Swaraj,* Gandhi's vision of nonviolent nationalism held out the promise of achieving personal liberation as well as political self-rule while avoiding both the passive constitutionalism of the Indian National Congress and the violent insurrectionism of a growing band of militant Indian nationalists.

CHAPTER OUTLINE

Having set the thematic stage of the present study, I conclude this introduction with a short chapter outline. Chapter 1 provides the ideological origins and historical context of Gandhi's dilemma. Examining various intellectual currents of nineteenth-century British liberalism and their perspectives on colonial India, the chapter surveys the topographical features of the discursive landscape that both constrained and enabled the development of Gandhi's nationalist thought. I especially highlight the significance of an exclusionary "ideology of difference," inserted into liberal doctrine by influential British thinkers. During his student years in London, Gandhi dealt with the mounting tension between the universalist promise of liberalism and its increasingly chauvinistic undertones by seeking refuge in the company of British vegetarians and "New Agers," whose orientalist views contributed to his early vision of

India as a glorious civilization devoted to vegetarianism and spiritual perfection.

Chapter 2 examines how Gandhi's attachment to European civilization and his attraction to the universalist promise of liberal theory were tested by the harsh reality of systematic racial discrimination in South Africa. The chapter explores the ways in which South Africa formed the "Indian" Gandhi, paying particular attention to his early attempts to construct the idea of "Indianness" from abroad. Opting for a legal strategy of constitutional protest against the government's discriminatory policies, Gandhi launched a collective "fight for national self-respect" in Natal and the Transvaal. Pleading with the colonial authorities for the recognition of full citizenship rights for all South African Indians, he struggled for the first time with the dilemma of moral principles and nationalist power. In order to gain a political advantage for the Indian community, he employed exclusivist ethnic categories linking the "Anglo-Saxon" and "Indian races" to a common "Indo-Aryan" identity. Ultimately, however, this strategy did little to advance his political cause, and a frustrated Gandhi resorted to the more radical approach of challenging the entire European civilizational paradigm.

Chapter 3 offers a close textual interpretation of *Hind Swaraj,* Gandhi's sole sustained treatise of political theory. This text is significant because it was conceived as a response to both the moderate nationalism of the Indian National Congress and the militancy of Indian nationalists who approved of violent means to further their political agenda. Providing the theoretical foundation of Gandhi's nonviolent nationalism, *Hind Swaraj* amounts to a fierce attack on "modern civilization" and its reliance on physical and psychological violence. Although he later modified his views to some extent, Gandhi never offered a wholesale rejection of the arguments he presented in this treatise. Gandhi's critique radically undermines the attempts of liberal ideologists of difference to link the universalist language of reason to the culturally specific norms of British society. Reversing the roles of "tutor" and "pupil" on which the colonial order in India depended, Gandhi implies that, rather than being considered the educators of the world, the British were morally underdeveloped aggressors who required the help of spiritual experts like himself in order to mend their corrupt ways.

Chapter 4 turns to Gandhi, the romantic cultural nationalist, whose vision of a regenerated India was based on the belief that it was actually possible to retain one's nonviolent principles in the effective pursuit of political power. I employ key passages in *Hind Swaraj* and other writings to trace Gandhi's construction of Indian identity as a bounded collectivity with certain essential qualities to an evolving literary discourse on nationalism and Indianness, both inside and outside of India. His emerging ideas of what constituted a "genuine nation" were thus already pre-interpreted in dynamic layers of unique and linguistic practices involving both the colonizer and the colonized. The chapter argues that Gandhi's nationalist vision relied on orientalist images of India as the homeland of spiritual purity and antimaterialist values. Pervaded by a host of problematic dichotomies inherited from the British nineteenth-century discourse on India, Gandhi's own version of "affirmative orientalism" employed exclusivist language in favor of the moral and spiritual superiority of an imagined "ancient Indian civilization." These arguments conflicted with his moral vision based on the core principles of *ahimsa*. Emphasizing irreconcilable differences and evoking suspicion of European "civilization" and cultural practices, Gandhi's narrative contributed to the hardening of the perceptual boundaries separating "Indians" from "the British."

Chapter 5 explores the connections between Gandhi's arguments for national self-rule, nonviolence, and his discourse of ethical self-sufficiency, which found its practical expression in a renunciative project of physical discipline and self-control. I argue that Gandhi's "experiments with truth"—involving dietary restrictions, fasting, naturopathy, and, most importantly, sexual abstinence—are closely tied to his nationalist imaginings of a "healthy" and "pure" India. Borrowing from Michel Foucault's important inquiry into the workings of disciplinary power and its normalizing effects of producing docile bodies, I question the allegedly nonviolent character of such processes of identity formation in which the body and its physical desires assume the status of a tainted Other that requires policing and domination by an ontologically superior, spiritual essence. Just as Gandhi sometimes cast the "British system" as devalued Other, so, too, did he construct a devalued Other in the "corrupted minds" of those of his countrymen who failed to adopt his technologies of self-discipline. The chapter argues that Gandhi cultivated an idealized higher self opposed to a vilified lower self in order to dominate the latter and so be assured of its purity. In spite of its emphasis on nonviolence, Gandhi's account of his struggle against the temptations of the body is frequently conveyed through images of war and battle. His consistent reliance on conceptual violence within a semiotic of self-control becomes especially apparent in his attempts to situate "femininity" and "women" within his nationalist discourse.

Chapter 6 considers the problematic relationship between Gandhi's moral vision and his political actions. I discuss in some detail the tension between his principles of nonviolence and the political imperatives of his nationalist agenda, as portrayed in three concrete scenarios: Gandhi's posture during the Great War and two previous wars in South Africa; his leadership in the 1920–22 noncooperation campaign; and his pivotal role in the 1942 Quit India movement. These three cases illustrate the dilemma Gandhi faced as he attempted to balance the moral claims of *ahimsa* with the nationalist movement's demand for effective political action. Hence, these cases provide further insight into the success or failure of Gandhi's claim to reconciling the diverging agendas of his philosophy of nonviolence and national liberation.

The theoretical and practical feasibility of a benign nationalism that fully conforms to the civic ideal has been widely discussed in contemporary social and political theory. My epilogue connects my concluding remarks on Gandhi's dilemma to such broader theoretical issues that are critical to the contemporary study of nationalism and collective identity formation. After wrestling with the question of whether it is indeed possible to construct a "benign" type of nationalism without relying on forms of conceptual and physical violence, I explore the promise of a cosmopolitan agenda.

Mohandas K. Gandhi's moral politics of redemptive love and nonviolence still represents an appealing vision for the dawning twenty-first century. Although this author concludes that its realization ought not be sought through the avenue of nationalism, the history of political thought has undoubtedly been enriched as a result of Gandhi's willingness to struggle with this dilemma. His commitment to truth and nonviolence and his desire for social justice shine forth in the darkness of an age of nuclear weapons and genocide. Mahatma Gandhi remains an inspiration to each new generation of thinkers and activists in the political tradition of nonviolence that bears his name.

1

THE PROMISE OF BRITISH LIBERALISM

ॐ

I hope that some of you will follow in my footsteps and after you return from England you will work wholeheartedly for big reforms in India.

—M. K. Gandhi[1]

We should not envy the nation [Britain], but emulate its example. Those who have faith in God recognize that the British do not rule over India without His will.

—M. K. Gandhi[2]

LIBERAL BRITISH IDEAS OF INDIA:
THE IDEOLOGICAL CONTEXT OF GANDHI'S DILEMMA

Hans-Georg Gadamer once observed that, "There are no propositions which can be understood exclusively with respect to the content that they represent. . . . Every proposition has presuppositions that it does not express."[3] Applying these hermeneutical insights to the subject of this book, then, I wish to commence my interpretive journey with an investigation of the unexpressed presuppositions in Gandhi's nationalist imagination. In his exemplary study on utopian experimentalism, Richard G. Fox, too, focuses on these conceptual forestructures of Gandhi's political thought. With much care, Fox's account unravels the development of new sets of cultural meanings as Gandhi originated his political vision from pre-existing cultural traditions and then proceeded to experiment with its key concepts. As he labored to implement new ideas, existing material conditions and cultural meanings defined, limited, but did not completely compel, the ultimate outcome.

Rather, these structural factors enabled him to contemplate still more cultural innovations that might be realized through purposeful actions.[4]

Hence, Fox's perspective contributes to a better understanding of how Gandhi's political ideas arose "in conversation" with established traditions as a mixture of agency and structure, the old and new, the dying and not-yet-born. Emerging slowly from a dynamic clash of ideas and goals, material interests and rhetorical strategies, Gandhi's dilemma of reconciling nonviolent principles with nationalist power represents both an extension of and a unique response to certain preconstituted cultural meanings, leading in the process to new conflicts involving ideas and political practices.[5] In my view, nothing simultaneously enabled and constrained Gandhi's reflections on the relationship between nonviolence and nationhood more than various nineteenth-century British liberal discourses on India.[6] Examined below, the various attitudes and values expressed in these ideologies of empire represent the most influential set of pre-existing cultural meanings that impacted Gandhi's nationalist imagination.[7]

It is hard to quarrel with the often-repeated assertion that the nineteenth century represents an epoch of liberal triumph in Britain. Still, the term "liberalism" meant different things to different people. As Richard Bellamy notes in his influential work on the subject, nineteenth-century British liberalism never congealed into a coherent philosophical doctrine. Rather, it constituted a loose collection of heterogeneous views and assumptions that tended to overlap on certain issues, such as the primacy of the individual, limited government, popular sovereignty, and social reformism.[8] Yet, as expressed in the writings of prominent liberals like Jeremy Bentham, James Mill, John Stuart Mill, Sir Thomas Babington Macaulay, and Sir Henry Maine—all self-consciously inspired by John Locke's political thought—liberalism became linked to a common reformist political project that contributed to the legitimation and the extension of the British empire.[9] In his recent study, Uday S. Mehta shows that conservatives like Edmund Burke were highly critical of British imperialism, whereas "liberalism and empire were tightly braided threads such that their separation would have resulted in the fraying of a well-woven mental and political tapestry."[10]

At first glance, however, Mehta's emphasis on continuity between liberalism and empire seems to run counter to the intuition that the growth of the British empire by means of conquest and authoritarian rule violated liberalism's normative commitment to universalism and therefore constituted a profound theoretical and practical problem for liberals. In order to avoid such glaring contradictions, anyone embracing the notions of representative democracy, the political equality of citizens, and the protection of certain inalienable human rights regardless of race or ethnicity, would also have to opt for a moral universalism resting firmly on the three pillars of the liberal creed: rationality, individual liberty, and human dignity. Consistent with these normative commitments there emerges, ideally, an ideology of *sameness* centered on an ethico-political imperative which categorically prescribes that the British would have to consider members of different cultures as equals, entitled to the same civil rights, subject to the same moral law, and therefore bound to universal principles of justice. Indians should therefore be deserving of the same kind of respect and fair treatment that Europeans would ideally extend to and expect from each other. This political, ethical, and epistemological universalism contained in liberal theory called for an emancipatory political program directed against despotism and domination, meaning that arbitrary justifications for various forms of social inequality be routinely challenged by political institutions born of the liberal spirit of essential sameness.

As Thomas Metcalf notes in his magisterial study on the ideologies of the raj, such an ideology of sameness did indeed manifest itself in colonial India through various rhetorical strategies emphasizing essential characteristics that Indians shared with their colonizers.[11] On one hand, the spread of this universalist ideology to indigenous elites could be seen as serving the instrumental purpose of generating popular support for an oppressive colonial regime. On the other hand, however, it might be interpreted as evidence for the sincerity and the enthusiasm some European idealists brought to their encounter with Asian cultures. It appears that both views contain important insights. After all, influential British myths of "fair play" and "impartiality of justice" based on the idea of essential "sameness" coexisted with grossly exploitative colonial practices. The most famous expression of the liberal ideology of sameness can be found in Queen Victoria's 1858 Proclamation, which affirmed that her majesty's Indian subjects were entitled to the same rights and privileges as their European counterparts:

We hold ourselves bound to the natives of our Indian territories by the same obligations of duty which bind us to all our other subjects, and those obligations, by the blessings of the Almighty God, we shall faithfully and conscientiously fulfil. . . . We declare it to be our royal will and pleasure that none be in anywise favoured, none molested or disquieted, by reason of their religious faith or observances, but that all shall alike enjoy the equal and impartial protection of the law. . . . And it is our further will that, so far as may be, our subjects, of whatever race or creed, be freely and impartially admitted to offices in our service, the duties of which they may be qualified, by their education, ability, and integrity, duly to discharge.[12]

Mohandas Gandhi, along with thousands of other young Indians educated in the second half of the nineteenth century in schools based on European curriculae, imbibed this intoxicating spirit of sameness behind the Queen's words. After all, the document promised Indians full political recognition. Growing up a generation after the bloody Anglo-Indian War of 1857–58, however, many of these young Indian intellectuals remained puzzled by the paradox of British legitimacy.[13] How could the European colonizers justify their violent conquest and subsequent rule over India without invalidating the moral universalism underlying liberal theory? As demonstrated with extraordinary clarity in Mehta's and Metcalf's respective studies, solving this potentially explosive dilemma of reconciling moral principles with colonial power did not necessarily result in the revocation of liberalism's commitment to universalism. Instead, many British liberals embraced the discursive strategy of emphasizing presumed qualities of *difference* of history, race, and society that allegedly separated Indian and British cultures.[14] To be sure, this emphasis on civilizational differences was already latent in eighteenth-century Enlightenment ideas of India, but it became more pronounced as the new century wore on. On the ideological level, it produced and reinforced a series of conceptual dichotomies and polarities that routinely privileged European civilization over the remaining "backward" regions of the world. Without dropping their liberal idiom, British liberals infused their universalism with a developmental logic of "civilizational stages" originally propagated by Adam Smith and other philosophers of the Scottish Enlightenment. As Megan Vaughan notes, such evolutionary schemes touted the West's moral and economic progress, but "were unable to contain any notion of difference that was not directly tied to the question of inferiority and the necessity of subordination."[15]

At the core of this liberal ideology of difference one thus finds crafty attempts to inscribe universalism with specific cultural practices sustained by contingent notions of history, civilization, and nationhood. This conceptual sleight of hand allowed liberals not only to confine their commitment to universalism to "mature societies," but also provided them with a seemingly benign justification for the existence of sustained patterns of political exclusion. Mehta traces the practice of linking the liberal language of rationality to the culturally specific norms of British society to John Locke's subtle invocation of politically exclusionary social conventions and manners. The British philosopher presented the supposedly universal and natural capacity to reason—which establishes the grounds for political inclusion—as a precise and detailed process of education dependent on a specific (English) set of cultural norms. Undermining his own universalist account of rationality, Locke suggested that people had to be inculcated with conventional norms in order to enjoy the very rights and privileges that are supposedly theirs by virtue of their natural attributes.[16]

Hence, British authoritarian rule in "undeveloped" regions of the world was a necessary first step along a path of "social reform." As Mehta notes, the sense of Western superiority displayed in this hubris of developmentalism suggests that many British liberals considered the experiences of non-European peoples as irredeemably provisional and incomplete—a condescending attitude that reveals the conceptual and normative bias inherent in the liberal ideology of difference:

> The empire as liberals conceived of it, and the terms in which they supported it, was premised on the idea . . . that in the face of this provisionality it was right, indeed even obligatory, to seek to complete that which was incomplete, static, backward, or otherwise regnant, and to guide it to a higher plateau of stability, freedom, and purposefulness—to hitch it to a more meaningful teleology. . . . As its corollary, the rights that liberals do assert are supported by a higher order of things: a superior knowledge, a more credible science, a more consistent morality, and a more just and free politics. These relative valuations all follow from, and undergird, the claim of the provisionality of other peoples' experiences.[17]

This patronizing posture was intertwined with an image of India as a vast social laboratory housing the greatest experiment the world had ever seen: the "improvement of the lower races." Note the remarkable conceptual shift in liberal theory: its transhistorical and transcultural principles assigning to all humans common characteristics like natural freedom, equality, and rationality—and therefore entitling them unconditionally to dignified treatment *in the present*—become a mere prospect of full recognition *in the future*. Categorical moral imperatives based on respect for human dignity turn into hypothetical expressions of intent. In order to get to the civilized "there," the colonized must pass continuous tests administered by the colonizers—a disciplinary steeplechase race resulting in the creation of docile bodies and minds. Imbuing sameness with difference blunts liberalism's self-critical edge by forcing "self-evident," timeless truths into a historicist framework that encourages invidious comparisons between "rational" European agents and "colonial children." As a result, imperialistic power interests can hide behind seemingly altruistic educational schemes, and the paternalism of colonial governments is made to appear as a progressive means to reach the noble end of public enlightenment. While the threat of open physical violence remains in the background as a punitive last-resort measure applied to "naughty children," the conceptual violence involved in allocating meanings of "superiority" and "inferiority" pervades the daily routine of colonial rule.

Seen in this light, Uday Mehta's insistence on fundamental continuities between liberalism and imperialism represents a rather sensible thesis. After all, the insertion of difference into the liberal discourse of universalism made the extension of empire no longer an embarrassment to theory. In fact, the growth of empire became the rational and moral mission of a compassionate nation dedicated to the improvement of humankind. A clear sign of the liberal-nationalist inclination to cast England as "God's Firstborn," this exclusionary logic of difference is particularly visible in the influential nineteenth-century utilitarian writings of James Mill and John Stuart Mill.[18] Both employed by the East India Company, father and son were fond of elaborating on India's "exceeding difference"—a convenient strategy that assured the subcontinent's indigenous peoples their position on the primitive end of their civilizational schema.

John Stuart Mill's philosophical support of these exclusionary tendencies is explicit in his famous remark in *On Liberty* that the universal principle of liberty had no application to "those backward states of society in which the race itself may be considered as in its

nonage." Referring explicitly to India as such an example of a re-
tarded civilization lagging far behind Europe, Mill argued that
British authoritarian rule was perfectly compatible with the dictates
of universal reason "provided the end be their [barbarians'] improvement." After all, Mill insisted, despotism was a legitimate mode
of government, reflecting a "natural" system of domination based
on the "lawful" subjugation of indigenous peoples: "Such is the
ideal rule of a free people over a barbarous or semi-barbarous
one."[19]

No doubt, Mill's claim that universal reason was reflected in the
towering achievements of British culture supported a number of
concrete political and economic practices. For one, insisting on the
universal applicability of their conventional practices, the agents of
the empire were able to justify their systematic program of economic exploitation as an "improvement" of indigenous methods of
production. Moreover, it gave them the moral authority to build a
coercive state apparatus that protected their material interests and
whose affiliated systems of knowledge reconstructed and transformed native modes of thought and practice. Promoting Western-
style education, the British raj claimed to fulfill its "civilizational
mission" of imparting breeding and rationality to select members of
the Indian elites.

In truth, however, there appears to have been no pressing need
for the recruitment of indigenous high-level administrative person-
nel; in the period from 1861 to 1910, only eighty Indians were admitted to the Indian Civil Service.[20] Dadabhai Naoroji, the "Great
Old Man of India" and member of British parliament, voiced his disappointment at the low probability of British-educated Indians finding employment with the colonial administration: "The thousands
that are being sent out by the universities every year find themselves
in a most anomalous position. There is no place for them in their
motherland."[21] Hence, it appears that the main purpose of the
British rhetoric of "imparting breeding" to Indians consisted less of
preparing them for self-rule and representative government than in
producing second-class colonial subjects. Lord Thomas Babington
Macaulay, the liberal architect of English education in India, implicitly corroborated this strategy when he acknowledged the importance of forming an educated class of "Indians in blood and colour"
whose English tastes, morals, and opinions would help protect
British colonial interests.[22]

In his recent study, the contemporary Indian historian Ranajit Guha shows how the liberal practice of casting British social conventions and cultural practices in a universalist language was essential to the colonial task of establishing popular conformity to European rule while also helping to legitimize the violence involved in "pacifying" unruly territories.

> Combined with a fair amount of force, it helped Britain to keep the antagonism of the subject population well under control despite the two extensive rebellions of 1857 and 1942 and many local uprisings. That peace between the rulers and the ruled was mediated to no mean extent by the indigenous elite. Thanks to the propagation of western-style education, they had imbibed the ideology of liberal-imperialism well enough to believe that "domination by the English would be conducive to the happiness of *projas*"—the prophecy which, at the conclusion of *Anandamath,* persuades its hero to withdraw from armed opposition to the raj.[23]

However, as the case of Gandhi shows, there was a limit to how much of this imperialist ideology of difference could be absorbed by indigenous elites without causing serious inflammation. To be sure, the internalization of European knowledge and its normative claims proved to be critical for the formation of colonial subjects, but such processes never resulted in the total acquiescence and conformity of the subjugated. British attempts to solve the dilemma of reconciling liberal principles with imperialist power often turned into major catalysts for the rise of Indian nationalism. As Ashis Nandy emphasizes, Indians did not remain simple-hearted victims of liberal imperialism, but became active participants in a moral and cognitive venture against colonial oppression.[24] In other words, the more British liberals allowed "difference" to penetrate their universalist theory—that is, the more liberalism turned into a chauvinistic and exclusivist doctrine celebrating European superiority—the more difficult it was for Indian intellectuals like Gandhi to retain their uncritical posture of acquiescence. Where, then, were the limits to the susceptibility of Indian elites to the liberal siren song of progress and development? How much difference could liberalism accommodate before it lost its emancipatory promise? As illustrated by the heated Ilbert Bill debates, there came a point where the sharpening rhetoric of difference would divide liberals into two contending ideological factions.

Liberalism and Difference:
The Ilbert Bill Controversy

In 1882–83, only five years before the young Gandhi left for London to study law, a bitter controversy erupted among British liberals on the extent and meaning of the alleged differences between European and Indian cultural spheres. Sir Courtney Ilbert, a liberal Law Member of Viceroy Ripon's colonial administration (1880–84), introduced a bill designed to remove racial distinctions enacted in 1872 that made it impossible for Indians in the British Judicial Service to preside over any cases involving Europeans. In other words, under the existing law, European-British subjects could be tried only by judges of their own "race." Lord Ripon agreed with Ilbert that there was no place for such bias in the British legal system. Having secured the Viceroy's consent, no member of the Executive Council in Calcutta anticipated any public protest against a measure whose object was "simply the effectual and impartial administration of justice," as Ilbert put it when he presented his bill to the Legislative Council.[25] Seemingly embodying the universalist spirit of Queen Victoria's 1858 Proclamation, Ripon and Ilbert's initiative was hailed with joy by the native press all over India.

As political pragmatists, however, both men supported a moderate ideology of difference which, situated within the framework of a liberal teleology of progress, envisioned that educated members of Indian society would in time emulate the superior moral worth and refined sense of justice of their colonial masters. As the historian and high-ranking Indian civil servant William Wilson Hunter put it, by passing the required examinations, the native members of the Indian Civil Service had overcome the "inertia of climate and the prejudices of their race," thus proving themselves to be "more English in thought and feeling than Englishmen themselves."[26] The professional achievements of British-educated Indians were integral to the political agenda of moderate liberals, because they confirmed the "truth" of their model of educational developmentalism: "[W]ith the removal of these disqualifications would disappear the arguments resting on privilege—arguments which are as unsound as they are invidious. The theory that an Englishman is entitled to the privilege of being tried exclusively by Englishmen, has . . . been manufactured for consumption in the Indian market. Imagine its being suggested to a Parisian magistrate on behalf of an English pick-pocket!"[27] With

Behari Lal Gupta, a senior Indian member of the service already waiting for his due promotion to the post of session judge in upper Bengal, Ilbert's initiative signaled the moderates' final resolve to give the promise of liberalism its legal expression.

Opponents of the bill thought otherwise. Thousands of British-born members of Calcutta's Anglo-Indian associations protested the measure vigorously, in the process organizing mass meetings, attacking the viceroy in newspaper ads and burning him in effigy, and arguing that "nigger natives" could never be the peers or equals of Englishmen.[28] Annette Beveridge, the wife of one of the most liberal European members of the Indian civil service, wrote an emotional letter to the Calcutta newspaper *Englishman* that serves as a clear example for the existing interpenetration of ethnonationalist notions of cultural difference and exclusivist hierarchies of race and gender. Beveridge's letter condemned the Ilbert Bill as a "proposal to subject civilized women to the jurisdiction of men who have done little or nothing to redeem the women of their race, and whose social ideas are still on the outer verge of civilization."[29] Choosing their words more carefully and claiming that they were moved not by unthinking racial prejudice, but by principle, other liberal supporters of the empire, like Judge James Fitzjames Stephen, a former law member of the Viceroy's council, used the controversy to push the ideology of difference to its logical extremes. Asserting that India, in its social organization, was fundamentally and unalterably different from Europe, Stephen found it absurd to try to enforce the moderates' commitment to European legal principles.[30] His letter to *The Times* on March 1, 1883, expressed his belief that the maintenance of firm legal distinctions between European and Indian were inherent in the nature of British colonial rule itself:

> It [the raj] is essentially an absolute government, founded, not on consent, but on conquest. It does not represent the native principles of life or of government, and it can never do so until it represents heathenism and barbarism. It represents a belligerent civilization, and no anomaly can be more striking or so dangerous, as its administration by men, who being at the head of a Government founded upon conquest, implying at every point the superiority of the conquering race, of their ideas, their institutions, their opinions and their principles, and having no justification for its existence except that superiority, shrink from the open, uncompromising, straightforward assertion of it, seek to apologize for their own position, and refuse, from whatever cause, to uphold and support it. . . . One great prac-

tical inference is that government in India must proceed upon principles different from and in some respects opposed to those which prevail in England, and which, since the outbreak of the French Revolution, have acquired in many parts of Europe something like the consistency and energy of a new religion.[31]

Stephen's argument that British power was founded primarily on conquest harkens back to similar views expressed in earlier European histories of India. Written by the likes of Alexander Dow and Warren Hastings, such historical narratives acknowledged the central role of physical violence without hesitation: "The success of Your Majesty's arms has laid open the East to the researches of the curious. . . . The British nation have become the conquerors of Bengal and they ought to extend some part of their fundamental jurisprudence to secure their conquest. . . . The sword is our tenure. It is an absolute conquest, and it is so considered by the world."[32] Stephen employed the same metaphor of the "sword" to repudiate the moderate liberal position that Britain's superiority derived from its reputation for fairness and rationality. His letter renders visible the formidable challenge posed by extremist ideologists of difference to both the universalist tenor of liberal theory and the condescending evolutionism animating exclusionary colonial practices. For a hard-nosed liberal *Realpolitiker* like Stephen, power always preceded liberty and therefore only the former could be considered as the foundation of any well-organized government.[33] Such political realism not only assailed as "unpatriotic" and "naïve" the educational optimism of moderate liberals, but it also exposed the latter's unwillingness to acknowledge the violent truth of imperialism, namely, that the right to rule India rested on superior physical force. Asserting that liberals like Ilbert had gone "soft" in their commitment to the empire by inviting Indians to share power, Stephen warned that they were jeopardizing European hegemony on the subcontinent.

Dismissing as mere "sentiment" the evolutionist talk of India's eventual transformation, significant sections of the British press echoed Stephen's extreme ideology of difference: "Those who take their stand upon some abstract theory or sentiment may, of course, exclaim *fiat justitia* after the magnificent manner of sentimentalists everywhere, but practical politicians will agree with us in thinking that the universal opinion of the European community cannot be thus lightly disposed of."[34] Exploiting to the fullest the moderates' theoretical inconsistency with regard to the limited reach of universalism, Stephen routinely employed orientalist stereotypes to postulate the existence of permanent differences separating East and West. In this view, Indian culture represented an inferior civilization in which "the whole of the population, with exceptions in point of number too trifling to mention, are ignorant to the last degree, according to any European standard of knowledge." The central practical suggestion emerging from his analysis was that British power ought to remain exclusionary and absolute, because the essential traits of Indianness—"idolatrous superstition, ignorance, enervation, indifference, and fatalism"—could never be removed by the grand educational schemes of moderate liberals. Pronouncing their abstract interest in liberty incompatible with concrete imperial power interests, Stephen predicted the emergence of Indian intellectuals who, frustrated by the unrealizable promises of liberal idealism, would eventually turn their backs on the empire and embrace an anticolonial nationalism. Hence, his letter closes with a strong disapproval of the Ilbert Bill:

> The most definite point on which I should disagree with the views about India which seem to become popular is that I do not share the view so often stated and insinuated in all kinds of forms, that it is a moral duty on the part of the English nation to try to educate the natives of India in English ideas in such a way as to lead them to set up a democratic form of government administered by representative assemblies. . . . [35]

The articulation of this extremist ideology of difference combined with the unrelenting pressure of British public opinion in both India and England eventually wore Lord Ripon down. Subjected to incessant personal attacks, he capitulated, ultimately agreeing to the gutting of the Ilbert Bill. Under the measure's revised provisions as finally enacted in 1884, accused Europeans secured the right to claim a trial by jury, at least half of whose members were to be European.[36] As Metcalf notes, in the Ilbert Bill controversy all the stereotypes that marked out India's inferiority were marshaled with a renewed intensity.[37] The damage to race relations was enormous as more and more Indian intellectuals could no longer rationalize the obvious failure of the British raj to live up to its promise of equal treatment for all Indian subjects. A Brahmin member of the viceroy's Legislative Council best expressed their growing disillusionment with the "emancipatory" rhetoric of liberal theory: "The [British] Indian Civilian does not wish us to rise. When we learn his language, understand his ideas, and attain his intellectual level, he regards this not as a homage which he should welcome, but as an encroachment to be resented."[38]

LIBERALISM AND INDIAN NATIONALISM

Yet a fair number of moderate British liberals, too, reacted strongly against the Ilbert Bill decision. Unwilling to cede ground to the defenders of European privilege, the retired Scottish civil servant Allan Octavian Hume pleaded with influential Indians not to abandon the great liberal experiment. He dedicated the rest of his life to spreading the liberal-nationalist message that the Indian educated elites should put their energy and patriotic pride into the creation of a new national organization devoted to the progressive task of facilitating the public discussion of social reform in India: "Whether in the individual or the nation, all vital progress must spring from within, and it is to you, her most cultured and intelligent minds, her most favoured sons, that your country must look for the initiative."[39] Supported by prominent Indian intellectuals like W. C. Bonnerjee or Surendranath Banerjea who, after his wrongful dismissal from the Indian civil service had created the Indian Association in Calcutta, Hume's message did not fall on deaf ears. Indeed, his tireless agitation contributed to the founding of the Indian National Congress in 1885, an organization dedicated to the "moral and political regeneration of the country." Over time, the Congress became the organizational vehicle for a moderate Indian nationalist movement clinging to the notion of modernization along European lines. Key passages of the inaugural speech of Dadabhai Naoroji, the second President of the Congress, reflect his unreserved commitment to a peaceful gradualism:

It is our good fortune that we are under a rule which makes it possible for us to meet in this manner. (*Cheers*) It is under the civilizing rule of the Queen and the people of England that we meet here together, hindered by none, and are freely allowed to speak our minds without the least fear and without the least hesitation. Such a thing is possible under British rule and British rule only. (*Loud Cheers*) Then I put the *question* plainly: Is this Congress a nursery for sedition and rebellion against the British Government (*cries of no, no*); or is it another stone in the foundation of the stability of that Government (*cries of yes, yes*)? There could be but one answer, and that you have already given, because we are thoroughly sensible of the numberless blessings conferred upon us, of which the very existence of this Congress is a proof in a nutshell.[40]

Expanding on the aims and methods of the new institution in a speech delivered at Allahabad in 1888, Hume likewise emphasized the Congress' task of promoting the "social, mental and moral progress of the nation." Its chief methods were to be the "quiet teachings and preachings throughout the greater part of the country of simple elementary political truths," among which Hume listed, most prominently, peaceful methods of reform and the towering achievements of European civilization.

[Indian people] are taught to recognize the many benefits that they owe to British rule, as also the fact that on the peaceful continuance of that rule depend all hopes for the peace and prosperity of the country. . . . The sin of illegal or anarchical proceedings are brought home to them, and the conviction is engendered that by united, patient, constitutional agitation they are certain ultimately to obtain all they can reasonably or justly ask for, while by any recourse to hasty or violent action they must inevitably ruin their cause and entail endless misery on themselves.[41]

Ending his speech before a select, but appreciative audience, Hume issued a stern warning to the defenders of an extremist ideology of difference:

Do you not realise that by getting hold of the great lower middle classes before the development of the reckless demagogues, to which the next quarter of a century must otherwise give birth, and carefully inoculating them with mild and harmless form of the political fever, we are adopting the only precautionary method against the otherwise inevitable ravages of violent and epidemic burst of the disorder? I know that both in these provinces and the Punjab there are many officials—good men and true though not far-seeing—who are publicly and privately doing their utmost to impede the progress and hinder the happy development of this great and beneficent [Indian national] movement; but, Gentlemen, as they are good men, acting, though ignorantly, in all good faith, they will be very sorry later for this, and they will regret that before opposing they did not first take the trouble of thoroughly understanding the movement. . . . [42]

In short, Hume attacked the very foundation of Judge Stephen's "realist" perspective by arguing that the calculated spread of a benign cultural nationalism based on the norms and values of a European moderate-liberal worldview would inoculate the British colonizers against future challenges by radical Indian nationalists. Harnessed to the political methods of constitutionalism, a mild form of cultural nationalism was not only extremely unlikely to oppose imperial domination, but it would also allow the raj to showcase British "tolerance" and "openness" toward "reasonable" forms of Indian self-expression. Hence, liberals like Hume considered the Indian National Congress an arena that allowed for the almost therapeutic release of existing political tensions. Moreover, the establishment of the Congress gave the representatives of moderate difference a great opportunity to counteract the extremist views within their own ideological camp while at the same time winning over new Indian constituencies for their version of liberalism.

While many Indian intellectuals, like the young Gandhi, were greatly attracted to the universalist promise of liberal theory, they nonetheless contemplated settling for such an ideology of bridgeable difference, for it offered them a unique sense of "Indianness" that did not conflict with sentiments of loyalty and affection for the British Empire. As late as 1907, G. K. Gokhale, Gandhi's mentor and one of the principal leaders in the Congress, expressed his fondness for such a British-Indian identity:

> I recognize no limits to my aspiration for our motherland, I want our people to be in their own country what other people are in theirs. . . . I want all this and I feel at the same time that the whole of this aspiration can, in essence and its reality, be realized within this Empire. . . . Despite occasional lapses—and some of them most lamentable lapses—despite prolonged reactions, inevitable in human affairs, the genius of the British people, as revealed in history, on the whole made for political freedom, for constitutional liberty.[43]

Like those of his mentor, Gandhi's early ideas about "Indianness" cannot be separated from the dominant nineteenth-century British discourse on India. Although ultimately mounting a formidable challenge to the entire liberal paradigm, Gandhi's core values and assumptions were built on a number of unexpressed presuppositions that are deeply rooted in the political tradition of J. S. Mill,

C. P. Ilbert, and A. O. Hume. Their moderate ideology of difference thus represents the most influential set of those preconstituted cultural meanings that helped to shape Gandhi's nationalist imagination, in the process spawning a host of specific themes, stereotypes, questions, and answers that eventually came to define his dilemma of nonviolent principles and nationalist power. Hence, there exists a common intellectual heritage connecting Gandhi's predicament to the conflicting ideas of India arising from a liberal tradition whose thinkers found themselves at odds over the meaning of "difference."

Indeed, the particular dynamics that characterize Gandhi's dilemma of reconciling nonviolent principles with nationalist power can be better understood if we consider them related to British liberalism's larger dilemma of reconciling its universalist principles with colonial power. As Uday S. Mehta puts it, if the supposed universal political vision governing liberalism could be swayed by historical considerations of difference, it meant that "either that vision had to be acknowledged as limited in its reach or those recalcitrant and deviant histories had to be realigned to comport with it."[44] Extremist ideologists of difference like Stephen opted for the former, moderate liberals like Hume for the latter option. Still, neither alternative resolved the dilemma, but rather bequeathed to young Indian intellectuals like Gandhi a host of obstacles and difficulties. Stephen's insistence on permanent difference meant that Indians could never be recognized as full human beings. Hence, the only way to shake off the colonial yoke would lie in countering imperial power with greater power. This was the road to independence through violent nationalism. The evolutionary logic inherent in Hume's ideology of moderate difference promised Indians full recognition in exchange for their willingness to help reform traditional India. This meant that Indians first had to be properly "Europeanized" and "modernized" in order to qualify for political self-rule. Like so many of his compatriots, young Gandhi opted for the latter alternative, jumping at the opportunity to prove himself worthy of receiving the benefits of European civilization.

GANDHI'S INFATUATION WITH "BRITISHNESS"

In his pioneering work on cultural nationalism, John Hutchinson notes that many notable nationalists started out as enthusiasts of universalist ideologies.[45] As pointed out above, Mohandas Gandhi was no exception. A firm believer in the universalist promise of British liberalism, young Gandhi saw himself as a true gentleman and loyal subject to Her Majesty Queen Victoria, having acquired flawless English manners and impeccable professional credentials. But long before he traveled to London for his legal training, the educational power of the British liberal tradition and its official version of English history had already instilled in the young man an admiration for the political and cultural achievements of the empire. "I thought to myself," Gandhi later explained, "[I]f I go to England not only shall I become a barrister (of whom I used to think a great deal), but I shall be able to see England, the land of philosophers and poets, the very center of civilization."[46] As his biographer Dennis Dalton points out, "Gandhi's high-school curriculum, dictated and dominated by English masters there and abroad, had induced in him an awe of British civilization."[47]

Still, the teenager's longing for Europe must have been of a rather general nature, for at no point in his revealing *Autobiography* does Gandhi recount specific incidences or encounters with Europeans that triggered his sudden passion for England. In fact, the suggestion to send him abroad came from a Brahmin family adviser who convinced his older brother Laxmidas that Mohandas's chances for a successful professional career in India would be greatly enhanced by the possession of a European college degree.[48] In his probing account of Gandhi's trip to England, V. S. Naipaul wonders about the youngster's motivation: "For a reason which he never makes clear—he was virtually uneducated, had never read a newspaper—he passionately wanted to go to England."[49] However, as I have attempted to show in my discussion of the power of the liberal British discourse on India, Gandhi's desire to know England was anchored in the unexpressed presuppositions that constituted his cultural framework. Once the topic of English education was broached, his conceptual forestructure found its conscious articulation and emotional expression. Indeed, judging by his own account, the boy's wish to travel to London was overwhelming and persistent, mixed with a good dose of ambition and curiosity: "I had a secret design in my mind of coming here to satisfy my curiosity of knowing what London was."[50] One finds many similar passages in Gandhi's writings where he openly confesses that while "sleeping, waking, drinking, eating, running, and reading, I was dreaming and thinking of

England and what I would do on that momentous day." Even his dreaded childhood cowardice seems to have "vanished before the desire to go to England, which completely possessed me."[51]

Likening himself to his mythical hero, Rama, "fighting the many heads of the evil giant Ravan," Mohandas's will grew even stronger as he resolved to confront the many obstacles blocking his passage to England.[52] Determined to prevail, he identified four major difficulties: taking leave of his wife and infant son for three years; receiving the consent of his mother and his uncle, the head of the Gandhi clan; raising a large sum of money to cover his expenses in England; and, finally, confronting the religious taboos against anyone of his caste traveling overseas. With much tenacity, he ultimately overcame the first three problems. Yet, the last hurdle turned out to be particularly daunting. As Judith Brown points out, venturing abroad was a dramatic cultural step for Gandhi, given that no member of his sub-caste of *modh banias* (middle-caste Gujarat traders and merchants) had visited Europe before.[53] The remarkable strength of religious tradition was still manifest in the powerful injunction to maintain spiritual purity at all cost; Gandhi's proposed journey to England violated the prohibition against traveling to foreign countries, and his endeavor would therefore inevitably result in ritual pollution.

While waiting in Bombay for his passage to London, Gandhi was summoned before the council of the *modh banias*. He later characterized as "indescribable" the pressure he had to withstand in this trial camouflaged as a "general meeting." Almost all of his caste fellows were in opposition and tried their best to prevent him from leaving India. Responding to the headman's charge that it was impossible to keep the caste's religious rules in England, Gandhi argued that he had already promised his mother under oath that he would refrain from having sex, consuming liquor and tobacco products, and eating meat. The headman remained unconvinced, but Mohandas was equally stubborn: "I cannot alter my resolve to go to England. . . . I think the caste should not interfere in the matter."[54] Forced to choose between an idealized British tradition filtered down through his colonial education and the much more tangible, but antiquated, tradition of his family clan, Gandhi chose the former without hesitation. His decision is impressive testimony to the vast reach of late nineteenth-century British ideas and Western modernizing tendencies in even the most distant and traditional parts of the subcontinent. In the end, young Mohandas showed himself willing to accept the harsh penalty for his disobedience. The headman announced that he would henceforth be treated as an outcast and that any family member helping him to realize his travel plans would be subject to a hefty monetary fine.

During his three years in London, Gandhi solidified his sense of attachment to England and British culture. Remarkably, except for a few casual allusions to events involving his vegetarianism, the sections in his *Autobiography* pertaining to his stay in London show no recorded personal experiences of racial discrimination. If Gandhi's recollections are correct, one can understand why it was not too difficult for him to slip into the liberal persona of a British gentleman. Yet, his first impressions surrounding his arrival in London proved to be rather sobering. Dressed in Bombay-style white flannels, the fledgling law student discovered that what he had considered to be an appropriate European style of dress was not only out of place in the continental climate but also entirely "unsuitable for English society." Seeing that he was the only person wearing such a suit, Gandhi was overwhelmed by intense feelings of shame and personal inadequacy that grew even more intense as he drew unwelcome glares from passers-by on his way to his hotel.[55] As a complete novice in the matter of English etiquette, he later recalled finding himself "between Scylla and Charybdis." His words poignantly attest to the young man's struggle between his embarrassment and his determination to succeed: "England I could not bear, but to return to India was not be thought of. Now that I had come, I must finish the three years, said the inner voice."[56]

Within weeks of his arrival, Gandhi's lingering emotional unsettlement prompted him to embark on a frantic quest for a new identity: "He was, after all, there to learn English law, in one of the great English institutions, the Inns of Court, which seemed to have endured forever."[57] Vowing to find out who and what he "really" was and wanted to become, the young law student "threw himself into an overt strategy of Westernization, attempting to learn all the skills and graces he thought befitted an English gentlemen. He started out on lessons in French, dancing, violin, and elocution. He even had an evening suit made in Bond Street. . . . [H]e struggled for ten minutes each day in front of a mirror to master the art of tying a tie, and to tame his unruly hair."[58] An acquaintance meeting him in Piccadilly Circus would be left in no doubt about the image the young man sought to project:

Gandhi was wearing at the time a high silk top hat 'burnished bright,' a stiff and starched collar (known as Gladstonian), a rather flashy tie displaying all the colors of the rainbow, under which there was a fine striped silk shirt. He wore as his outer clothes a morning coat, a double-breasted waistcoat, and dark striped trousers, and not only patent-leather shoes but spats over them. He also carried leather gloves and a silver mounted stick, but wore no spectacles. His clothes were regarded as the very acme of fashion for young men about town at that time, and they were largely in vogue among the Indian youth prosecuting their studies in law at one of the Four institutions called the Inns of Court. The Inner Temple, the one in which Gandhi enrolled, was considered by Indians the most aristocratic.[59]

Though Gandhi's intense period of infatuation with English finery lasted only for a few months, his fastidiousness in dress and his infatuation with "Britishness" persisted long after his arrival in South Africa. Dennis Dalton speaks with good reason of Gandhi's "obsessive emulation of English values in his twenties and thirties"—the bulk of his years in England and South Africa.[60] Undoubtedly, these values were liberal in essence as Gandhi began to speak with much reverence and admiration of the British constitution and its regard for civil rights and religious pluralism. Moreover, the young law student was greatly impressed with the official heroes of liberal reformism, particularly Gladstone. As James Hunt emphasizes, "Politically, he [Gandhi] seems to have been a Liberal imperialist; believing of course that Indians should have increased participation in government, but that England and India were to continue joined in the Empire, and that the effect of English civilization on India was generally admirable."[61] Indeed, London's small Indian community was closely connected to the liberal cause; in 1890 a group of Liberals launched a campaign to elect Dadabhai Naoroji as the first Indian Member of Parliament. Gandhi was introduced to Naoroji and became an avid reader of *India,* Dadabhai's journal for the discussion of Indian affairs.[62]

Complementing his formal education with daily readings of *The Daily Telegraph,* the *Daily News,* and the *Pall Mall Gazette,* Gandhi readily absorbed liberal England's tales of her material and moral greatness. Throughout his life, he retained a Victorian concern with evangelical notions of truth and duty, particularly the idea that truth required sacrifice. As his studies drew to a close, he had become quite comfortable in his adopted home: "So much attached was I to London and its environments; for who would not be? London with its teaching institutions, public galleries, museums, theatres, vast commerce, public parks and Vegetarian restaurants, is a fit place for a student and a traveller, a trader. . . ."[63]

LIBERALISM AND VEGETARIANISM

As it turned out, London was also a fit place for "faddists," as vegetarians like Gandhi were called by their critics. Martin Green argues convincingly that it is virtually impossible to overestimate the influence various British vegetarians and theosophists exerted on the young law student.[64] In fact, one could make the reasonable claim that Gandhi's mature views on morality and politics derive in large part from his contacts with British "New Age" circles. Arguments like those presented in vegetarian pamphlets such as *A Plea for Vegetarianism,* written by Henry Salt, gave ideological substance to Mohandas's formalistic abstention vows to his mother. By 1891, the London Vegetarian Society had become a second home to the law student, offering him his first organizational experience (he was elected to its executive committee), and giving him the opportunity to hone his literary skills and discover his own voice. At the time, the agenda of the vegetarians in England went far beyond that of a single-issue movement; it exhibited an organizational vigor and evangelical zeal that was deeply rooted in Christian humanitarian and universalist ideas reminiscent of Emerson and Thoreau's transcendentalism. Moreover, there were strong formal and social ties among various vegetarians, theosophists, nonconformists, Unitarians, liberal idealists, spiritualists, moralists, purity campaigners, nature-cure experts, romantic nationalists, naturalists, pacifists, and many other New Age groups. (Like the New Age movement of today—which has its origins in earlier New Ages, particularly late Victorian England—this New Age stressed spirituality, environmental care, pacifism, and vegetarianism.) Most importantly, as a center of gravity for much innovative social thinking and action in London, organized vegetarianism was linked to Indian culture and religions in crucial ways. As Thomas Trautmann puts it, "Indomania" found a place in British society under the aspect of "eccentricity."[65] Prominent vegetarians like Edwin Arnold and Edward Carpenter were leading "orientalists"—European writers and scholars who discovered in "ancient India" a glorious civilization devoted to physical, mental, moral, and spiritual perfection. Indeed, it was through Arnold's translation of the *Bhagavad Gita* and other orientalist writings on India that Gandhi began to rediscover and reimagine his "own" tradition.

Thus it is rather ironic that young Gandhi, who knew very little about Indian food and cookery and had read only a few standard works about Indian culture and history, soon emerged as the London Vegetarian Society's chief interpreter of the "Indian mind."[66] In the first few months of 1891, he authored a series of ten articles on Indian foods and cultural festivals for the organization's official journal, *The Vegetarian,* edited by Josiah Oldfield. His short essays on "Indian Vegetarians," as well as his more substantial article on "The Foods of India," are especially important for our subject, because they provide the reader with some insight into the first systematic construction of Gandhi's idealized vision of India—a fantastic image comprised of liberal, orientalist, and folklorist fragments. In addition, these early essays also supply clear evidence for Gandhi's painful search for identity in an environment dominated by the liberal ideology of difference.

Essay IV, "Indian Vegetarians," opens with a consideration of the "hollow" and "baseless" arguments advanced by the extremist proponents of cultural difference regarding the "weak constitution of the Vegetarian Hindus."[67] Although Gandhi affirms the European stereotype of the "notoriously weak Hindus," he also claims that this "proverbial weakness" is attributable to causes other than their vegetarian diet, such as "the wretched custom of child marriages and its attendant evils." In order to illustrate the main point of his article—that vegetarianism is perfectly compatible with bodily strength—Gandhi invents a fabulous picture of the "shepherds in India" who represent "a good example of how strong an Indian Vegetarian can be where other opposite agencies are not at work." What follows reads like a description of an exotic hero in an orientalist fairy tale:

> An Indian shepherd is a finely built man of Herculean constitution. He, with his thick, strong crudgel, would be a match for any ordinary European with his sword. Cases are recorded of shepherds having killed or driven away tigers and lions with their crudgels. . . . [T]he Vegetarian shepherd would be equal to, if not more than a match for, a meat-eating shepherd. . . . From the above facts it is easy to see that Vegetarianism is not only not injurious, but on the contrary is conducive to bodily

strength and that attributing the Hindu weaknesses to Vegetarianism is simply based on a fallacy.[68]

Although he claims to have met a shepherd who was over a hundred years old just before departing for England, it is highly unlikely that Gandhi had sustained personal contacts with real-life Indian pastoralists. Indeed, his descriptions hardly reflect the harsh reality of pastoral life in late nineteenth-century India. His insistence on "facts" notwithstanding, it appears that the purpose of his vegetarian morality tale lay less in providing historically accurate description than in the affirmation of an orientalist image of purity designed to influence the dietary habits of his audience.

For example, in essay V, Gandhi proceeds to describe in much detail the daily schedule and habits of Indian shepherds. As it turns out, their daily routine is not unlike that of a committed European vegetarian in late Victorian England. According to Gandhi, the Indian shepherd gets up at five o'clock in the morning, and, after offering some heartfelt prayers to God, he performs his toilet, which includes washing his hands and face as well as brushing his teeth. After a fine vegetarian breakfast consisting mainly of millet cakes and clarified butter, he goes to the pasture about three miles outside of town, where "he has the unique advantage of enjoying the freshest air with natural scenery thrown in." After a hearty lunch consisting of millet cakes (again), vegetables, and "fresh milk directly taken from the cow," he takes a short nap under a shady tree. At six he returns home and has supper; this time rice is added to the usual menu of millet cakes and vegetables. After completing some household chores, he indulges in a "pleasant chat with the family members," and retires at ten o'clock. Weather permitting, the shepherd sleeps in the open air. "His, in many respects, is an ideal mode of life. He is perforce regular in his habits, is out of doors during the greater part of his time, while out he breathes the purest air, has his due amount of exercise, has good and nourishing food and last but not least, is free from many cares which are frequently productive of weak constitutions."[69]

As the chapters below will show, it is remarkable how little Gandhi would alter the basic elements of this early vision in the course of the next half-century. In particular, his acceptance of the orientalist idea that modern Indians had become "weak" or "degenerate" would supply the rationale for his call for the moral regeneration of the nation. Indeed, his vision of a return to a healthy community reflecting the simple virtues of Indian villagers became the main theme of his cultural nationalism. At the same time, Gandhi's idyllic picture already contained the revolutionary idea of a morally superior India. In 1891, the radical potential of this vision was still buried beneath old layers of European educational propaganda. Yet, the influence of British vegetarians and their orientalist imagination slowly began to put a crack in his wholesale acceptance of the moderate liberal model presenting England as India's tutor in all areas of human activity.

Returning once more to the topic of Indian vegetarianism in his concluding essay, "The Foods of India," Gandhi approaches the vexing problem of cultural difference in a highly ambiguous fashion. Conceding that the dietary habits of Indian and English people were currently "quite different" from each other, he nonetheless expresses much confidence in the notion that their separate paths were gradually converging:

> . . . I further hope the time will come when the great difference now existing between the food habits of meat-eating in England and grain-eating in India will disappear, and with it some other differences which, in some quarters, mar the unity of sympathy that ought to exist between the two countries. In the future, I hope we shall tend towards unity of custom, and also unity of heart.[70]

Once the question of food was resolved, Gandhi seemed to argue, "some other differences" would gradually wither away as well, and the two countries would move ever closer toward a "unity of custom." However, his articulation of a common future for India and Britain begs a crucial question: Who would learn from whom? For British liberals, the answer was obvious, and Gandhi himself had previously emphasized that Indians had much to learn from British civilization. Yet, given the alternative values and the New Age lifestyle endorsed in his fanciful tale of the Indian shepherds, it was no longer clear what Europe had to offer its colonies. Much in the vein of Rousseau's critique of modernity, Gandhi's tale challenged the very idea of backwardness upon which the liberal notion of British superiority was based. Though never explicitly laid out, the ramifications of Gandhi's logic are no mystery: the differences between "meat-eating England" and "grain-eating India" would presumably have to be resolved by universalizing vegetarianism and its alternative worldview. This meant that Gandhi's India—imagined as a vegetarian haven populated by simple village folk—emerged as the true bearer of the universalist promise.[71] The social and political realization of this promise required, therefore, a reversal of the liberal one-way tutor-pupil relationship then in place in India. In other words, Gandhi struck upon a conceptual model that challenged British colonial domination without changing the underlying evolutionary framework of the moderate liberals' ideology of difference. A nonexploitative future—Gandhi's "unity of heart"—depended on nothing less than the wholesale moral transformation of Europe, starting with spiritually advanced citizens emulating Indian food habits. Hence, Gandhi's revealing conclusion in his last article for *The Vegetarian,* written a few months before his departure to Bombay: " . . . I carry one great consolation with me that I shall go back without having taken meat or wine, and that I know from personal experience that there are so many Vegetarians in England."[72]

Can we therefore deduce with V. S. Naipaul that Gandhi's three-year stay in England turned him from a creature of instinct into a self-searching vegetarian and "Hindu by conviction?"[73] I think not, because almost everything the young Gandhi absorbed about "Hindu" culture and religion can be traced back to European orientalist sources. Moreover, it is unlikely that he was fully aware of the tremendous political implications contained in his commitment to a romantic vegetarianism rooted in orientalist imagery. When he left England, a wistful Gandhi saw himself, first and foremost, as a reformer and modernizer in the nineteenth-century British liberal sense of the term: "And then, as I was a reformer, I was taxing myself as to how best begin certain reforms [in India]."[74]

Once reunited with his family, he made sure to introduce European items of clothing and furniture into his home. Nevertheless, the increasing tension between his acquired New Age values and his legal work as a wig-wearing advocate of the Bombay High Court began to show itself in his shy reluctance to perform basic courtroom duties such as the conduct of witness cross-examinations. Longing to escape what he experienced as his "confining routine" in India once again, the young barrister grasped at the unexpected opportunity to do a few months of legal work in South Africa. It was in this novel environment where Gandhi's attachment to "British civilization" and his attraction to the universalist promise of liberal theory would be tested by the harsh reality of systematic racial discrimination.

2

CONFRONTING DIFFERENCE
AND EXCLUSION

૨૦

Gandhi's Struggle for Recognition in South Africa

*My first contact with British authority in that country [South Africa] was not
of a happy character. I discovered that as a man and an Indian I had no rights.
More correctly, I discovered that I had no rights as a man because I was an
Indian.*

—M. K. Gandhi[1]

Yet in several crucial ways South Africa made the Indian Gandhi.

—Judith M. Brown[2]

AN INDIAN IN SOUTH AFRICA

Confronting South Africa's exclusionary system of racial discrimination, Mohandas Gandhi entered the world historical
stage at the turn of the century as both cultural nationalist
and archetypal protagonist of nonviolence. What eventually became
the Mahatma's comprehensive vision of nonviolent nationalism
began in Natal as a shy outsider's struggle against the colony's pervasive racist practices. To borrow from the terminology of Latin
American liberation theology, Gandhi's traumatic experiences in
South Africa served as the catalyst for his political conscientization.

As he awakened to the plight of the local Indian immigrants, the Anglophile lawyer slowly realized how the liberal construction of cultural difference according to European criteria legitimized exclusionary colonial practices that imposed on Asians the inferior identity of second-class citizens. Subjected to frequent racial slights, threats, beatings, and other forms of violent rejection, the young barrister eventually resolved to remain in South Africa and direct most of his legal work at achieving full recognition for all local British-Indian subjects in strict accordance with the universalist spirit of Queen Victoria's 1858 Proclamation. However, when his persistent constitutional efforts yielded only meager results, he began to experiment with alternative, nonviolent methods of confronting the physical and epistemic violence embedded in the harsh technologies of European colonial rule.

At the same time, Gandhi greatly expanded his earlier ideas of India and its moral values, in the process developing powerful orientalist myths of nationhood based on essentialist notions of "Indianness." Letting himself be drawn more and more deeply into the alternative lifestyle he had merely speculated about in London, he began to doubt Western civilization's claims to moral superiority, and pointed instead to the profound gulf between liberal pretensions to impartiality and fairness and imperial practices of racial discrimination. Emphasizing the importance of Gandhi's censure of liberalism as the result of his painful encounters with empire's violence, Raghavan Iyer, one of his main intellectual biographers, notes that the young Indian barrister "laid down the foundations of his thought during the pioneering days of his campaigns in South Africa," and returned to India in 1915 as "a mature man of forty-five who had done his essential thinking on morals and politics."[3] Iyer's assessment has been substantiated by more recent studies which have explored the transforming effects of Gandhi's South African years.[4]

For the purposes of this study it is not necessary to provide the reader with all the details involving Gandhi's gradual transformation from an apolitical British-Indian barrister into a passionate advocate of political rights for Indian immigrants in South Africa. This story has been told by both Gandhi himself and his principal biographers, and thus need not be repeated here in its entirety.[5] It is important, however, that this chapter provide some key illustrations of this remarkable transformation in order to emphasize the connection between the young lawyer's growing disaffection with British liberalism and an ensuing identity crisis that could only be assuaged by the eventual adoption of a new conceptual framework. As Judith Brown notes, South Africa compelled the young lawyer "to confront fundamental questions about being Indian; to ask what was central to Indian identity. . . . In particular, the experiences of Africa forced him to ask what bound Indians together and constituted their essential unity."[6]

Furthermore, by focusing on Gandhi's unexpected discovery of his subordinate status as an Indian Other, this chapter attempts to convey a sense of why and how he embarked on his political quest for full recognition. The culmination of this engagement—his full-blown 1909 critique of liberalism and its underlying views on modern civilization—will be taken up in the next chapter. Finally, Gandhi's struggle for Indian civil rights in South Africa also confronted him for the first time with the existing tension between political power and ethical principles. Accepting the challenge, Gandhi spent the rest of his life searching for a solution to his own version of this dilemma.

GANDHI'S TURBAN

Throughout human history, clothes have exerted much symbolic power, conveyed through politically and socially salient meanings which people use to consolidate social relations and mobilize political constituencies. As Jane Schneider and Annette Weiner point out, one such important domain of meaning projected by clothing involves the uses of dress and adornment to reveal and conceal identities and values.[7] In the colonial systems of the nineteenth century, styles of dress were of great importance in symbolically representing the differences between the rulers and the ruled. As noted by Bernard S. Cohn, clothes in India were part of a system of codes of conduct that clearly demarcated "Britishness" from "Indianness" and thus reinforced a sense of distance between the colonial masters and their subjects.[8] In the wake of the 1857–58 Anglo-Indian War, the British rulers expanded their control over their imperial subjects by making them conform to their conception of what Indians of a particular status were supposed to wear for various official and semi-official occasions. Based on their ideology of difference, the British constructed unequal rules governing the wearing and non-wearing of shoes and headdress. Whereas Europeans were free to disregard Indian customs, Indians had to conform to English ideas of what constituted proper Indian dress and behavior.[9] At the same time, consistent with their overall technology of colonial rule, the British encouraged Western-educated Indian elites and members of the urban middle classes to express their loyalty to the empire through the adoption of certain articles of European clothing and home furnishings.

As the indigenous elites began to internalize the dress code of the colonial order, their appetite for European clothes increased exponentially. Cohn observes that many of the wealthier Bengalis believed that the adaptation of a European style of dress could bring them the coveted material benefits of modernity: "The thousands of clerks and functionaries who worked in the Government and commercial offices of Calcutta and Bombay had by the late nineteenth century developed a distinctive form of dress, a mixture of Indian and European."[10] The wearing of at least some pieces of European dress by Indians signified not merely their rising social status, but also demonstrated the "truth" of liberal developmental schemes: properly educated and dressed, Indians, too, could rise to the same "civilized" status as their English tutors. Although originally functioning as markers of exclusionary privilege, European clothes began to signify the universalist promise of liberalism to be realized at some unspecified point in the future. As discussed in the previous chapter, native claims to the full privileges of British citizenship were encouraged by Queen Victoria herself when she stated that among the European-educated Indian classes, "[T]here are to be found gentlemen whose position and attainments fully qualify them for all the duties and privileges of citizenship."[11]

When Gandhi landed on the wharf of Durban, the major port city of Natal Colony, he considered himself such a "gentleman." Naturally, his attitude was reflected in his dress. Throughout his life, Gandhi would remain extremely sensitive to the connection between costume and social status, perceiving that changes in social position required changes in dress.[12] Indeed, his changing ideas about self and nation were always reflected in dramatic transformations of his clothing style. Upon his arrival in South Africa, he wore a starched white shirt, a black tie, meticulously pressed, striped trousers which matched his fashionable black frock coat, gleaming black patent leather shoes, and a huge black turban, an imitation of the Bengali *pugri*. As Martin Green puts it, the young attorney was the "very picture of an Anglicized babu [intellectual], a son of the empire."[13] Greeted by his local employer, Dada Abdulla, an elderly local Muslim merchant held in high esteem by the commercial Indian immigrant community, Gandhi quickly realized that his fine attire set him squarely apart from other Indians in South Africa and made him stand out among whites and nonwhites alike: "Those who looked at me did so with a certain amount of curiosity."[14] To some extent, the circumstances surrounding his 1893 landing in Durban harbor mirrored those of his arrival in London five years earlier. Again, according to local custom, Gandhi's style of dress seemed to be strangely out of place. This time, however, the young attorney had so deeply internalized the assumed identity of a British-Indian gentleman that the flagrant racist slurs hurled by South African whites at disembarking Indian passengers seemed inexplicable. Yet, demeaning terms like "sammi" were a common appellation for all Indians in South Africa, and, much to his surprise and consternation, Gandhi observed from the very first minute of his visit "that Indians were not held in much respect."[15]

On the second or third day after his arrival, he was taken to the Durban Court to watch the proceedings and familiarize himself with the legal tasks that the trade firm Dada Abdulla & Co. had hired him to perform. Wearing the same outfit, the young attorney was subjected to the hostile glares of the officiating English magistrate, who, stating that he was merely enforcing a rule of court, finally asked him to remove his turban. Dada Abdulla later explained the rules to his young employee. Those wearing a Muslim costume had to bow but were allowed keep their turbans on, while, on entering the courtroom, all other Indians were required to bow and remove their headdress. In this provincial courtroom far away from Europe and India, Gandhi was finally brought face to face with the inflexible system of exclusion based on a hardened ideology of difference dividing South African Indians into different categories according to specific criteria.

Although colonial regimes never entirely relinquished the use of physical violence as a central means of control, their continued rule depended on a permanent process of ordering and classifying their overseas acquisitions according to European epistemological standards, thus paving the way for the conceptual violence of creating and controlling the Other as a knowable object. As noted by

Bernard S. Cohn and Nicholas Dirks, these more indirect forms of violence fortified British control through the objectification of the colonized according to European modes of representation. This host of investigative modalities included the delineation and reconstruction of systematic grammars for vernacular languages, the introduction of English legal practice, the biomedical-scientific discourse of studying the Other, and the representation of colonial control through the mastery and display of archeological memories and religious texts.[16] To be sure, such practices involved some blurring of pure positions of self and other through the borrowing and lending of ideas in both directions.[17] But as Ania Loomba emphasizes, colonial knowledge was ordinarily built upon the fundamental difference between Europe and its Others. Cultural "crossovers" were rare, partly because not all that took place in various contact zones could be monitored and controlled, and partly as a result of deliberate colonial policy: "One of the most striking contradictions about colonialism is that it both needs to 'civilize' its 'others,' and to fix them in perpetual 'otherness.'"[18]

Thus, empire's violence was structurally embedded in a vast network of colonial norms and rules which, through the meticulous regulation, dissection, and reallocation of time and space, imbued "Indianness" with essential qualities and definitive traits. Assigning proper names and authoritative meanings to all phenomena, authoritative colonial discourses employed invidious notions of difference to validate elaborate cultural, racial, and religious classification schemes that reified the sharp boundaries separating the colonizer from the colonized. Pejorative terms such as "coolie" signified the immigrant Indians' particular location within the parameters of linear time and physical, psychological, symbolic, and discursive space set by South African whites. To be "Indian" meant, among other things, to partake in a particular historical record assembled by Europeans; to belong to an assigned ethnic category; to speak an identifiable language or dialect; to be affiliated with a classified religion; to live in a physical place named by the colonizers; and to follow customs and traditions duly registered by colonial authorities. On the level of daily experience, it meant that Indians were expected to know their inferior place in the colonial system and to validate this knowledge through public reenactments of submissive behaviors like removing one's turban at court. Among the many obligatory performances expected from Indians were the acceptable ways of

addressing Europeans; appropriate gestures and looks; correct manners of dress; and, of course, the strict adherence to a long list of
forbidden acts and excluded spaces. In short, Indian identity in
South Africa was the indelibly marked result of technologies of rule
that incessantly reenacted the "truth" of Oriental cultural inferiority, thereby making humiliation and low self-esteem a permanent
feature of "Indianness."

Unsurprisingly, Gandhi's coveted identity as a "British-Indian
gentleman" remained largely unacknowledged. In the eyes of the
Durban magistrate he was merely a "coolie barrister" whose skin
color and turban marked his inferior position at an official place of
colonial regulation. For the young lawyer, however, turbans were not
like hats. Gandhi did not experience the order to remove his turban
as a gesture of deference; rather, it was a positively demeaning request. From the eighteenth to the twentieth century, the British and
Indians had fought an extended symbolic battle over the nature of
Indian headdress. For most Hindus, the turban was more than a
functionalist piece of cloth protecting a person from the heat of the
sun. The head was the locus of power and knowledge, and to place
a turban at the feet of conquerors was a sign of complete surrender,
indicating the willingness on the part of the vanquished to become
their slave.[19] Susan Bean puts it in a nutshell: "The sartorial requirements of the Empire forced Indians to humiliate themselves, and revealed the true relationship—of master and slave—between the
English and the Indians."[20] At the time, Gandhi might not have been
aware of all the historical and symbolic connotations of the magistrate's request, but he clearly understood that he was denied recognition as an equal citizen merely on the grounds of his Indianness.

Gandhi soon recognized that his cultural and ethnic heritage
constituted a constant source of conflict. Still, he was willing to negotiate his identity to the point where he would drop *some* claims to
his cultural particularity. Yet, since difference in South Africa was
maintained through hard boundaries of exclusion, his new environment would not allow even hybrid forms of identity. As Ania
Loomba emphasizes, the underlying premise of the colonial system
was, of course, "that Indians can mimic but never exactly reproduce
English value, and that their recognition of the perpetual gap between themselves and the 'real thing' will ensure their subjugation."[21] Was Gandhi prepared to negotiate other markers of his
Indianness, such as his choice of foods and his headdress? Recalling

the turban incident three decades later as the Mahatma and undisputed leader of the Indian nationalist movement, Gandhi conveys a decidedly combative posture: "This [removing his turban] I refused to do and left the court. So here too there was fighting in store for me."[22] However, a perusal of relevant secondary sources leaves the reader with a much less defiant impression. While he was clearly stung by the magistrate's insulting request to the point of walking out of the court, Gandhi soon had second thoughts about the appropriateness of his response and later indicated to Dada Abdulla his willingness to wear an English hat in future court appearances. Much to Gandhi's surprise, it was his seemingly submissive employer who advised him to adhere to his original action: "If you do anything of the kind, it will have a very bad effect. You will compromise those insisting on wearing Indian turbans. And an Indian turban sits well on your head. If you wear an English hat, you will pass for a waiter."[23]

Still shaken by his experience in the Durban courtroom and groping to find his place in the hostile South African environment, Gandhi discovered that the turban incident had been reported in the local newspaper under the heading "An Unwelcome Visitor." Writing to the *Natal Advertiser* the same day in order to explain his actions, Gandhi expressed, once again, a rather accommodating attitude:

> It is true that on entering the Court I neither removed my head-dress nor salaamed [bowed], but in so doing I had not the slightest idea that I was offending His Worship, or meaning any disrespect to the Court. Just as it is a mark of respect amongst Europeans to take off their hats, in like manner it is in Indians to retain one's head-dress. To appear uncovered before a gentleman is not to respect him. In England, on attending drawing-room meetings and evening parties, Indians always keep the head-dress, and the English ladies and gentlemen generally seem to appreciate the regard which we show thereby. In High Courts in India those Indian advocates who have not discarded their native head-dress invariably keep it on."[24]

Obviously, Gandhi's references to English conventions were meant to teach his uncouth audience a lesson in "real" British manners. The flaunting of his intimate knowledge of English social etiquette was supposed to provide his courtroom behavior with some authoritative backing while conveying to his readership that, in spite of his Indianness, he had been a sophisticated and fully accepted member of society in London. The message was unmistakably clear: Gandhi wanted to highlight the demeaning discrepancy between British and South African society with regard to their respective treatment of Indians. Still, he ended his letter by striking a reconciliatory chord: "Lastly, I beg His Worship's pardon if he was offended at what he considered to be my rudeness, which was the result of ignorance and quite unintentional."[25]

Over the next few months, Gandhi became the target of further insulting acts of racial discrimination by white South Africans, like the police constable who threw him out of the first-class cabin of a train bound for Maritzburg, the barber in Pretoria who refused to cut the hair of a "bloody coolie," or the pedestrian who pushed him off the sidewalk. While his British mannerisms and his fine clothes would at times allow him access to spaces that were closed to ordinary South African Indians, he could not manage to escape racial violence. Yet, such incidents made him understand that his initial passive strategy of pleading ignorance and showing good intentions would not save him from further ill-treatment. Torn between his wounded pride and the desire to settle his employer's law case quickly, Gandhi found himself in the throes of an intense identity crisis that shook his naive faith in the political institutions of his host country: "I saw that South Africa was no country for a self-respecting Indian, and my mind became more and more occupied with the question as to how this state of things might be improved."[26] Slowly, he shook off his political passivity and began to contemplate his personal responsibility for initiating social change:

> I began to think of my duty. Should I fight for my rights or go back to India, or should I go on to Pretoria without minding the insults, and return to India after finishing the case? It would be cowardice to run back to India without fulfilling my obligation. The hardship to which I was subjected was superficial—only a symptom of the deep disease of colour prejudice. I should try, if possible, to root out the disease and suffer hardships in the process.[27]

Thus, the "turban incident" proved to be the first chapter in the remarkable story of Gandhi's transformation. Confronted with externally imposed barriers blocking the enactment of his coveted identity as a British-Indian gentleman, he resolved to confront the South African system of difference and exclusion while at the same time maintaining his overall trust in the universalist ideals of liberal theory. His 1894 "farewell party" turned into the first meeting of an ad-hoc working committee of the incipient Natal Indian Congress which would be dedicated to the preservation and extension of the civil rights of Indians. Staying on in his adopted country, he resolved to address the existing injustices through constitutional methods. "Thus God laid the foundations of my life in South Africa and sowed the seed of the fight for national self-respect."[28]

As might be expected, Gandhi's eventual emergence as a public figure in South Africa was accompanied by significant changes in his dress and his lifestyle. As the years wore on and the political struggle intensified, his expensive English outfit was slowly replaced by simple, homespun Indian garments. His fashionable Bengali turban was ultimately transformed into the plain "Gandhi cap," defiantly worn by most participants in the first full-scale Indian non-cooperation campaign of 1920–22.

PLEAS FOR INCLUSION

As he shouldered the tedious onus of drafting long petitions to various colonial authorities, Gandhi's debilitating shyness gave way to confidence in the providential calling through which God had selected him to become the servant of a pressing moral cause. His dedication to this higher calling is evident in his 1894 correspondence with Dadabhai Naoroji, in which the young attorney expresses his newly-found confidence in his leadership qualities: "A word for myself and [for what] I have done. I am yet inexperienced and young and, therefore, quite liable to make mistakes . . . [but] I am the only person who can handle the question."[29] Erik Erikson rightly argues that Gandhi's unshakable conviction that he was "the man of the hour" constitutes an important feature of the personal transformation he underwent in South Africa.

> In spite of being a "coolie barrister" he saw the whole matter at first as an affront to his own class, which was learning to emulate the white man. . . . And so the young barrister also became the conscience of his nation only when—inadvertently at first—he found his body on that line which marks the difference between retreat and irreversible commitment. . . . There is every reason to believe that the central identity which here found its his-

torical time and place was the conviction that among the Indians in South Africa he was *the only person equipped by fate* to reform a situation which under no condition could be tolerated.[30]

During this initial phase of his "fight for national self-respect" in South Africa, Gandhi opted for a strategy of persistent, but polite constitutional protest: " . . . Nor is there any heroic sacrifice required by communities living under British rule; well-sustained, continuous and temperate constitutional effort is the main thing needed."[31] However, given the mounting evidence of London's reluctance to interfere with the blatantly racist policies of its South African colonies, Gandhi's remaining loyalty to the empire is rather striking and indicates the extent to which he had internalized the structures of colonial knowledge. Judith Brown puts it well:

> It is a strange contrast: the heroic rebel of the 1930s and 1940s who ulti-mately challenged the British to quit India, and the devoted imperialist of the turn of the century who sang the national anthem with gusto, planted a tree to celebrate Queen Victoria's Diamond Jubilee and helped to circu-late to Indian children in South Africa in 1901 a memorial souvenir of the late Queen which would not have been out of place in any patriotic schoolroom in Britain. He was at this stage convinced that the British im-perial connection with India was providential: the work of God which would ultimately be for India's good. . . . The hinge of this loyalty to the empire was a deep-rooted belief that its fundamental values were those of the British constitution, and he was not swayed from this by local practice in parts of the empire or temporary aberrations which seemed at variance with these basic values. Looking back from the 1920s he thought he had probably not known anyone who cherished such loyalty to the British constitution as he did then. . . . Those basic values of the constitution in-cluded love of justice, fair dealing, equality and liberty; and he spoke and wrote of them continuously in connection with the empire, despite evi-dence to the contrary in South Africa.[32]

Gandhi's numerous petitions to various colonial authorities drawn up between 1894 and 1906 reflect his overall political ob-jective of bringing South African laws in line with the inclusive promise of liberalism by changing existing discriminatory policies against the Indian community and preventing the passage of such legislation in the future. For example, in his very first petition ad-dressed to the Natal Legislative Assembly, he objected to the racially motivated attempt to disenfranchise the colony's mere 250 eligible voters of Indian origin. Typically, Gandhi's petitions would start out by criticizing existing or proposed restrictive legislation on the basis of the injustice involved in drawing "invidious distinctions between one class of British subjects and another." The young attorney often ended his pleas for inclusion by reminding the colonial authorities that acts of racial discrimination conflicted not only with "the best British traditions," but also with "the principles of justice and morality" and "the principles of Christianity."[33] Indians, he argued, were entitled to full civic recognition in accordance with the universalist spirit of liberal theory. "Having, then, taken stock of the principal grievances of the British Indians in South Africa, and shown, we believe, conclusively, that the unreasoning and unreasonable colour prejudice is generally at the bottom of them,"[34] Gandhi went on to cite with gusto the relevant portions of the 1858 Royal Proclamation that inveighed against the curtailment of the liberties and rights of Her Majesty's Indian subjects. Consistent with the developmentalist schemes advocated by moderate liberals, his petitions and articles sought to justify the gradual extension of political rights to previously excluded populations. After all, Gandhi noted, in addition to possessing "the ability to understand representative institutions," Indians everywhere had proven themselves to be "loyal subjects of the Crown" as well as "sober, industrious and law-abiding citizens." Hence, Gandhi insisted that "the Indians' fitness for an equality with the civilized races" was self-evident.[35]

From the very beginning, Gandhi made sure that his pleas for inclusion were also heard by audiences back home in India. In 1896, he combined his brief trip to India for the purpose of fetching his wife and children with a large-scale lecture tour in major cities designed to inform Indians about the indignities to which their compatriots were being subjected in South Africa. In addition, Gandhi intensified existing connections between his own Natal Indian Congress and the Indian National Congress, visited prominent Indian leaders like Gopal Krishna Gokhale and Bal Gangadhar Tilak, and pitched his political cause to influential members of the Indian press. His efforts soon resulted in the publication of a pamphlet, titled *The Grievances of British Indians in South Africa,* consequently known as the Green Pamphlet because of the color of its cover. The initial run of ten thousand copies could not keep up with the demand, and it became necessary to print a second edition. Quickly noticed by the press, a much shortened version of Gandhi's essay was cabled to London. A few days later, the Reuters' London office sent a still briefer three-line summary to Natal: "A pamphlet published in India declares that Indians in Natal are robbed and assaulted, and treated like beasts, and are unable to obtain redress. *The Times of India* advocates an inquiry into these allegations."[36]

A simplified summary of the pamphlet, containing the name of its author, was subsequently printed in South African newspapers, and upon his return to Durban, an incensed crowd of white settlers gathered at the wharf prepared to "hang old Gandhi on the sour apple tree."[37] True, the document contained graphic examples of racist violence in South Africa, such as the burning of Indian stores by whites without the slightest provocation, but it is equally important to emphasize its conciliatory tone and its expression of loyalty to the empire. For example, Gandhi quotes at length from a sympathetic article written by a veteran Natal journalist in order to confirm the sporadic existence of "true British character" with its love of justice and fairness "even in South Africa."[38] Further evidence of Gandhi's continued faith in the promise of liberalism is reflected in his persistent efforts to maintain a cordial relationship with such important British personalities as Sir William W. Hunter, the India editor of the London *Times,* or Joseph Chamberlain, the British Secretary of State for the Colonies. In fact, it was at Gandhi's request that a small deputation of the Natal Indian Congress was sent to England in 1897 with the express purpose of establishing firm contacts with influential figures in London.[39]

Yet, in many ways, his long years in South Africa made Gandhi an outsider to both Indian and English society.[40] He was no longer a naive law student, uncritically absorbing the wonders of British civilization, nor was he interacting on a daily basis with English vegetarians, theosophists, and orientalists. But he had also turned his back on his former life as a fledgling attorney hoping for a legal career in Bombay. Finally, he was also an outsider in his adopted South Africa—a despised Asian immigrant who had stirred up enough trouble to nearly get himself lynched. Realizing his growing distance from both Europe and India, Gandhi struggled to turn his sense of alienation into a political opportunity by claiming for himself the mantle of a sophisticated mediator sympathetic to both worlds:

If European colonialists can believe me, I beg to assure them that I am here,
not to sow dissensions between the two communities, but to endeavor to
bring an honourable reconciliation between them. In my humble opinion,
much of the ill-feeling that exists between the two communities is due to
misunderstanding of each other's feelings and actions. My office, therefore,
is that of an humble interpreter between them.[41]

Indeed, solemnly pledging the allegiance of the "Indians residing
in British South Africa" to His Majesty Edward VII, King-Emperor of
"the great Anglo-Saxon race," the first issue of his newly-founded
weekly, *Indian Opinion,* emphasized that "there will be nothing in our
programme but a desire to promote harmony and good-will between
the different sections of the *one* mighty Empire."[42]

THE APPEAL TO INDO-ARYAN IDENTITY

Gandhi's programmatic statement in *Indian Opinion* raises troubling
questions with regard to at least two issues. First, by purporting to
speak for all Indians residing in British South Africa, he conjured up
the politically useful, but empirically false, notion that there existed
a unified Indian immigrant community. Second, his reflexive genu-
flection to "the great Anglo-Saxon race" underlines the importance
of his frequent appeals to a common "Indo-Aryan" identity, supposedly uniting not only all Indians, but Indians and their colonizers as
well. To be sure, such narrow appeals to a deeper, encompassing ethnic identity conflicted with the moral universalism underpinning his
pleas to the colonial authorities for recognition and inclusion. For
the first time, Gandhi encountered the dilemma of ethical principles
and political power. His propagation of the myth of Indian unity and
his appeal to an Indo-Aryan identity are related issues and will be
examined in turn below.

With regard to the former, it is useful to remember that
Gandhi's arrival in the Natal Colony coincided with the rapid transformation of South Africa's pastoral and agricultural economy into a
modern capitalist economy mostly based on mining.[43] These new
economic realities attracted immigrants with very different socioe-
conomic backgrounds. Deep social, economic, and cultural cleavages
separated old commercial elites—chiefly made up of Gujarat Muslims who had emigrated to South Africa at their own expense—from

a vast underclass of mostly low-caste Hindus who subsisted as in-dentured laborers and servants.[44] When Gandhi became deeply in-volved in South African politics in 1894, Natal Muslim merchants had already established separate political organizations to protect their businesses. They were fully aware that their commercial inter-ests were threatened by a new wave of racially discriminatory activ-ities and pending anti-immigration bills. These measures, epitomizing the rising tide of economically motivated hatred against all "colored," originated in the Orange Free State and the Transvaal and quickly spread to Natal. Driven by the urgent need for a full-time political organizer with an appropriate professional back-ground, Indian merchants in Natal actively recruited the young Gujarat lawyer—himself a member of a commercial caste—for their political cause.

Maureen Swan has made a strong case for Gandhi's suitability to the merchants' needs from the point of view of linguistic and legal qualifications, as well as his ideological compatibility: "As their hired representative he ensured the continuity of merchant political phi-losophy and practice between 1891 and 1906."[45] Gandhi's successful legal and political work on behalf of his wealthy employers made it rather easy for him to attach himself to the world of the commercial elites. Moreover, his close confidant and spiritual advisor, the Jain di-amond trader and religious philosopher Shrimdad Rajchandbhai, exhorted his pupil to follow his moral duties within the framework of his existing obligations to the merchant caste.[46] As a result, Gandhi's main political strategy of constitutional protest remained for a long time tied to the commercial interests of the merchants, as did his weekly journal and his communal settlement at Phoenix, near Durban.[47] Hence, the implicit assumption that the views ex-pressed in *Indian Opinion* were reflective of a unified Indian com-munity in South Africa might be a good example of Judith Brown's observation that Gandhi's peripheral position as a "critical outsider" did not automatically generate penetrating insight, but could also breed fantasy based on ignorance or wishful thinking.[48]

It was only after 1906 that Gandhi began to realize the crucial importance of reaching out to the lower classes if he was to heighten the political pressure on the newly constituted Transvaal government to reconsider the social status of Indians in South Africa. His attrac-tion to politics, together with his growing sentiment of moral oblig-ation to the poor, led him to undertake several legal representations on behalf of the disadvantaged. These activities, in turn, encouraged him to become more involved with the political and economic goals of an underclass whose objectives, in many cases, ran contrary to the merchants' material interests. Downplaying the reality of economic, religious, and cultural differences in the South African Indian community, Gandhi clung to his increasingly ineffective slogans emphasizing "Indian unity." The tension between his insight into the political importance of the lower classes and his unwillingness to acknowledge the weakness of a commonly shared identity among local Indians came to define Gandhi's final years in South Africa. Preaching social harmony to the poor and moral obligation to the rich, he ultimately failed to forge the existing plurality of highly stratified communities into one political community.[49]

Whenever discriminatory legislation directed against Indians in general thwarted the interests of the commercial elites, Gandhi quickly engineered short-lived alliances with parts of the underclass. Even at the height of the mass-based struggle in Transvaal between 1908 and 1914, Gandhi continued to appeal to the merchants' patriotic feelings and purses by stressing the nationalist character of his *satyagraha* campaigns: "Money too will be needed for such an agitation; for this regular provision should be made. If every Indian does his duty and performs the community's task in the same spirit that he does his own, it will not be surprising to see India being forged into a nation in South Africa."[50] By 1913, however, it become clear that Gandhi's emphasis on Indian unity had done very little to garner support from the commercial elites. As a result, he was forced to further broaden his mobilization efforts in the direction of the upwardly mobile strata of the lower classes while at the same time accepting questionable ethical compromises such as minimizing the central idea of self-sacrifice by assuring merchants that possible jail sentences resulting from their participation in *satyagraha* campaigns would be brief and that their engagement would not endanger their private property, resident permits, and businesses.[51]

Turning now to Gandhi's affirmation of an Indo-Aryan identity, it is not difficult to grasp how such a project might have served to distract South African Hindus and Muslims from divisive religious issues and instead unite them behind the idea of a common Indian ethnicity. Of course, the same logic of generating ethnically-based feelings of solidarity also underpinned Gandhi's attempts to link the "Anglo-Saxon" and "Indian races" to the "same Aryan stock."[52] How can one explain the apparent ease with which he employed the Victorian idiom of race? For one, the issue must be put within its proper context. After all, the young lawyer was burdened with the unenviable task of having to respond to vicious claims by many South African whites that Indians were greedy invaders who belonged to the "uncivilized races of Asia."[53] Hence, Gandhi's dangerous acceptance of the particularistic narrative of ethnic identity reflects in part the constraining power of the dominant discourse that forced him to counter such blatant expressions of race prejudice. For this purpose, he turned to available "factual information" provided by European orientalists.

Indeed, much of Gandhi's supposed knowledge of so-called Aryans—a mythical people who were said to have migrated south into the Indian subcontinent from Central Asia about the same time as Doric Greeks moved westward—can be traced back to the writings of European intellectuals like Max Mueller, W. W. Hunter, and Henry Sumner Maine. Dubbed "Orientalists" by their "Anglicist" counterparts who rejected orientalist romanticism and idealism in favor of their own utilitarian and empirical-positivist inclinations, Mueller and his colleagues achieved quick fame in European academic circles for positing the existence of an intimate connection between language and race. As Daud Ali notes, "It should not surprise us, then, that the classification of languages in the nineteenth-century philology was related to a new systematic racial taxonomy."[54] Orientalists argued that as the Sanskrit-speaking, fair-skinned Aryans moved into Northern India, they encountered and subdued a race of darker, shorter people with a very different language and culture. Soon the term "Dravidian" came to denote all of these "non-Aryan" peoples of India, and the history of the subcontinent increasingly became the ground upon which these two racial essences, the Aryans and the Dravidians, interacted. In short, it was through the orientalists' "discovery" of nordic Aryans that Victorian racial science gained a foothold in Indian historiography—one that has been difficult to dislodge.[55] Daud Ali offers convincing evidence that orientalist scholars created the influential myth of the inherent superiority of the warrior-like Aryans over the agricultural Dravidians. Popularized versions of this story contributed to the success of the idea that "the Aryans carried in their veins the same racial stock as the Doric Greeks, bestowing on them the values of classical civilization in the West: rationality and virility."[56]

There is little doubt that the race theories of European orientalists critically impacted indigenous attempts to construct India as a nation. In Bengal, for example, Aryan racial identity became an overarching theme for nineteenth-century nationalists.[57] As Susan Bayly notes, the concepts of "Aryans" and "Dravidians," together with other inventions of European race theory, were increasingly enlisted by Indian nationalist leaders to prove that their nation possessed a deep, authentic unity that could override its all-too-visible diversities of caste, language, and region:

> Thus although it has been usual to think of Third World nationalism, especially in India, as deriving from liberal, secular traditions of Western constitutional politics, it is important to recognise how powerful ethnological concepts of race appealed to spokesmen for nationalist organizations in India, and indeed in many other parts of the colonial world. Consciously or not, and however divided on other matters, South Asian nationalists invoked ethnological themes in their visions of recovery of Indian greatness through spiritual, physical and moral regeneration.[58]

Gandhi was no exception. While struggling against unjust policies of racial exclusion in South Africa, he nonetheless borrowed heavily from orientalist race theories. As is evident in his eager subscription to W. W. Hunter's idea of an Aryan racial bond between Britons and Indians, a number of Gandhi's petitions draw explicitly on the authority of the influential English journalist: "This nobler race (meaning the early Aryans) belonged to the Aryan or Indo-Germanic stock, from which the Brahman, the Rajput, and the Englishmen alike descend. . . . The forefathers of the Greek and Roman, of the Englishman and the Hindoo, dwelt together in Asia, spoke the same tongue, and worshipped the same gods."[59] For many orientalists it was no conceptual stretch to connect the idea of common racial origins to the developmentalist framework supplied by the moderate liberal ideology of difference. For example, John Beames of the Bengal Civil Service, suggested that the British empire had a moral responsibility to uplift their fellow Indo-Aryans and help restore the stagnant civilization of their distant racial cousins to its former greatness.[60]

It is not a pleasant task to unearth some of the troubling assumptions contained in the early conceptual boundaries of what would eventually come to define Gandhi's nationalist vision. More evidence for the influence of orientalist ideas on his ambitious plans for a moral regeneration of the Indian nation will be offered in later chapters of this study. For the present, the above discussion should suffice to show how Gandhi's ethnic appeals served two main objectives: first, the shoring up of his pleas for the political inclusion of South African Indians with a theory of common Aryan origins; and, second, the evocation of strong feelings of belonging to a cohesive national community in Indian immigrants. Even his choice of mild constitutional protest can be explained with reference to his orientalist ethnic categories. If Britons and Indians indeed shared a common Aryan stock, then it made rhetorical sense for the latter to opt for a political style that was peaceful and acceptable in Western politics. After all, by choosing such "rational" constitutional methods, Indians could reinforce their claim to be the civilized equals of white citizens of the empire.[61]

On the other hand, Gandhi's discursive alliance with orientalist-ethnic narratives clearly conflicted with his universalist ideals. How could he accuse South African colonial governments of introducing inhuman legislation, if he himself spread questionable ideas of ethnic superiority? Was he simply unaware of the existing contradiction between his moral universalism and his uncritical acceptance of the alleged inferiority of other ethnic groups? Or did he intentionally refuse to deal with this tension? Unfortunately, an examination of relevant textual passages does not yield an unequivocal answer to these questions. Peter Robb, for example, argues that Gandhi consciously sought to preserve Indians as a distinct entity in order to prevent the sharing of achieved benefits with other groups: "In Gandhi's case it is interesting that, while recognising that both 'dark' and 'brown' races were suffering from a 'colour bar,' he centered his South African campaigns (except for a few Chinese) wholly around 'Indians'—though from all regions and classes, Hindu and Muslim."[62]

Seen from such an instrumentalist perspective, it is indeed obvious why Gandhi's various political strategies of coalition-building never included solid alliances with other Asian immigrant populations, not to speak of trying to rally blacks behind the cause of racial discrimination.[63] One is hard-pressed not to acknowledge Gandhi's deep involvement in the calculating activities of self-interested social groups seeking to extend their political power. How else is one to make sense of his strong objections to the widespread use of the general category "Coloured," which included not only blacks and

mixed-race groups, but Indians as well? Note, for example, the instrumentalist tone in his cool comments on a large 1906 meeting of
the Association of Coloured People in Pretoria:

> This Association of Coloured people does not include Indians, who have
> always kept aloof from that body. We believe that the Indian community
> has been wise in doing so. For, although the hardship suffered by those
> people and the Indians are almost of the same kind, the remedies are not
> identical. It is therefore proper that the two should fight out their cases,
> each in their own appropriate way. We can cite the Proclamation of 1857
> in our favor, which the Coloured people cannot.[64]

Clearly, any attempt to find comprehensive explanations for such a
detached posture would greatly benefit from sophisticated instrumentalist models that stress the maximization of material benefits
through strong social mechanisms of inclusion and exclusion.[65]

On the other hand, explanations stressing only instrumentalist
factors can hardly account for the full range of motives fueling
Gandhi's attitude toward black Africans. There is very little doubt
that, in addition to his willingness to follow instrumentalist imperatives, he also shared some of the quite irrational prejudices of his
class concerning black people: "In this respect he became a segre-
gationist, albeit a liberal one, arguing for a special status for his own
people while objecting to the treatment given to the Black
Africans."[66] Indeed, the effects of such exclusionary emotions on
the formulation of new discriminatory policies is obvious in the
following revealing incident cited by James Hunt. One of the first
political "victories" of the Natal Indian Congress, which Gandhi
helped to establish, was the creation of a third separate entrance to
the Durban Post Office: "The first was for the Whites, but previously Indians had to share the second with the Blacks. Though they
would have preferred to enter with the Whites, they were satisfied
with achieving a triple segregation."[67]

Gandhi's patronizing attitude toward the "underdeveloped Kaffir" indicates the degree to which his own conceptual orientation
had been shaped by the moderate liberal ideology of difference and
its underlying sentiments of racial superiority. In his speeches to Indian audiences as well as in his petitions to the colonial authorities,
Gandhi consistently protested the "degradation sought to be inflicted upon us by the [South African] Europeans, who desire to de-

grade us to the level of the raw Kaffir whose occupation is hunting, and whose sole ambition is to collect a certain number of cattle to buy a wife with and, then, pass his life in indolence and nakedness."[68] While considering Indian civilization far superior to that of black South Africans, he nonetheless emphasized the natives' right to be treated with dignity. During the 1906 Zulu Rebellion, Gandhi organized a small Indian ambulance platoon that extended its services to wounded Zulus when no other British unit was willing to tend to black African casualties in the war. In his book *Satyagraha in South Africa,* written in India in the 1920s, Gandhi argued that Zulus "are not the barbarians we imagine them to be"[69] At the same time, he qualified such statements by stressing that "civilization is only gradually making headway among the Negroes," thus accepting Victorian cultural prejudices in the construction of the "primitive" Other. As Peter Robb observes, even when he was writing in praise of Zulus, Gandhi "could still call them 'innocent children of nature,' 'timid' and 'not used to hard work.'"[70]

As late as 1909—well into his nonviolent *satyagraha* campaigns against South Africa's racist laws—Gandhi observed "with regret" that some Indian prisoners were "happy to sleep in the same room as Kaffirs." "This is a matter of shame to us [Indians]," he concluded, since "we cannot ignore the fact that there is no common ground between them and us in the daily affairs of life."[71] While these vivid examples of Gandhi's exclusivist stance vis-à-vis blacks are not sufficient to establish his complicity in proto-apartheid policies, they are nonetheless clear indicators of the psychological violence inherent in his construction of the African Other. As will become even more obvious in subsequent chapters, such persistent patterns of conceptual and cultural forms of violence in Gandhi's nonviolent nationalism cast some doubts on his professed ability to resolve the dilemma of reconciling ethical principles and political power.

Overall, then, the textual evidence assembled in this chapter suggests that Gandhi's early reliance on hard boundaries of inclusion ("us") and exclusion ("them") should not be read as an example of Indian racial prejudice encouraged by tendencies in pre-existing, non-European modes of identity.[72] Rather, his participation in a racially-based discourse of superiority draws consistently on images and ideas lodged in nineteenth-century European traditions that tend to justify the oppression of one people by another by ideal constructions of nation and race. As Robert Ross emphasizes, "racist ideologies clearly in part derived from the experience of Europeans in colonizing and exploiting the overseas world."[73] According to this reading, then, Gandhi's subsequent attempts in *Hind Swaraj* to construct an Indian national identity on the basis of morality, culture, and geography derived to a large extent from "some of the most naive cultural essentialisms of Orientalist thought."[74]

MORE DISAPPOINTMENTS

Predictably, Gandhi's emphasis on an Indo-Aryan identity shared in common by Indians and Britons did little to advance his political cause. In fact, the situation in South Africa grew worse as the Transvaal government prepared a new Asiatic Law Amendment Ordinance ("Black Ordinance") in 1906, requiring all Indians to be fingerprinted and carry a certificate of registration at all times. Gandhi was incensed at this new attempt to humiliate Asian immigrants. Up to this point, he had believed that, by and large, British rule in India and South Africa was beneficial and had brought order and security of life and property to the colonized. He had argued that most of the "defects" and "temporary aberrations" of colonial rule could be overcome by persistent expressions of loyalty on the part of its Indian subjects. Emphasizing the alleged "inborn loyal spirit of the [Indian] people," Gandhi had consistently placed himself within the developmentalist paradigm of moderate liberals like Ilbert, Hume, and Gokhale, hoping that the principle of racial equality would be put into effect completely once the colonial authorities saw their Indian subjects expressing their loyalty through such extraordinary acts as volunteering to serve in the Indian ambulance corps organized by Gandhi during the British War efforts in the 1899–1901 Boer War and the 1906 Zulu Revolt. Moreover, South Asian immigrants had proven their faith in the imperial order by rejecting violent or extraparliamentary methods of protest against discriminatory laws.[75]

However, after a decade of rather fruitless constitutional agitation in Natal and the Transvaal, an exasperated Gandhi began to doubt whether the British were really prepared to live up to the egalitarian pretensions of liberal theory. Having previously praised the British sense of justice, "even if its full realization will take a long time," he now openly announced in *Indian Opinion* that London's passivity in the face of systemic injustices in South Africa made "a permanent estrangement between India and the Colonies merely a question of time, and however insignificant India may appear in the estimation of the Colonies at the present moment, a time must shortly come when they will recognize the mistake; only it may then be too late."[76] The new threat to Indian civil rights in Transvaal posed by the Black Ordinance greatly facilitated the radicalization of Gandhi's political outlook. In a mass meeting held in Johannesburg's Empire Theatre on September 11, 1906, three thousand Indian immigrants from every corner of the Transvaal solemnly declared that they would never submit to this demeaning ordinance.[77] Ascending the rostrum, Gandhi explained to his receptive audience the wide-ranging implications of their oath in breaking this unjust law:

> We may have to go to jail, where we may be insulted. We may have to go hungry and suffer extreme heat or cold. Hard labor may be imposed on us. We may be flogged by rude warders. We may be fined heavily and our property may be attached and held up to auction if there are only a few resisters left. Opulent today we may be reduced to abject poverty tomorrow. We may be deported. Suffering from starvation and similar hardships in jail, some of us may fall ill and even die. In short, therefore, it is not at all impossible that we may have to endure every hardship that we can imagine, and wisdom lies in pledging ourselves on the understanding that we shall have to suffer all that and worse. If some one asks me when and how that struggle may end, I may say that if the entire community manfully stands the test, the end will be near. If many of us fall back under storm and stress, the struggle will be prolonged. But I can boldly declare, and with certainty, that so long as there is even a handful of men true to their pledge, there can only be one end to the struggle, and that is victory.[78]

At last, Gandhi had come to the conclusion that the racial equality promised by the 1858 Proclamation would only be extended to those who were prepared to fight for it. The central question revolved around the choice of appropriate means for the struggle. Vowing to remain committed to nonviolence, Gandhi nonetheless contemplated for the first time taking his efforts for racial justice beyond constitutional methods of protest.[79] Yet, before embarking on such defiant acts against colonial authority, he urged that all legal and constitutional methods be exhausted to prevent the Black Ordinance from becoming law. After a few weeks of bombarding the government with long memorials and petitions, the Transvaal British Indian Association authorized Gandhi and the Muslim merchant

H. O. Ally to travel to England to present Lord Elgin, the Secretary of State for the Colonies, with a petition urging that London withhold its assent to the ordinance. On October 20, 1906, Gandhi stepped ashore at Southampton, returning to England for the first time since leaving the country as a newly qualified barrister fifteen years before. Reluctantly adopting the dress and manners of an English lobbyist, he marshaled support among respected British public figures, presenting London with a message delivered in the acceptable vocabulary of the British constitution.[80]

After three months of exhausting negotiations, Gandhi returned to South Africa, confident that his efforts had been successful. It soon became evident, however, that Lord Elgin had engaged in a shrewd strategy of deception. In order to placate the Indian petitioners, he had notified the Transvaal Commissioner in London that the King would disallow the registration ordinance, knowing full and well that Transvaal would cease to be a Crown Colony in a few months. The new self-government could then reenact the ordinance, making royal assent a mere formality.[81] Led by Louis Botha, the Transvaal government proceeded to do just that, and Colonial Secretary J. C. Smuts made sure that the Asiatic Law Amendment Bill was rushed through the newly constituted legislature. Known as the "Black Act," the law took effect on July 1, 1907, requiring all Indians to register within a month. Condemning Lord Elgin's "crooked policy," which he now saw had helped pave the way for these developments, a frustrated Gandhi called for the organization of nonviolent acts of "passive resistance" or *satyagraha* ("firmness to a truthful cause") through which Indians would express their refusal to obey the stipulations of law. Over the next two years, Gandhi's prediction of ensuing hardships for the nonviolent protesters came to pass. Repeatedly arrested and fined, he was eventually sentenced to several prison terms lasting up to six months, some of which included hard labor.

While still remaining committed to peaceful negotiations with the Transvaal authorities, the combative attorney had lost much faith in the British Constitution as applied in practice. His understanding of loyalty had been altered to the point where he assumed that a general sense of allegiance to the Crown was compatible with his heightened nationalist feelings, his discovery of *satyagraha,* and his growing rejection of modern civilization: "My notion of loyalty does not involve acceptance of current rule or government, irrespective of its righteousness or otherwise. Such a notion is based upon the belief—not in its present justice or morality—but in a future acceptance by Government of that standard of morality in practice which it at present vaguely and hypocritically believes in, in theory."[82] As P. H. M. van den Dungen points out, Gandhi no longer harbored loyalty to the empire in the ordinary sense of the word, and certainly not to the extent that he had expressed it before 1906: "The most vital point, however, is that his loyalty, however sincere, placed not the least restraint on his nationalist aspirations or his desire to offer satyagraha in India. Gandhi's formulation of loyalty in these terms was something of an achievement. It satisfied the needs of the South African struggle, it assuaged Gandhi's conscience and gave ample scope to his idealism."[83]

But the one irritation Gandhi's new understanding of loyalty could not soothe was his burning desire to be acknowledged as an equal to Her Majesty's European subjects. Seen from this angle, then, his lengthy confrontation with South Africa's exclusionary system of difference had not achieved its primary objective of securing full political recognition for Indians. By 1909, London's rather indifferent attitude toward the plight of South Asian immigrants in Natal and the Transvaal had turned Gandhi from a strong supporter of the British empire into a cultural nationalist who dreamed of the moral regeneration of India's "ancient civilization." The argument that such anticolonial nationalist visions are largely the products of uprooted, discontented intellectuals torn between the conflicting forces of tradition and modernization is not a new one. Elie Kedourie and other scholars of nationalism have provided incisive examples of indigenous intellectuals who initially embraced an apparently superior Western civilization and its ideals of impersonal merit and impartial justice, but then became bitterly disappointed as they found themselves unable to escape persistent patterns of exclusion and racial discrimination. Ultimately, their ensuing self-doubt and identity crisis gave way to a search for theoretical and political solutions to their alienation.[84]

Gandhi's career in South Africa fits Kedourie's analysis to a remarkable degree. Having rejected the traditional expectations and demands of his caste, the young professional had imbibed British manners and ideas only to discover that his willingness to assimilate into Western ways would never be rewarded with the recognition he so craved from his European counterparts. Growing in his role as a "critical outsider," the disaffected attorney eventually expressed his mounting frustration with the European paradigm in *Hind Swaraj,* his sole sustained treatise of political theory. The genesis of this highly influential monograph, together with the examination of Gandhi's comprehensive critique of liberalism and its underlying assumptions about the superiority of Western civilization, will be the subject of the next chapter.

3

GANDHI'S CRITIQUE OF LIBERALISM

❧

Exposing the Immorality of Modern Civilization

*The condition of England at present is pitiable. I pray to God that India may
never be in that plight. . . . If India copies England, it is my firm conviction that
she will be ruined. . . . It is not due to any particular fault of the English people, but the condition is due to modern civilization.*

—M. K. Gandhi[1]

When Gokhale saw the translation [of Hind Swaraj*], he thought it so crude
and hastily conceived that he prophesied that Gandhi himself would destroy the
book after spending a year in India.*

—D. G. Tendulkar[2]

NATIONALIST STIRRINGS:
GANDHI'S ROAD TO *HIND SWARAJ*

As emphasized in the previous chapter, it was not until the
middle of the first decade of the twentieth century that
Gandhi became openly critical of British liberalism and its
cultural ideals. Gradually, he allowed himself to express his nationalist feelings in stronger terms than ever before. The Russo-Japanese
war of 1904–5 heralded this new period in his life and focused his
sympathies entirely toward the new Asian power. P. H. M. van den
Dungen observes that this conflict contributed greatly to Gandhi's

"first great emotional espousal of nationalism" as he held up Japan's national sentiment and unity as an example to be followed by Indians.[3] For one already committed to the ideal of nonviolence, Gandhi sounded strangely enthusiastic, reporting to the readership of *Indian Opinion* that in spite of the "utter destruction" of over a hundred thousand men on both sides, "courage and endurance have not been wanting under any test."[4] Further pursuing this line of argument, he claimed that "Japan has been able to take the fort of Port Arthur only because she has been fighting with fervour. Fervour is as necessary in other tasks as it is in war, and it is a positive virtue."[5] Repeatedly praising Japanese soldiers for their acts of bravery and self-sacrifice, Gandhi pointed to the relevance of these qualities for his own ongoing struggle in South Africa:

> What, then, is the secret of this epic heroism? We have repeatedly to ask ourselves this question and find an answer for it. The answer is: unity, patriotism and the resolve to do or die. All the Japanese are animated by the same spirit. . . . They think of nothing else but service to the nation. They have so identified themselves with their motherland that they consider themselves prosperous [only] if they bring prosperity to the country in which they are born. . . . This unity and patriotic spirit together with a heroic indifference to life [or death] have created an atmosphere in Japan the like of which is nowhere else to be found in the world. Of death, they do not entertain any fear. To die in the service of their country, they have always regarded as wholly good. If, after all, one has to die some day, what does it matter if one dies on the battle-field? . . . But how will these thoughts avail us? What have we to learn from them? We do not find the requisite unity even in the minor struggle we are carrying on in South Africa; splits occur every day. Instead of patriotism, we see more of selfishness everywhere. . . . Our life is so dear to us that we pass away while we are still fondling it. . . . This is the condition most of us are in. Our reading of the account of the Japanese War will have been fruitful only if we emulate to some extent at least the example of Japan.[6]

Written only a year before the first major *satyagraha* protest in Transvaal, this passage reaffirms not only Gandhi's burning desire to forge Indians into a unified body required for effective political action, but it also shows his growing attraction to the notion of individual self-sacrifice for the sake of the nation. Gandhi seems to have assumed in rather uncritical fashion that the patriotic qualities of soldiers could be utilized as well by the participants in a nonviolent campaign. Throughout his life, he would remain fascinated by "the valour and patriotism often displayed by persons in arms."[7] Indeed, as will be discussed in chapter 6, he adopted the soldierly resolution to "do or die" as his favorite slogan during the 1942 Quit India movement.[8]

In the early fall of 1905, shortly after the victory of Japan, Gandhi received the exciting news of a large-scale *swadeshi* (things pertaining to one's own country; self reliance) campaign directed against the planned partition of Bengal according to Viceroy Curzon's orders. Tilak, Gokhale, Lala Lajpat Rai, the leader of the Hindu revivalist organization Arya Samaj, and other nationalists were convinced that the partition was a deliberate ploy to destroy their Hindu power base in Bengal. Urging people to boycott and burn British clothing and other goods, the *swadeshi* movement gathered so much strength throughout India that it even led to a revival of the old Indian cottage industry of hand-spinning and weaving.[9] Although the movement came more and more under the control of the Congress's radical faction led by Tilak, Gandhi readily supported the weapon of boycott, convinced that "Great Britain will be put to great loss; and the Government can have no means of dealing with it. They cannot compel the people to carry on trade. The method is very straight and simple."[10]

As during the Russo-Japanese War, Gandhi harped on the theme of patriotism and self-sacrifice, emphasizing that the success of *swadeshi* in India depended on whether Indians would maintain the requisite unity and whether merchants would be willing to curb their material interests and suffer for the good of the country: "If we can answer both these questions in the affirmative, India can be said to have truly woken up."[11] Increasingly accusing the British raj of ruling India in an oppressive manner, Gandhi linked the political events in South Asia with the erupting 1905 revolution in Russia. In uncharacteristically harsh language, he pointed to similarities between the autocratic Czarist government and the British colonial government in India, warning that, "We, too, can resort to the Russian remedy against tyranny. The movement in Bengal for the use of *swadeshi* goods is much like the Russian movement. Our shackles will break this very day, if the people of India become united and patient, love their country, and think of the well-being of their motherland disregarding their self-interest."[12]

In addition to playing a crucial role in fueling the South African lawyer's growing nationalist aspirations, the means employed by the leaders of the Bengali *swadeshi* movement also exerted a tremendous influence on the development of Gandhi's own nationalist thought as well as on his nonviolent method of *satyagraha*. Ideally, *swadeshi* was touted as a way of resisting the sense of cultural inferiority inculcated by European domination without hurting the colonizer. In the popular imagination, however, it was often tantamount to the wholesale rejection of Western styles and habits and an emphasis on the superiority of Indian customs.[13] This uneasy coexistence of universalist and exclusivist impulses in the philosophy of *swadeshi* prefigured to some extent Gandhi's own dilemma.

Evidence for the ways in which these inherited tensions compelled Gandhi's conceptual universe can be detected in something as trivial as his views on national anthems. He reported to the readers of *Indian Opinion* that millions of *swadeshi* followers had gathered in various Indian cities and sung *Bande Maataram* ("I bow to Thee O Mother"), a poem composed by the famous Bengali novelist Bankimchandra Chattopadhyay, which describes India as the land of flowing rivers, fertile fields, and lush forests. These images in themselves were not as problematic as the concept of bowing to the Mother. In fact, Bankimchandra's poem is part of *Anandamath* (1882), a novel that contains strong anti-Muslim language. For example, it describes Hindu warriors dressed in saffron robes who ride out to do battle with the enemy by first bowing to Mother India. The terms used to refer to the "enemy" are often words like *yavan,* which were employed to refer to Muslims and other "foreigners" in the past, such as the Greeks. Moreover, "Mother India" was commonly anthropomorphized by Hindus to resemble one of the Brahmanic goddesses.

Naturally, Indian Muslims had serious problems with Bankimchandra's poem and its symbolism. The deification and anthropomorphizing of Mother India violated Islamic religious norms, as did the imperative to bow before any god but Allah. Given his close relationship with Indian Muslims in South Africa, Gandhi must have been aware of these reservations. Still, he suggested that *Bande Maataram* might serve as a fitting national anthem for India. Pulled along by the exclusivism of Bengali upper-caste nationalism, he added the following invidious comparison: "It [Bankimchandra's song] is nobler in sentiment and sweeter than the song of other nations. While other anthems contain sentiments that are derogatory to others, *Bande Maataram* is free from such faults. Its only aim is to arouse in us a sense of patriotism."[14] In other words, the Bengali song was superior to other countries' national anthems because it supposedly praised the virtues of the "Motherland" in a more inclusivist language! As has been pointed out above, however, there was little "inclusivism" in the song. In fact, the Indian National Congress rejected it in favor of a more inclusive poem composed by Tagore. To this day, *Bande Maataram* has remained the rallying anthem of Hindu nationalists. In the 1990s, a common slogan hurled at Muslims by Hindu nationalists was, "*Agar is desh mein rehna hoga, to vande maataram kehna hoga*" ("If you are to stay in this country then you will have to sing *Bande Maataram*").[15]

As Gandhi adjusted the terminology of patriotism and war to suit the purposes of his own nonviolence campaigns of 1907–8, the broader implications of his agitation in South Africa began to dawn on him. Seeing his civil rights struggle in Natal and Transvaal from this larger perspective of India's liberation from its colonial masters, Gandhi conceived of his political environment as constituting more than a mere sideshow to the great political events of his time. If South African Indians could be persuaded to subsume their ethnic, religious, and economic differences under a common identity, then such a show of unity might well send a powerful message to their compatriots at home. For Gandhi, the prospect of playing an important role in the "awakening of India" pointed to the exciting possibility that his homeland might "be forged into a nation in South Africa."[16] Addressing the task of building a strong sense of national identity, he refined his views on Indian nationalism: "The great need of India is that national characteristics should be fostered and improved. If the resolve to use only Indian goods, as far as possible, be maintained, it will be no small help in developing the national spirit."[17]

The final event which contributed to the systematic formulation of Gandhi's nationalist sentiments in *Hind Swaraj* was his unsuccessful mission to England in 1909.[18] Seeking to safeguard the interests of South African Indians, a two-man deputation consisting of himself and the Muslim merchant Haji Habib departed for London in order to prevent the incorporation of various anti-Indian policies into the new federal Union of South Africa, planned to take effect in 1910. From the beginning, Gandhi's mission suffered from the charged atmosphere created by the assassinations of Sir William Curzon-Wyllie, a political aide to the Secretary of State for India, and

Cawas Lalkaka, a Parsi doctor who was killed in his attempt to save Curzon-Wyllie's life. Madanlal Dhingra, the perpetrator of the crime, belonged to a revolutionary Indian student group led by Vinayak Damodar Savarkar, a young Hindu nationalist who advocated the use of violence in the struggle against the British raj.[19] On a previous visit to London in 1906, Gandhi had established loose contacts with the followers of Shyamji Krishnavarma, the founder of the India House in Highgate and radical editor of the nationalist monthly, *The Indian Sociologist*. While admiring the patriotism of the young revolutionaries, Gandhi had dissented vociferously from their violent blueprints for social change. In turn, the revolutionaries disliked his adherence to constitutionalism and his close contacts to Gokhale and other moderate nationalist members of the Indian Congress.[20] Moreover, they considered his method of "passive resistance" effeminate and humiliating.[21]

Still, the news surrounding Gandhi's ongoing struggle in Transvaal sufficiently piqued their interest to invite him to a festive dinner, at which he politely disagreed with Savarkar on whether the Hindu epic *Ramayana* taught violence or not. Having resolved beforehand to avoid a potentially explosive discussion of current events, both men nonetheless managed to convey to the audience their respective positions on Indian politics. There is almost unanimous agreement among scholars that Gandhi's meetings with the Indian revolutionaries living in London at the time proved to be a powerful motivating force for writing *Hind Swaraj*.[22] Written during his stay in London, his seminal letter to Lord Ampthill, the former Governor of Madras and president of the South Africa British Indian Committee, already contains a preview of his subsequent arguments in *Hind Swaraj*. While sharply critical of English rule in India, Gandhi nonetheless left no doubt about his intention to continue preaching to the revolutionaries the efficacy of nonviolence: "Opposed as I am to violence in any shape or form, I have endeavoured specially to come into contact with the so-called extremists who may be better described as the party of violence. This I have done in order to convince them of the error of their ways."[23] Moreover, Gandhi admitted to being greatly distressed about his discovery that "among the majority it [national consciousness] is in a crude shape and there is not a corresponding spirit of self-sacrifice." Already firmly linking the theme of self-sacrifice to his method of *ahimsa,* he lamented that he had hardly met any Indian in London who "believes that India can ever become free without resorting to violence."[24]

As his stay in England dragged on without producing any tangible results, Gandhi descended into a gloomy mood that was further aggravated by his reading of Edward Carpenter's *Civilization: Its Cause and Cure.* The British author's extremely negative views of modern civilization as constituting a "kind of disease which the various races of man have to pass through" echoed many of Gandhi's own New Age values, including his dogmatic vegetarianism. It also dovetailed with the conservative spirit of John Ruskin's *Unto This Last*—another book condemning the moral depravity of modern life—which Gandhi had eagerly devoured a few years earlier. Suddenly, the mighty European metropolis appeared to him no longer in the bright colors of his student years but assumed the outward manifestation of an inner spiritual and moral void: "Looking at this land, I at any rate have grown disillusioned with Western civilization. The people whom you meet on the way seem half-crazy. . . . I am definitely of the view that it is altogether undesirable for anyone to come or live here."[25]

A combination of factors—including Gandhi's nationalist sentiments, intensified by the Russo-Japanese War and the partition of Bengal; his close encounters with the Indian revolutionaries; the disappointing course of his negotiations on behalf of the South African Indians; and his tremendous attraction to Carpenter's moralistic arguments—finally pushed him to present in writing a coherent summary of his nationalist views. As Partha Chatterjee notes, *Hind Swaraj* is one of Gandhi's few existing texts in which he can be seen attempting a systematic exposition of his ideas on state, society, and nation.[26] Surprisingly, however, some scholars today are reluctant to base their evaluations of Gandhi's political thought too heavily on the booklet, claiming that he later dropped some of its rather exclusivist language in favor of a more universalistic approach.[27] The main problem with this argument, however, lies in the existence of contradictory textual evidence. Even if one concedes that Gandhi later qualified some of his most extreme attacks on modern civilization, the fact remains that he never explicitly renounced the overall thrust of his 1909 pamphlet. Quite to the contrary. As late as 1938, he maintained that "after the stormy thirty years through which I have since passed I have seen nothing to make me alter the view expounded in it [*Hind Swaraj*]."[28] Only two years before his death, he reaffirmed this judgment in a letter to Nehru: "I fully stand by the kind of governance I have described in Hind Swaraj. . . . My experience has confirmed the truth of what I wrote in 1909."[29] For this reason, the present study not only acknowledges the central place of *Hind Swaraj* in Gandhi's oeuvre, but also makes generous use of arguments contained in this seminal piece.

Returning from his disillusioning experience in London, the forty-year-old Gandhi completed the eighty-page monograph in only ten days on board the S. S. *Kildonan Castle*. Written as a dialogue between two fictional characters—a newspaper "Editor" representing Gandhi's perspective and a radical "Reader" whose political position is modeled after the views of Savarkar and Dhingra—the booklet is divided into twenty chapters, plus two appendices featuring some "testimonies by eminent men" in support of Gandhi's thesis that "the ancient Indian civilisation has little to learn from the modern."[30] All but one of the twenty-two personalities listed are European authors, including philosophers like Plato and Cousin, orientalists like Mueller and Maine, romantics like Schlegel and Ruskin, New Agers like Carpenter and Blount, and nationalists like Mazzini. The sole Indian "authority" mentioned in *Hind Swaraj* is the prominent politician Dadabhai Naroroji, who had been residing in London for decades. As Anthony J. Parel points out, Gandhi's pamphlet is addressed to a wide and disparate audience that includes not only Indian nationalists greatly attracted to violent methods of social change, but also moderate members of the Indian National Congress, ordinary Indians in Asia and South Africa, and "the English."[31]

For analytical purposes, it is useful to separate the arguments made in *Hind Swaraj* into two distinct but related discourses. Most importantly, there is Gandhi's vision of an independent nation, morally regenerated by a nonviolent nationalism that would draw heavily on the values of India's "ancient civilization;" this will be further elucidated in the next chapter. This constructive part is intertwined with his passionate indictment of British liberalism and its underlying framework of modern civilization. As previous explications have shown, a textual interpretation of *Hind Swaraj* might proceed from a variety of entry points. My own preferred reading begins with an examination of his arguments against liberal political institutions. Slowly working its way through successive layers of his criticism, my interpretation arrives at what I consider to be the core of his critical project: the attack on modern civilization and its accompanying violence. For Gandhi, modern civilization constitutes a de-based moral framework for the nation-state. In order to address some conceptual problems emerging from his exposition, it is also necessary to touch upon his views on human nature and moral autonomy.

AGAINST LIBERAL INSTITUTIONS:
PARLIAMENT AND THE MARKET

Given his long-standing admiration for the British Constitution and its underlying values, it is astonishing to see how Gandhi reserved some of his most scathing criticism for the European system of representative government, touted by Western political thinkers from Locke to Mill as the crowning political achievement of the liberal tradition. Calling British parliament "a sterile woman and a prostitute," the Editor insinuates that, like the former, "Parliament has not yet of its own accord done a single good." Moreover, like a prostitute, it is "under the control of ministers who change from time to time," acting only through the application of "outside pressure."[32] Responding to the Reader's objection that Members of Parliament are, after all, elected by the people and therefore bound to be sensitive to public pressure, the Editor embarks on a long monologue, the central message of which amounts to a stunning repudiation of petitioning, lobbying, and other constitutionalist practices that Gandhi himself had engaged in over a period of fifteen years. As he puts it in another section of the booklet: "Mere petitioning is derogatory; we thereby confess inferiority."[33]

In a nutshell, then, the Editor's arguments proceed along the following lines: As the elected servants of the people, members of parliament ought to consider themselves the guardians of the public weal. Hence, they should apply the highest moral standards to their pivotal tasks of preparing, debating, and passing legislation. Following only the dictates of their conscience, the legislators' deliberations therefore ought to be free of the spur of petitions or any other outside pressure. In Gandhi's view, parliament's "work should be so smooth that its effect would be more apparent day by day." However, the Editor also concedes as a "matter of fact" that today's politicians are hypocritical, lazy, and selfish. Echoing Thomas Carlyle's pejorative remark about parliament being the "talking-shop of the world," Gandhi proceeds to lambaste legislators for making empty speeches and allowing their moral autonomy to be restricted by the instrumentalism of party discipline. In particular, the Editor singles out the office of the Prime Minister as the clearest example of the failure of liberal political institutions. More concerned with his power than with the welfare of the people, the Prime Minister "buffets about like a prostitute." Reluctant to "do the right thing," he focuses solely on the success of his party. While the polished rhetoric of parliamentarians may sound patriotic and honest, it is in reality only a thin veil hiding their willingness to put private interests over the good of the nation: "I do not hesitate to say that they have neither real honesty nor a living conscience." On the other hand, the English electorate is deliberately manipulated and deceived by the media, particularly by "dishonest newspapers." Thus the voters are fickle and easily swayed by powerful orators who substitute appearance for substance: "As are the people, so is their Parliament." In the end, then, the Editor seems to suggest that ordinary people and their political leaders are morally bankrupt, hence there is not much in the British system of representative government that is worth salvaging: "The Parliament is simply a costly toy of the nation."[34]

At this point, it is important to raise an obvious question: Which factors does Gandhi consider to be most responsible for allowing the British people and their political leaders sink to such depths of moral depravity? Following Hobbes, Madison, and other liberal political thinkers writing in a "realist" vein, one possible response would advance the essentialist argument that selfishness and estrangement are sewn into the very fabric of human nature. Such theorists would therefore stress the importance of creating prudent constitutional designs, which, at best, might prevent the escalation of unavoidable conflict and violence. Even a cursory look at Gandhi's position regarding human nature reveals that he never explicitly involved himself in the old debate in Western political thought on whether people were naturally good or evil. Still, his views on the subject rely on an ontological perspective that married Hindu religious concepts drawn mainly from the *Bhagavad Gita* with elements of Hellenic philosophy—particularly the elevation of the spiritual aspect of human existence over its mere physical dimension.[35] Arguing that human souls were unique yet at the same time one with the cosmic spirit, Gandhi considered humans to be essentially spiritual beings, implying that each person harbored at the inner core a deep tendency toward good.[36] However, as Bhikhu Parekh notes, this does not mean that Gandhi held that human beings always loved and pursued good, "for they often lacked true self-knowledge, were subject to the body-based illusion of particularity, and their *swabhava* [unique psychological and moral constitution] might dispose them to do evil. All it meant was that human beings had a deep-seated capacity to perceive and pursue good and would act on it *if* that capacity were to be awakened and activated."[37]

What kind of answer does Gandhi's theory of human nature yield to our question about the source of human moral corruption? It appears that there are a number of possible candidates. First, the successful activation of the good tendencies in human beings might depend on examples set by persons who are morally and spiritually more developed than the rest of society. For that reason, Gandhi emphasized time and again the importance of spiritual leadership, arguing that the real purpose of life—manifested in one's striving for ever greater realizations of "truth" through dedicated service to the poor and marginalized—would be greatly facilitated by capable moral guides. As the Editor puts it in *Hind Swaraj,* "If the money and time wasted by the Parliament were entrusted to a few good men, the English nation would be occupying today a much higher platform."[38] Second, Gandhi's philosophical anthropology also allows the conclusion that the awakening of people's goodness by ethical leaders was impossible without the existence of a conducive external environment reflected in just political institutions, an other-regarding economy, and a tolerant culture. Indeed, *Hind Swaraj* puts a strong emphasis on the pivotal role played by structural forces in improving or corrupting public morality. Finally, one might also argue the exact opposite, namely that Gandhi's theory of human nature implies, first and foremost, an abiding commitment to the notion of moral autonomy.[39] Highlighting the individual's obligation to resist selfish desires and the lure of materialism, he frequently reminded his followers that moral agents must assume ultimate responsibility for the activation of their good tendencies: "A moral act must be our own act. . . . How can a man understand morality who does not use his own intelligence and power of thought but lets himself be swept along like a log of wood by a current?"[40]

Obviously, each of these possible answers implies a different remedy for the moral corruption of society. For example, the emphasis on individual responsibility would appeal to a personal project of reform, while highlighting the role of external forces would suggest the importance of structural change. Unfortunately, Gandhi's writings on the subject of social change are ambiguous at best and contradictory at worst, never indicating clearly which of these paths he considered to be most promising for the moral improvement of humans and their political institutions. Throughout the pages of *Hind Swaraj,* he employed all of the above options either separately or, at different times, in combination. Consequently, the Editor fails to give consistent answers to questions that are of immense practical importance for any emancipatory project: Who are the agents of social change? Where does one start in the process of "awakening the nation"? In an age characterized by widespread moral corruption and violence (*kali yuga*), how does the individual break through the barriers of ignorance fostered by a hegemonic "Satanic civilization"?

On the final page of *Hind Swaraj,* the Editor assures his readers that he bears no enmity toward particular individuals or the English people as such, but only toward the social system they represent.[41] One cannot help but wonder at such statements. Was Gandhi simply unaware that he was contradicting his own belief that the ultimate foundation of any system was always comprised of real people bound to specific moral duties?[42] Or was he perhaps intentionally depersonalizing his critique of liberalism for fear of possible political repercussions? Both these possibilities contain serious problems for Gandhi. The former opens the door for people to blame structural forces for their moral inadequacies, meaning that individuals can no longer be held accountable for their actions. This can hardly be reconciled with Gandhi's belief in moral autonomy, which forms the backbone of his theory of nonviolence as presented in the introduction to this study. After all, *satyagrahic* action is conceivable only within a philosophical framework that emphasizes a person's responsibility to choose an ethical course of action even in an immoral environment. Raising once again the specter of instrumentalism, the latter possibility is equally disconcerting, for it would suggest that Gandhi allowed his ethical principles to be overpowered by cold political calculations. If this was indeed his intention, he failed to achieve the objective.[43]

These caveats are not intended as a wholesale rejection of Gandhi's understanding of human nature. For example, as Parekh observes, by stressing both human identity and difference, it "left ample ontological space for autonomy and diversity."[44] Still, the conceptual versatility contained in Gandhi's rejection of the split between the personal and the social is offset by its vagueness with regard to the origin of human corruption. It is as though he seems to be saying that, removed from their roles and their environments, the good tendencies in human beings always shine forth; however, in their concrete embodiments as "lawyers" or "politicians," people tend to fall prey to their selfish tendencies.[45] As will be shown in chapter 6 of this study, Gandhi's idealist vision of human goodness abstracted from the evils of materiality was bound to clash with the contingencies of the political arena.

In the end, then, *Hind Swaraj* provides no clear answer to the question of which factors are ultimately responsible for the moral depravity of British politicians and their system of representative government. However, one is on safe ground in asserting that large portions of the booklet highlight the impact of impersonal structures on the moral status of the individual. Engaging in such a structuralist analysis, the Editor continues his critique of liberalism with a broadside against the economic system underlying British political institutions. For him, the most severe flaw of capitalism consists in divorcing economic activity from moral considerations. Even worse, it allows people to celebrate their selfish and material impulses as the necessary engine for "progress" measured purely in terms of "luxuries that money can buy." Noting that the capitalist search for profit has threatened traditional ways of life based on moral precepts, the Editor fears an ensuing conversion of the whole world into a vast market for consumer goods.[46]

Providing a concrete example of how the economics and politics of liberalism join hands to keep people "enslaved by the temptation of money," the Editor reminds the Reader that the political domination of South Asia began with British attempts to open the Indian market to European trade: "Napoleon is said to have described the English as a nation of shopkeepers. It is a fitting description. They hold whatever dominions they have for the sake of their commerce. Their army and their navy are intended to protect it."[47] Recounting the exploits of the East India Company, he continues his train of thought: "That corporation was versed alike in commerce and war. It was unhampered by questions of morality. Its object was to increase its commerce and to make money."[48] The result of these efforts was the establishment of the British empire and the destruction of small, self-sufficient village communities that used to be perfectly capable of producing enough goods to satisfy their basic needs. Instead, capitalism encourages the formation of large urban centers full of "gangs of thieves and robbers, prostitution and vice"—modern cities that artificially multiply people's materialistic tendencies at the expense of their spiritual health and moral uprightness.[49]

Finally, echoing a central theme in Marxist thought, the Editor speaks of the fundamental alienation that accompanies the limitless expansion of capitalism. Having been enticed by their capitalist environment to judge everything and everyone in terms of money, people treat each other merely as means to a materialistic end. In particular, Gandhi focuses on the professional classes, who, instead of setting a moral example for the rest of society, have eagerly exchanged a genuine concern for community for an isolated life of luxury. For example, medical doctors, in alliance with modern pharmaceutical industries, encourage people to indulge their appetites in order to make them dependent on expensive medication and treatments: "It is worth considering why we take up the profession of medicine. It is certainly not taken up for the purpose of serving humanity. We become doctors so that we may obtain honours and riches."[50] Likewise, it is self-interest and greed that induce otherwise capable persons to become lawyers, "not in order to help others out of their misery, but to enrich themselves. It is one of the avenues of becoming wealthy, and their interest exists in multiplying disputes." In the case of India, the selfishness of indigenous lawyers also contributes to the power of English authority. After all, "without lawyers, courts could not have been established or conducted, and without the latter the English could not rule." Business people, too, contribute to the strength of the empire: "I fear we have to admit that moneyed men support British rule; their interest is bound up with its stability."[51]

Indeed, the intended targets of the Editor's critique of the unfettered market were both British and Indian capitalists: "And those who have amassed wealth out of factories are not likely to be better than other men. It would be folly to assume that an Indian Rockefeller would be better than the American Rockefeller."[52] Being an attorney himself, Gandhi was obviously willing to shoulder his share of the blame. By engaging in such an admirable act of self-criticism, he implicitly acknowledged that he, too, was suspended in the web of alienation spun by the political and economic institutions of liberalism. But in order to escape the threads of self-interest that kept them in perpetual captivity, Indians had to go beyond the furious thrashing about of the revolutionary nationalists. True liberation from British domination meant unsettling the very foundation that gave the web its stability, and thereby its power to enmesh new victims. In short, the attainment of *hind swaraj* depended on the transformation of modern civilization.

AGAINST MODERN CIVILIZATION
AND ITS RELIANCE ON VIOLENCE

As pointed out by Mark Francis, the nineteenth century saw a major shift in the European discourse of "civilization." Victorian thinkers gradually jettisoned old eighteenth-century associations between civilization and refinement of manners and between civilization and social order in favor of a new meaning of the term that portrayed the accumulation of material wealth as a rational quality supposedly lacking in an indigenous people. By the turn of the century, this understanding of civilization according to criteria of wealth and technology had become even more dominant, often complemented by extreme forms of racism.[53] Rejecting this narrow identification of rationality with material progress, Gandhi argued that civilization was primarily a moral concept. It referred to an ethical way of life, guided by a "mode of conduct which points out to man the path of duty. Performance of duty and observance of morality are convertible terms. To observe morality is to attain mastery over our mind and our passions. So doing, we know ourselves. The Gujarati equivalent for civilisation means 'good conduct.'"[54] This definition conveys the Editor's conviction that it was indeed possible to assign positive or negative value to human actions according to whether a person made "bodily or spiritual welfare the object of life."[55] Building on his central idea that humans were essentially spiritual beings exposed to the pernicious influence of material forces, Gandhi's critical enterprise contained at its core a fundamental dualism that saw the world in terms of an epic struggle between Rama and Ravana, good and evil, hopefully ending in the victory of spirit over matter. From this fundamental dichotomy flowed many other binaries he employed so generously in *Hind Swaraj;* most importantly, the crucial distinction between "ancient" and "modern" civilization.

As opposed to the former, which connoted for Gandhi an ethos of truth, purity, righteousness, and nonviolence, the latter implied the presence of materialistic tendencies and *adharma* (irreligion). Hence, much like civilization, the Editor conceives of modernity not merely as a concept capturing objective phenomena in the world or describing a particular historical period, but a deluded state of mind fostering an uncaring attitude toward the self and the cosmos. Dedicated only to the multiplication of bodily pleasures and the accumulation of material possessions, modernity enslaved both colonizers and the colonized. Once again veering away from the idea of moral autonomy, the Editor argues that individual members of British society should not be blamed for the pitiful conditions brought about by modern civilization. In fact, "they rather deserve our sympathy. They are a shrewd nation and I, therefore, believe that they will cast off the evil. They are enterprising and industrious, and their mode of thought is not inherently immoral. Neither are they bad at heart. I, therefore, respect them. Civilization is not an incurable disease, but it should never be forgotten that the English people are at present afflicted by it."[56] Relying more on rhetorical hyperbole than reasoned argument, the Editor never pauses to explain to his audience how the Europeans' "shrewdness" and "industry," which brought about modernity, might also be the causes for the opposite trajectory.

In the fiery language of the Editor, the term "modern" turns into a synonym for a plethora of incriminating adjectives ranging from "warlike" and "diseased" to "evil" and "satanic." In other words, "real" civilization, understood as "good conduct," is inconceivable within the framework of modernity, because the latter "takes note neither of morality nor of religion." Nurturing people's selfish tendencies and worldly ambitions, modernity entices humans to turn their backs on the divine principle that pervades the whole universe. Human desires are thus no longer limited by moral injunctions that derive from the acknowledgment of the underlying oneness of all beings. Instead, in the crowning act of human hubris, "reason" is shorn of its moral essence and celebrated as value-free science operating through a detached calculation of means and ends. It comes as no surprise, then, that the Editor pours much of his moral outrage into elaborate tirades against railroads, tramways, airplanes, cloth-mills, and other articles of machinery created by the forces of technology and industry: "Machinery is the chief symbol of modern civilisation; it represents a great sin. . . . It is necessary to realise that machinery is bad. We shall then be able gradually to do away with it."[57] In Gandhi's view, instead of providing a less onerous life for all members of society, technology and industry invited inequality and misery in the form of "structural violence," to use a felicitous term introduced by Johan Galtung some time ago. "The workers in the mills of Bombay become slaves. The condition of the women working in the mills is shocking. When there were no mills, these women were not starving. If the machine craze grows in our country, it will become an unhappy land."[58]

Most importantly, then, Gandhi argued that modern civilization was an intrinsically violent phenomenon, for it violated the natural hierarchy of being as expressed in his postulation of the primacy of the spirit. According to the Editor, the exercise of "brute force" always contains great spiritual harm, because it confirms and propagates the deluded view that the physical dimension of human existence represents the ultimate good.[59] The British reliance on violence in their conquest of India should therefore not be considered as proof of the superiority of their modern civilization, but rather as a symptom of "the disease that is eating into the vitals of their nation."[60] The Editor even goes so far as to suggest that the seemingly ethical struggle of British liberals to extend the vote and other political rights to previously excluded segments of the population was tainted by the violent means employed in the process. Preaching the immorality of separating means and ends, he instead conveys his view that "real rights are a result of performance of duty; these rights they have not obtained. We, therefore, have before us in England the farce of everybody wanting and insisting on his rights, nobody thinking of his duty."[61] Obviously, the duty referred to in this passage alludes to the primary spiritual obligation to abstain from the use of violence.

Finally, in a powerful passage that connects the practice of nonviolence to the virtue of courage, the Editor suggests that only ignorant people can confuse the cowardice inherent in the application of brute force with bravery. Seen from Gandhi's "higher" spiritual perspective, which provided the rationale for his *satyagraha* campaigns, real fortitude involved nothing less than the voluntary sacrifice of life and limb in defense of moral principles. Rejecting the Reader's revolutionary argument that only brave patriots are prepared to take up arms in the struggle to free the nation, the Editor explains the link between nonviolence and courage in more detail: "Wherein is courage required—in blowing others to pieces behind a cannon or with a smiling face to approach a cannon and be blown to pieces? Who is the true warrior—he who keeps death always as a bosom-friend or he who controls the death of others? Believe me that a man devoid of courage and manhood can never be a passive resister."[62] As Ved Mehta observes, what an astonishingly violent defense of nonviolence![63]

To be sure, the debate between the Editor and the Reader involves more than just the elucidation of a philosophical principle. Indeed, the former intends to undermine the claim of revolutionary Indian nationalists that the British could only be forced to leave the country by violent methods, including terror, assassinations, and guerrilla warfare.[64] Gandhi's discussion of violence within the framework of his critique of modern civilization reveals, therefore, not only his rationale against the *weltanschauung* of the European colonizers, but also the ultimate reason for his rejection of both the extremists' radicalism and the moderates' constitutionalism. Both factions, in their own ways, betrayed their attachment to an immoral, "foreign" paradigm. The revolutionaries' fervent advocacy of violence made them adherents to the same gospel of materialism as their enemies. For Gandhi, they merely "want English rule without the Englishman. You want the tiger's nature, but not the tiger; that is to say, you would make India English. . . ."[65] Employing the same brute force as their masters, the revolutionaries—even if successful—would merely create another "Englistan." Thus, an independent India born of violent resistance would have failed to build its national identity on a necessary break with modern civilization.

While disavowing the methods of the extremists, the moderates, too, embraced the evils of modern civilization in their willing acceptance of the developmentalist scheme of liberalism. By admitting that British rule was indispensable until Indians had recreated themselves in the image of their masters, moderates like Gokhale mistakenly acknowledged the superiority of the European model and its ideology of difference. For the Editor, such a thoughtless embrace of the materialistic ethos of modern civilization amounted to the sin of blasphemy, the "denial of the Godhead."[66] Forged by the adharmic spirit of the moderates, an independent India would merely recreate the immoral political and economic institutions of European liberalism: "Parliaments are really emblems of slavery."[67] In that sense, then, the new nation could be called "free" only if one acceded to the corrupted vocabulary of modern civilization.

CONCLUSION

As pointed out in chapter 1, education was one of the ways in which liberalism and empire sought to maintain their hegemony in overseas colonies. The objective was to shape the minds and bodies of an indigenous intellectual elite in such a way that they would come to understand reality according to European concepts of "development." Such views were perhaps best expressed in a 1905 speech given by Lord Curzon at Calcutta University, where he declared that "the highest ideal of truth is to a large extent a Western conception" and that "undoubtedly truth took a high place in the moral codes of the West before it had been similarly honoured in the East, where craftiness and diplomatic vile have always been held in much repute."[68]

By 1909, Gandhi, the former assimilationist and "son of the empire," had produced an angry response, repudiating the moral superiority of the West. Echoing some of the powerful sentiments associated with a long line of Romantics from Tolstoy to Rousseau, he served notice to his masters that he was no longer in awe of their achievements. His critique exposed the immorality of modern civilization, implying that modern nation-states were built on a shaky foundation. As a result, *Hind Swaraj* radically undermined the attempts of liberal ideologists of difference to link the universalist language of reason to the culturally specific norms of British society, thereby allowing the latter to claim for itself the maturity and the knowledge necessary to dispel the clouds of ignorance hovering over the world's "undeveloped" regions. Emphasizing that the experiences and cultures of non-European peoples were far from being provisional and incomplete, Gandhi ultimately undermined the moral and political authority of the empire, suggesting that the British had never been in a position to judge at what point a particular colony had achieved a sufficiently high level of development to be permitted to rule itself.

Representing a total moral critique of modern civilization, *Hind Swaraj* suggests that its author did not seek to reform the social relationships of modernity; he rejected modernity itself.[69] Modernity, in short, becomes the source of evil as technology, machinery, and the modern state are brought into play as alienating modes of instrumental thinking: individual conscience degenerates and conformity increases. In spite of his harsh rhetoric, Gandhi claimed to steer clear of personal attacks, instead launching a comprehensive assault against the impersonal workings of an "evil system." Although he conceded that modern civilization had been born in Europe and that countries like England were responsible for spreading it to every corner of the earth, Gandhi often portrayed ordinary British citizens as ignorant and weak-willed victims of materialism. In other portions of the text, however, one can detect his return to notions of moral autonomy and the individual's responsibility to resist evil—a model that was more consistent with his theory of nonviolence. Such passages portrayed the British as brutal invaders who had never learned to rule over their selfish tendencies, and thus failed to understand the "inner," moral meaning of *swaraj*. This deplorable lack of self-discipline on the part of the British had led to the strengthening of their materialist interests, which, in turn, were responsible for the personal and structural violence at the heart of imperialism. Anchored in ignorance and brute force, the expansion of the empire signified, therefore, neither the victory of rationality nor moral progress, but the ominous spread of a serious "disease," which was destroying the spiritual health of both colonizer and colonized.

By establishing the Editor as a Socratic spiritual doctor who, after determining the causes of the disease, proceeded to pronounce it—in principle—as curable, Gandhi radically reversed the roles of tutor and pupil on which the colonial order in India depended. For him, the British were incapable of imparting genuine "breeding." They were not the educators of the world, but moral infants requiring the help of a wise older tutor specializing in moral affairs. Moreover, England's grand idea of India as a vast social laboratory waiting to be imbued with the spirit of modern rationality was but a childish fantasy to be corrected by an example set by a truly ethical nation. Its ancient civilization contained all the necessary ingredients for the moral advancement of the West. Examined in more detail in the next chapter, this constructive part of *Hind Swaraj* thus calls for the moral regeneration of a nation presently corrupted by the vices of modernity. If successful, this process of purification would give India the moral authority to lead the British and the rest of the (modern) world in a march of atonement for past sins toward the goals of moral transformation and the establishment of a true universalism. Given that moderate and radical forms of nationalism were unsuited for the task of bringing about genuine *hind swaraj,* the only viable alternative lay in the creation of a nonviolent nationalism whose methods of *satyagraha* would be politically effective while at the same time preserving the moral compatibility of means and ends. Reflecting the metaphysical "truth" of the oneness of all being, this reconciliation of principles and power would usher in a truly virtuous chapter in human history—a New Age characterized by social harmony, religious pluralism, and economic welfare for all.

4

IMAGINING INDIA

୧ல

Gandhi's Construction of Nonviolent Nationalism

But I must confess that I am not so much concerned about the stability of empire as I am about that of the ancient civilisation of India which, in my opinion, represents the best that the world has ever seen.

—M. K. Gandhi[1]

His [Gandhi's] social utopia was an idealization of ancient Hindu civilization that had no more reality than Rousseau's natural man.

—Octavio Paz[2]

THE IDEA OF INDIA

It was not until 1899 that an Act of Parliament converted "India" from a name given to a cultural region into a geographically bounded, political territory. However, this does not mean that India emerged *ex nihilo* as a pure invention of British colonial administrators or South Asian nationalists. Rather, as Sunil Khilnani observes, it suggests that the subcontinent's existing cultural matrix was in the process of being shaped and reshaped by the fundamental agencies and ideas of modernity—European colonial expansion, the state, nationalism, democracy, economic development, and so on.[3] The indigenous sculptors of the idea that India could be united into a single, independent community were largely members of "India's modern, educated, urban elite, whose intellectual horizons were extended by these modern ideas and whose sphere of action was expanded by these modern agencies."[4] By now, it should be obvious that there existed among the nationalist elite diverse and often contending definitions of what exactly constituted "Indianness" and of how *swaraj* was best to be achieved. Moreover, they employed different styles of imagining their ideal community.[5] These competing ideas of India all attempted to address the paramount question of the day, namely the relation between several cultural communities and to which community the "Indian nation" actually belonged.[6] Following their own intuitions, the midwives of Indian nationalism had to invent and fashion their public selves in interaction with their respective traditions and audiences. To borrow from Khilnani's insight once again:

> They had to make themselves Indian according to their own ideas of what exactly that meant. The presence of a foreign Raj had ensured that an Indian identity could not be assumed as a natural condition. Some, of course, chose to devise an ostentatiously "traditional" self; others declared for a more stridently Western or modern one. But all had to make themselves out of the intimidations and possibilities posed by the West's modernity.[7]

Previous chapters of this book sought to give the reader a good sense of how, influenced by the British liberal discourse on India and orientalist countercultural views flourishing in the New Age circles of London, the young Gandhi transformed himself from a liberal assimilationist into a fierce critic of the empire and its underlying modern civilization. The present discussion turns to Gandhi, the romantic cultural nationalist, whose vision of a regenerated India was based on the belief that it was actually possible to adhere to nonviolent principles in the effective pursuit of political power.[8] Unlike political nationalists, who typically strive for the creation of an autonomous state based on common citizenship, cultural nationalists generate influential discourses of the nation beyond politics, which distrust state-centered models and their legal-rational roots in modernity. They emphasize the cultural realm of "the people" as a permanent life force that enunciates a popular "truth" in spite of domination and the corruption of elites. In India, this discourse appeared eminently meaningful to large sections of the colonial mid-

dle classes.[9] Although the goals and techniques of cultural nationalists differ from those of their political counterparts, the former often
become active in the political movements they inspire. As John
Hutchinson points out, cultural nationalists usually act as moral innovators who, "at times of crisis when society is polarized between
traditionalist and modernist groups, construct new matrices of collective identity and directions for collective action." Perceiving a
unique and differentiated civilization at the core of their nation, cultural nationalists typically employ a wide variety of the following
strategies to make their case: idiosyncratic interpretations of popular
myths and their projection to a wider audience, suggestions for new
educational strategies, the construction of emotionally compelling
images of the nation, the ordering of multiple symbols, and so on.[10]

How exactly did Gandhi assemble his vision of India? Which elements and features did he consider to make up "genuine Indianness"? Was his construction of national identity compatible with the
moral inclusivism expressed in his nonviolent philosophy? As I seek
to demonstrate in this chapter, *Hind Swaraj* contains a number of
central assumptions that supply the basic foundation of Gandhi's
nonviolent nationalism. Imagining an ancient Indian civilization as
the morally pure Other to "modern civilization," he employed a set
of mythic patterns that include a golden age of cultural splendor, the
fall into a dark age, and a period of regeneration beginning in the
present.[11]

THE MORAL CONDITION OF INDIA:
GANDHI'S AFFIRMATIVE ORIENTALISM

Perhaps the best starting point for the exploration of Gandhi's vision of India is a passage in *Hind Swaraj* in which the Reader strug-
gles to make sense of the Editor's blanket condemnation of modern
civilization: "If [modern] civilisation is a disease, and if it has attacked the English nation, why has she been able to take India, and
why is she able to retain it?" The response comes without hesitation: "The English have not taken India; we have given it to them.
They are not in India because of their strength, but because we
keep them."[12] In other words, the Editor argues that many Indians
have accepted foreign rule for purely materialistic reasons: "[W]e
keep the English in India for our base self-interest. We like their

commerce, they please us by their subtle methods, and get what they want from us. To blame them for this is to perpetuate their power."[13] Gandhi adopted this line of reasoning from Count Leo Tolstoy, who asserted in his *Letter to a Hindu* that the only possible explanation for the strange phenomenon of 30,000 "rather weak and ill-looking" Britons enslaving 200 millions of "vigorous, clever, strong, and freedom-loving people" was that Indians had come to embrace the materialist values of their colonizers. Not only had Indians accepted their "enslavement" with good grace, but they had actively connived with their enslavers for the sole purpose of advancing their own material interests.[14]

This position underlies Gandhi's firm belief that all political efforts to achieve Indian home rule had to be accompanied by a rigorous program of moral reformation aimed at restoring the spiritual health and integrity of the individual. As Partha Chatterjee points out, Gandhi's entire political project of national liberation can therefore be understood as predicated upon his commitment to identify, address, and rectify the moral failure on the part of modern Indians.[15] Indeed, the Editor never hesitates to drive his stern message home, accusing his fellow citizens of having become indolent and "effeminate." Nurturing selfish thoughts of personal material gain generated by the perverted ethos of modern civilization, modern Indians habitually surrendered to their cravings for pleasure. Contented to hand over control of their nation to the foreign exponents of a materialistic lifestyle, they had turned into sly sycophants and willing servants of the empire, thereby proving to the world that they were morally "unfit to serve the country."[16] While bemoaning India's wholesale adoption of the Western civilizational paradigm, the Editor nonetheless discusses the moral corruption of his compatriots within a historiographical framework developed by European orientalists, particularly their linear model of India's decline from a classical "Golden Age" to its present "degenerate condition." Pleading for a reversal of this trend, the Editor argues that a successful recovery of the authentic values of the past depends upon India's ability to fix its gaze up on its glorious ancient civilization and its eternally valid moral standards.

Only a few weeks before Gandhi wrote *Hind Swaraj,* G. K. Chesterton raised the pivotal question of what constituted "authentic Indianness" in a widely discussed article published in the *Illustrated London News.* In a nutshell, the British author put forth the rather orientalist thesis that modern Indian nationalists of both the radical and the moderate persuasion were neither "genuinely Indian" nor "truly nationalist." After all, Chesterton suggested, their nationalist imagination was thoroughly indebted to European political concepts and philosophical categories. Consequently, their ambitious blueprints for the creation of their own nation-state amounted to little more than shallow imitations of Western political arrangements. Closing his essay with a biting passage of cultural criticism, Chesterton emphasized that he was not at all opposed to the right of Indians "to live as Indians," provided they were prepared to advocate forms of self-rule that grew organically from their native customs and traditions and could therefore be counted as "authentic" expressions of "Indianness."

> There is a great difference between a people asking for its own ancient life and a people asking for things that have been wholly invented by someone else. Suppose an Indian said: "I wish India had always been free of white men and their works. Everything has its own faults and we prefer our own. . . ." Suppose an Indian said that, I should call him an Indian nationalist. He would be an authentic Indian, and I think it would be very hard to answer him.[17]

Agreeing with the essay's central message, Gandhi exhorted the readers of *Indian Opinion* to "reflect over these views of Mr. Chesterton and consider what they should rightly demand. What is the way to make the Indian people happy?"[18] For Gandhi, the obvious conclusion was that neither the passive acceptance of colonial rule nor a Western-style nationalism would achieve that goal. Following Chesterton's logic, he instead saw as the first step toward building a genuine Indian nationalist movement a general appreciation of the unique and differentiated classical civilization at the core of the nation. The only way to reverse India's decline and shake off its self-imposed yoke of dependency was to bring about the moral regeneration of self and nation through the reappropriation of a virtuous way of life without parliaments, machinery, lawyers, and large cities. To be sure, the Chesterton-Gandhi view of the "authentic" for India was shot through with cultural stereotypes such as the notions that popular elections and parliaments were inherently foreign to India or that Westernized Indians were fundamentally decultured and unrepresentative. As Richard Fox puts it, "Confronting the domination encoded in Chesterton's stereotype, Gandhi can achieve an authentic Indian nationalism only by rejecting Englistan. Chesterton also enables Gandhi, however. By saying what the goal of an authentic Indian nationalism cannot be, Chesterton gives Gandhi the space to say what it can be: if not Englistan, then a Wisdom-land utopia built on the ancient cultural essentials."[19]

Building on the vision of German nationalists like J. G. Herder and J. G. Fichte, the romantic discourse of cultural authenticity constituted a very influential stream within orientalist scholarship that did not remain confined to Europe but spread rapidly to the rest of the world.[20] Notions of a recuperation of past glory and the latent spirituality of India occupied a prominent position in the works of European orientalists like Chesterton, Mueller, Hunter, and Maine, as well as early Indian nationalist experimentalists like R. Roy, Swami Vivekananda, Sister Nivedita, Aurobindo Ghose, and Annie Besant.[21] At this point, it is useful to recall that chapter 2 of this study explored Gandhi's intellectual debt to European orientalists, arguing that his emerging ideas of an existing Indo-Aryan identity should not be understood as objective, self-contained entities, but as always already pre-interpreted, dynamic layers of unique discursive and linguistic practices involving both the colonizer and the colonized. Aptly described by Edward Said and others as "orientalism," such practices defined the conceptual landscape of the colonial world and made it susceptible to certain kinds of management and manipulation.[22]

Likewise, Gandhi's idea of India in *Hind Swaraj* as referring to a bounded collectivity with certain essential qualities reflects historically situated perspectives and specific cultural prejudices. His acceptance of Chesterton's critique indicates how deeply Gandhi's arguments for Indian self-rule were imbued with what Richard Fox calls "affirmative Orientalism."[23] In contradistinction to its negative version, which categorizes India as passive, otherworldly, superstitious, chaotic, caste-dominated and despotic, morally degraded, and hopelessly backward, nineteenth-century forms of affirmative orientalism essentialized India as the mystical home of ancient spirituality and antimaterialism. Feeding on an existing religious discourse carried on by a rising Brahman elite and reacting to the pro-Western posture of the early Bengali literary renaissance, a new generation of Indian intellectuals had begun to reify Hindu culture as exemplars of an ancient Sanskrit civilization characterized by "'Hindu spirituality,' borne by the Hindu nation, which was superior to [the] 'Western materialism' [that had been] brought to India by an aggressive and arrogant 'British Nation.'"[24]

This increasingly popular mixture of affirmative orientalism, anticolonial nationalism, and religious dogmatism rested on the assumption that ancient spirituality constituted the "inner," more genuine dimension of Indianness. As Partha Chatterjee explains, "The spiritual . . . is an 'inner' domain bearing the 'essential' marks of cultural identity. The greater one's success in imitating Western skills in the material domain, therefore, the greater the need to preserve the distinctness of one's spiritual culture. This formula is, I think, a fundamental feature of anticolonial nationalisms in Asia and Africa."[25] This bifurcation of the world into a material and a spiritual domain made it easier for Indian intellectuals to acknowledge the predominance of the West in the "outer" areas of economics, law, administration, science, and technology while at the same time insisting on the inherent superiority of the East in the more important "inner" aspects of civilization. Gandhi always rejected the extremism of Hindu orthodoxy, but he, too, was tremendously attracted to the notion that timeless truth resided in an ancient Indian civilization and its spiritual wisdom.

THE MYTH OF INDIA'S ANCIENT CIVILIZATION

Drawing on deep symbolic resources contained in the language and images of the "Golden Age," the Editor in *Hind Swaraj* describes the purported character of India's ancient civilization in glowing terms. Most importantly, he sees it as a spiritual civilization, a "land of religion" inhabited by a moral people who had the wisdom to set limits to physical indulgences: "They saw that happiness was largely a mental condition. . . . Observing all this, our ancestors dissuaded us from luxuries and pleasures."[26] Rejecting large urban centers as "snares and useless encumbrances" that corrupted a natural sense of simplicity, they lived in small, self-sufficient "village communities." Signifying cooperation and harmony, these communities constituted the basic building blocks of Gandhi's model of Indian nationhood. Ancient villagers formed intimate face-to-face relationships based on mutual trust and support, and political and economic decisions were made collectively in direct-democratic fashion.[27] Reminiscent of Socrates's view of justice as performing one's own tasks according to one's capacities, the Editor imagines ancient Indians as familial people who were content with their place in the community. They were happy to follow their own occupations and trades without engaging in much competition, consciously embracing the same basic technologies of production handed down to them by their ancestors: "They saw that our real happiness and health consisted in a proper use of our hands and feet. . . . A nation with a constitution like this is fitter to teach others than to learn from others." Relying on a time-tested educational system that bypassed abstract schooling in the sciences in favor of a more concrete program of "character-building," the Indians of old enjoyed "true home rule," understood as the observance of morality in order to attain mastery over mind and passions.[28]

Only rarely does Gandhi allow the radical Reader to interrupt the Editor's idyllic portrayal of this seemingly ageless society based on the values of an unchanging natural order. On one occasion, however, the Reader does offer a sensible critique of the rather oppressive nature of some of these "ancient traditions," such as child marriage, child prostitution, and animal sacrifice. Dismissing these practices as "regrettable mistakes," the Editor warns his young counterpart not to confuse such "later aberrations" with the lasting achievements of ancient civilization. A much more serious and sustained disagreement between the two interlocutors emerges only when the Reader, praising the heroic deeds of Garibaldi and Mazzini for leading Italy's struggle for national liberation against Austria, endorses a similar strategy of violent resistance to British rule. Accepting the challenge, the Editor argues that arming India would be imitating the instrumental methods of a European civilization based on "brute force." Unsurprisingly, he rejects this option and launches into a long monologue on ancient India's special relationship to the practice of *ahimsa*.

With moral considerations once again at the core of his exposition, the Editor introduces several examples designed to prove that any civilization worth the name ought to insist on the correspondence of means and ends: " . . . I wish only to show that only fair means can produce fair results, and that, at least in the majority of cases, if not, indeed, in all, the force of love and pity is infinitely greater than the force of arms. There is harm in the exercise of brute force, never in that of pity."[29] In its ignorant reliance on violence, modern European civilization has failed to grasp the significance of this superior "love-force." Conversely, ancient Indian civilization was organized around the nonviolent principles of self-sacrifice and passive resistance. Singling out imaginary lives of solidaristic peasants in much the same way Gandhi had sung the praises of the simple Indian shepherd almost twenty years earlier, the Editor suggests that faint traces of these virtuous practices of old could still be detected in contemporary India:

> The fact is that, in India, the nation at large has generally used passive resistance in all departments of life. We cease to co-operate with our rulers when they displease us. This is passive resistance [*satyagraha*]. I remember an instance when, in a small principality, the villagers were offended by some command issued by the prince. The former immediately began vacating the village. The prince became nervous, apologized to his subjects and withdrew his command. Many such instances can be found in India. Real home rule is possible only where passive resistance is the guiding force of the people. Any other rule is foreign rule.[30]

However, when prompted by the Reader to consult existing records that suggest that violence has always been part of Indian history—and that concrete examples of nonviolent direct action are therefore "nowhere to be found in history"—the Editor retreats to a rather elusive view on the validity of historical evidence:

> But you ask for historical evidence. It is, therefore, necessary to know what history means. The Gujarati equivalent means: "It so happened." If that is the meaning of history, it is possible to give copious evidence. But, if it means the doings of kings and emperors, there can be no evidence of soul-force or passive resistance in such history. You cannot expect silver-ore in a tin-mine. History, as we know, is a record of the wars of the world, and so there is a proverb among Englishmen that a nation which has no history, that is, no wars, is a happy nation. How kings played, how they became enemies of one another, and how they murdered one another is found accurately recorded in history, and, if this were all that happened in the world, it would have been ended long ago. . . . The fact that there are so many men still alive in the world shows that it is based not on the force of arms but on the force of truth or love. Therefore, the greatest and most unimpeachable evidence of the success of this force is to be found in the fact that, in spite of the wars of the world, it still lives on. . . . History, then, is a record of an interruption of the course of nature. Soul-force, being natural, is not noted in history.[31]

There are two distinct arguments here. One entails a quite sensible critique of history as an elitist enterprise that merely records the deeds of a select few. The other is less convincing, asserting in rather general fashion that acts of great compassion or solidarity rarely find their way into the history books. The Editor seems to imply that as a result of this omission, adherents to "soul-force" are morally obliged to set the historical record straight by reconstructing the missing parts of the story without the benefit of hard empirical evidence. Are we thus to understand that Gandhi consciously advocates fabricating timeless morality tales about India's ancient civilization? Given the imputed impossibility of offering a balanced historical account of India's past, does he assign to the Editor the task of creating a persuasive cultural ideal that bestows upon the nation essentialist characteristics such as nonviolence and spirituality?

As Partha Chatterjee notes, this interpretation commands ample textual and contextual support. Throughout his writings, Gandhi let it be known that he felt it to be entirely unnecessary to even attempt a historical demonstration of the possibilities he was trying to point out. On several occasions he admitted to "being an indifferent reader of history."[32] Objecting to the historical mode of reasoning as being quite unsuitable, if not irrelevant, for his purpose, he even declined to regard his beloved *Mahabharata* and its *Bhagavad Gita* portion as a historical narrative. In his view, the epic's historical underpinnings were merely a literary device helping the reader to understand a universal truth that transcended history. The central message of this unchanging truth was the "eternal" moral imperative to live a decent life based on nonviolence and altruism.[33] Similar to Chatterjee's interpretation, Ashis Nandy argues that Gandhi rejected historicism in favor of myth as a vehicle much more suitable to moving public consciousness in the desired direction. Activating certain memories while deleting others, myths offer the advantage of allowing the narrator to break out of the determinism of history, thus accessing processes that constitute history on the level of the here and now: "Consciously acknowledged as the core of culture, they [myths] widen instead of restrict human choices. They allow one to remember in an anticipatory fashion and to concentrate on undoing aspects of the present rather than avenging the past."[34]

Such readings of Gandhi as a myth-maker who negated history altogether strike me as too extreme. A master of shifting back and forth between the historical and mythical, he readily employed the language of "empirical" history when it suited his moral message. At one point in *Hind Swaraj,* for example, the Editor tells the Reader that concrete manifestations of the old civilization can still be seen in contemporary India: "I would certainly advise you and those like you who love the motherland to go into the interior that has not yet been polluted by the railways, and to live there for six months; you might then be patriotic and speak of Home Rule."[35] Once this qualification is taken under advisement, however, Nandy's point appears to be on the mark. As one of South Asia's leading cultural nationalists, Gandhi confronted his audience with the myth of India's ancient civilization in order to introduce an alternative to present forms of nationalism. The goal was to create new patriotic values that nonetheless bore the stamp of age-old "authenticity." Imported into India and imitated by the Indians, Europe's shallow "obsession with history" was, according to Gandhi, responsible for the modern explosion of greed and disharmony that betrayed India's inherited tradition of elevating the unchanging moral truths over the fleeting achievements of history. Indeed, Gandhi's morality tales of ancient India performed most of the functions typically associated with political myths: the strengthening of group solidarity in the face of major challenges, the supply of compelling arguments for the abolition of undesirable institutions or conditions, the inspiration of group members with confidence in their destiny, the glorification of their past achievements, and the inauguration of a new symbolic order that engenders a sense of awe and fascination in true believers. Naturally, successful myths also bestow power and authority on its creators.[36] As Henry Tudor puts it, political myths offer "an account of the past and the future in the light of which the present can be understood. And as we would expect, this account is, not only an explanation, but also a practical argument."[37]

Affirmative orientalist imagery contributed greatly to the popular appeal of Gandhi's myth. Enshrining India's ancient spiritual wisdom as the core of its national identity, it inspired in a nascent public consciousness a sense of trust in his alternative model of a nonviolent nationalism. As Richard Fox notes, "Otherworldliness became spirituality, an Indian cultural essential that promised her a future cultural perfection unattained in the West. Passiveness became at first passive resistance and later nonviolent resistance; the age-old Indian character thus provided a revolutionary technique by which to bring that future perfection."[38] More sensitive to the condition of the masses than any previous Indian leader, Gandhi relied on political myths and popular legends to conjure an ideal nation that was receptive to the problems of the present while at the same time cognizant of its ancient moral mission. Articulating this vision in a liberal language of (moral) progress and development, he reversed not only the dominant colonial meanings of "ancient" and "modern," but also radically undermined the European idea of a necessary connection between modernity and the viability of the nation. Yet, as Gyan Prakash points out, Gandhi's tales of ancient India derived from his rereading of the colonial archive:

> It was by rescuing the premodern from its assigned space in history, from its designation as colonialism's self-confirming other, and by inserting it in the same time as the modern that Gandhi was able to formulate his concept of the nonmodern. By such a reinterpretation of the premodern as the nonmodern, by realigning categories aligned by colonialism, Gandhi was able to produce a postcolonial text that made the violent critique of the colonial discourse speak with nonviolent meanings.[39]

CONJURING THE IDEAL NATION

In his important essay on Gandhi's nationalist thought, Anthony Parel emphasizes that Gandhi regularly used the Gujarati word "*praja*" as the equivalent of the English term "nation." As opposed to the more common term "*rashtra,*" which emphasizes the dimension of state power, *praja* carries the strong denotation of "people" or "cultural community."[40] The value of this distinction is readily apparent when considering the Editor's seemingly anachronistic claim that, "We were one nation before they [British] came to India. One thought inspired us. Our mode of life was the same."[41] In this crucial passage, Gandhi reacted strongly against the colonial assertions that India never constituted a proper nation and that it would require a long time before it became one. For the Europeans, of course, nationhood was inextricably linked to modernity in the assumption that the modern nation-state constituted the only legitimate container for a common set of cultural and political properties. From a British perspective, India had neither sufficiently matured to sustain the operations of a modern nation-state on its own, nor had it developed such a common cultural framework. Hence, it could not lay claim to "nationhood." Championing a conception of the nation as *praja, Hind Swaraj* contests the justificatory grounds of this colonial claim. Firstly, the Editor challenges the view that modernity represents the ultimate standard for deciding whether or not a given collectivity qualifies as a "nation." Secondly, he seeks to establish the alleged age-old existence of common "Indian" cultural properties.

The Editor supports his claim to India's existing "nationhood" by pointing to the combination of geography and religion as the basis for the evolution of an all-India consciousness. Traveling throughout India either on foot or in bullock-carts, religious pilgrims realized that, "India was one undivided land so made by nature. They, therefore, argued that it must be one nation. Arguing thus, they established holy places in various parts of India, and fired the people with an idea of nationality in a manner unknown in other parts of the world."[42] His essentialist emphasis on the spiritual origins of the Indian nation leads the Editor to introduce yet another invidious comparison: "Any two Indians are one as no two Englishmen are."[43] Immediately, the Reader raises a common Hindu objection designed to get his conversation partner to reconsider his position in light of existing tensions between Hindus and Muslims: "Has the introduction of Mahomedanism not unmade the nation?" The Editor's response has often been taken as a clear sign of Gandhi's commitment to religious tolerance and cultural pluralism: "India cannot cease to be one nation because people belonging to different religions live in it. The introduction of foreigners does not necessarily destroy the nation, they merge in it. A country is one nation only when such a condition obtains in it. That country must have a faculty for assimilation. India has ever been such a country."[44] Arguing that the phrase "inborn enmity between Hindus and Mahomedans" represents an invention of the British designed to divide the colonized, the Editor does not hesitate to shore up his construction of "tolerance" as one of the essences of Indian spirituality with an emotional appeal to common ethnicity: "Should we not remember that many Hindus and Mahomedans own the same ancestors, and the same blood runs through their veins? . . . Is the God of the Mahomedan different from the God of the Hindu? Religions are different roads converging to the same point."[45]

However, as both Peter van der Veer and Thomas Blom Hansen point out, one of the main problems with Gandhi's "pluralist" proclamation of an all-embracing Indian spirituality as the defining

characteristic of the nation is that his ecumenical language and syn-
cretic religious practices usually retained a recognizable Hindu
idiom.[46] His emphasis on the tolerant and pluralist character of ancient India notwithstanding, the Editor's discussion of the Hindu de-
votional practice of cow protection not only upholds the nationwide
validity of the cow as the "the protector of India," but also seems to
take for granted that "Our Mohamedan brethren will admit this."[47]
Given Gandhi's obvious awareness of existing Islamic dietary habits,
his elevation of the notion of protecting the cow as "India's mother"
implies the spiritual superiority of the Hindu tradition. Thus, his interpretation of Hinduism as a universal religion did not fail to alien-
ate Muslims who had their own discourse on universal religion:

> Gandhi's pluralism therefore did not make much sense from the point of
> view of many Muslims. . . . Gandhi's message was that of a "spiritual Hin-
> duism" that would include other religions, albeit given the common ac-
> ceptance of such cherished Hindu notions as cow worship and
> vegetarianism. The steps he took to transform Hindu discourse and prac-
> tice were considerable, but, in the final analysis, have to be understood
> within that tradition. Despite his attempts to formulate a message of toler-
> ance and pluralism, his idiom remained Hindu and thus contributed sub-
> stantially to Hindu nationalism.[48]

If Gandhi's attempts to bolster India's claim to nationhood on
the basis of a shared spiritual and geographical space retained such
problematic elements that undermined his vision of *praja,* then what
about his arguments against using modernity as the standard for deciding whether or not a given collectivity qualifies as a "nation"? As
discussed in the previous chapter, Gandhi conceived of modernity
not merely as a description of objective phenomena, but also as a deluded state of mind characterized by selfishness and violence. As the
embodiment of such exercise of "brute force," the modern nation-
state thus stood in the way of a true *praja* based upon the principles
of communal love and *ahimsa*. The exercise of violence was not only
out of tune with the spirit of Indian traditions as Gandhi read them,
but it was also a visible sign that genuine nationhood had not yet
been achieved. In a complete reversal of the dominant colonial discourse, Gandhi thus implied that it was the morally underdeveloped
European countries that had not yet earned the distinction of being
true nations. In fact, genuine nationhood became impossible under

conditions of modernity. The assumed link between the virtues of nonviolence, tolerance, morality, and "genuine nationhood" also explains Gandhi's persistent injunction to "drive out Western civilization" in order to return India to its nation-bestowing spiritual essence.[49] Moreover, this link provides the justification for his rejection of the "suicidal policies" of Indian radical nationalists who have mistakenly adopted "modern civilization and modern methods of violence to drive out the English."[50] In accordance with the ideal of the *praja*-nation, the achievement of Indian home rule depended upon the transformation of (Western) modernity by means of a different kind of nationalism, one that was not anchored in modern civilization and its reliance on brute force. The political purpose of such a nonviolent nationalism was certainly not to give birth to yet another modern nation-state à la Britain, but to build an exemplary, decentralized nation of virtuous Indians guided by their own premodern tradition of performing duty and observing morality: "Real home-rule is self-rule or self-control."[51]

Aside from pointing to the connection between physical violence and nationalism, the strength of Gandhi's discourse on the ideal nation lies in its recognition of the extent to which existing nationalist narratives routinely utilized violent images, words, and symbols. *Hind Swaraj* consistently highlights the historical tendency of modern nationalisms to forge exclusivist collective identities through the construction of hard conceptual boundaries. However, Gandhi's insight into the workings of modern nationalism does not guarantee the absence of conceptual violence in his own nationalist imaginings. While concurring with Anthony Parel's reading of Gandhi as rejecting "the *modern* concept of the nation in so far as the latter is based on the notions of brute force, the priority of national interest, and a principle of exclusiveness based either on religion, or language or race," I am reluctant to leave matters at that.[52] In order to assess the plausibility of Gandhi's constructive claim of offering an alternative nationalism that steers clear of exclusivism, it is imperative to turn the Editor's critical eye on his own constructive efforts.

THE VIOLENCE OF GANDHI'S NONVIOLENT NATIONALISM

At this point, it is important to remember that Gandhi himself insisted that a proper definition of violence ought not be limited to its

physical dimension but should also include more subtle psychological and conceptual forms of harm embedded in words, images, and
thoughts.[53] As emphasized in the introduction of this study, the rules
of immanent critique prescribe that my evaluation of his nonviolent
nationalism proceed according to his own standards for what
counted as "violence." In order to verify his claim that his nationalist discourse actually conformed to his general idea of *ahimsa,* one
would reasonably expect him to do his best to avert systemic patterns of conceptual violence such as those involving the drawing of
invidious comparisons, the construction of hostile antagonisms, the
fostering of polarizing attitudes, the demonization of "enemies," the
creation of exclusivist images, and so on.

Yet the existence of such instances of conceptual violence is evident throughout the pages of *Hind Swaraj.* As Gyan Prakash observes, "The specific content of his [Gandhi's] criticism is less
relevant than the mode in which the creed of a nonmodern and
nonviolent Indian struggle for freedom is crafted out of a violent de-
nunciation of the modern civilization. There is . . . the irony that the
philosophy of nonviolence is overwritten by a language bristling
with violent criticism."[54] Hence, Gandhi's construction of nationhood appears to be incompatible with his professed moral universalism. Linking his celebration of Indian spirituality with his populist
assertion of an overriding antagonism between India and the West,
the Editor situates his account of what he considers to be India's ancient civilization within a conceptual framework prone to spawn invidious comparisons and foster exclusivist attitudes.[55] His depiction
of social and political realities frequently occurs in hostile terms that
convey the idea of unbridgeable differences, ultimately portraying
the contending civilizational modes—ancient and modern—as mu-
tually exclusive: "The tendency of Indian civilization is to elevate
the moral being, that of Western civilization is to propagate immorality. The latter is godless, the former is based on a belief in God.
So understanding and so believing, it behooves every lover of India
to cling to the old Indian civilization even as a child clings to its
mother's breast."[56] The Editor's claim to "true morality" seems to ex-
clude everyone and everything that does not fit in with the central
principles of ancient civilization. Indeed, his strident assertion that
"ancient Indian civilization represents the best that the world has
ever seen" occurs at several strategically important sections of the
text and harbors the core of an essentialized national identity based

on India's moral and spiritual superiority.[57] Given that Gandhi's mouthpiece even goes so far as to suggest that India "has nothing to learn from anybody else," it would be implausible to read such remarks merely as innocent expressions of encouragement meant to bolster the self-confidence and pride of his readers.[58] Insisting that all modern forms of nationalism bear the marks of a sinister modernity, the Editor finds it unnecessary to look for guidance to recent European models of national unification. "The condition of India is unique. Its strength is immeasurable. We need not, therefore, refer to the history of other countries. I have drawn attention to the fact that, when other civilizations have succumbed, the Indian has survived many a shock."[59]

Commenting on the exclusivist tone that emanates from these passages, Richard Fox rightly identifies as one of its underlying causes Gandhi's acceptance of orientalism "thrust upon [him]—that India was, had always been, and would always be radically different from the West—and then [he] claimed a superior nationalism and a more humane society as the possible outcomes of this India, spiritual and organic."[60] Yet there were formidable obstacles in the way of these goals, the foremost being the contemporary Indian nationalists, who, like the radical Reader, had lost sight of the "true India"—a moral community firmly anchored in its ancient civilization with unique cultural attributes of spirituality, diversity, and tolerance. The conceptual violence contained in Gandhi's language of invective directed against these nationalists is especially apparent in a passage where the Editor implores the Reader to stop considering such "half-Anglicized Indians" as "good specimens of the real Indian nation."[61] Indeed, he explicitly refers to those who want to change India's ancient ways as "enemies of the country and sinners."[62]

Dependent upon the notion of an inferior Other for his construction of a superior Indian collective identity, Gandhi failed to realize that by defining these Others as "evil" or "satanic," it was he himself who created the very threat to the purity of his imagined civilization. As a result of his fairly essentializing and unequivocal cultural ascription, the necessity arises to police, control, dominate, and appropriate the Other. Ultimately, it has to be made to disappear, or be "transformed," to use Gandhi's kinder term. Rather than being recognized as an equal moral partner subscribing to a different perspective on modernity, the Other is branded as being morally ignorant and wrong, and consequently must be subjected to proper moral instruction. Although Gandhi always maintained that such strategies of persuasion ought always rely on nonviolent means ("conversion" rather than "condemnation"), the bellicose implications of these procedures should be rather obvious. At a minimum, such a position entailed the taking of a missionary attitude toward Others who did not share his principles, allowing, therefore, for a morally condescending relationship with any individual, group, or system that refused to adopt his principles. What Gandhi advertises as a humble search for truth rests nonetheless on the presumed inequality of struggle. As Leela Gandhi notes, "[I]t relies on the *satyagrahi*'s conviction that she/he is already in possession of greater knowledge, in fact, of truth itself. Hence, the *satyagrahi*'s specific acts of resistance against contesting or authoritarian discourses begin with the knowledge that the moral victory has already been resolved in his/her favor."[63] Indeed, such "knowledge" of the Other's moral corruption fueled Gandhi's critique of contemporary Indian nationalists, European colonizers and their civilization, self-interested Indians who drew material benefits from modernity, and, ultimately, any impure mind held captive to the ceaseless appetites of the physical body.

At no point in the dialogue does the Editor pause and reflect on the significant amounts of conceptual violence that pour into the construction of these threatening Others. In the end, then, Gandhi's construction of an alternative, nonviolent nationalism does not live up to his own high standards with regard to *ahimsa,* for he failed to see that his essentialist vision of a superior Indian spirituality as the defining feature of the *praja* and the indispensable precondition of *swaraj* was itself born in conceptual violence. In other words, the project of the moral regeneration of the nation was marked by violence at its origin, thus reproducing some of the essentializing qualities of the very modernity he sought to fight.[64] Both confined and enabled by the potent combination of orientalism and the British liberal ideology of difference, Gandhi's construction of Indianness represents a sort of mirror image of the European nationalist discourse with its conceptually violent assumptions of moral superiority, culturally specific claims to a universal truth, and invidious comparisons.[65]

Most importantly, his nationalist language adopted liberalism's practice of inscribing universalism with particular cultural practices—except that here, these subtle invocations of exclusionary social conventions and manners were spoken in a decidedly Gandhian idiom. In order to qualify as a truly universal phenomenon, the human capacity to think and act had to pass a rigorous test, the design of which reflected a culturally specific set of moral norms. Gandhi's nonviolent nationalism was meant to be a universal solution as well, applicable as much to the countries of the West as to nations such as India. Yet, fed a steady diet of Enlightenment rationalism, British liberals, too, had long claimed that their norms applied universally. Challenging these claims, the radical critiques of anticolonial nationalists like Gandhi ignited for the first time a controversy over which nation/culture had developed a "better" understanding of universalism. Of course, this contest was only resolvable within the broader context of an ongoing political struggle between the contending "nations."[66]

Thus, while switching the criteria used for the definition of cultural preeminence from "material" to "spiritual" matters, the ideas expressed in *Hind Swaraj* nonetheless retained the language of progress and development. Replacing one form of superiority with another, the Editor proposed to replace alien tutelage with the tutelage of Gandhian morality. This project mirrored the concerns of the liberal ideology of difference by seeking to morally "improve" the Other. As Leela Gandhi emphasizes, "[A]*himsa,* which he [Gandhi] defends as the corrective force of the soul and as an alternative system of improvement, also becomes a way of "re-civilizing" the colonizer."[67] To put the matter in rather provocative terms: Gandhi, the Indian nationalist, never abandoned the conceptual framework of liberalism. Although based ostensibly on the resolute rejection of the ills of liberalism, his alternative vision of nonviolent nationalism nonetheless bore the marks of the renounced paradigm. Merely inverting liberalism's logic of progress and reversing the roles of the major antagonists, Gandhi remained firmly tied to old conceptual categories that distinguished between superior and inferior cultures, referred to necessary stages of development, and suggested proper educational schemes. To be sure, he offered creative reinterpretations of the "Indian tradition," and he experimented with innovative social designs, but both his vision of a morally regenerated nation and its related understanding of what constituted genuine "Indianness" remained profoundly influenced by the views of Western antimodernists.[68]

I am not implying here that Western traditions represent the apex of all human thought and action. Nor do I mean to "colonize the imaginations of anticolonial resistance," or deny a certain degree of interdependence, or "hybridity," between colonizer and colonized.[69] Instead, to borrow from Sunil Khilnani's insight, my argument is "simply a recognition of the profound historical impress of these ideas upon the practical experience of India and of the non-Western world in general"[70] Leela Gandhi seconds this opinion: "One aspect of this Gandhian reversal of the logic of colonialism is his induction or appropriation of seminal Western writers and thinkers into the service and ideology of *ahimsa*." Hence, her perspective highlights the "interpretive maneuvers whereby Gandhi and some of his nationalist contemporaries were able to transform productively and, as it were, bring to insurgency the cultural and political productions of foundational Western thought."[71] Even such defenders of Indian traditionalism as Ashis Nandy, who often argue that Gandhi's opposition to modernity derives from his place outside the "West," concede that his "Hinduism included many recognizable Western elements which he saw as necessary for contemporary Hinduism." Nandy further reports that Gandhi himself publicly admitted that he was "ill-acquainted with Indian traditions."[72]

Struggling against the hegemonic ideological claims of British colonialism, Gandhi responded with his own form of spiritual imperialism, culminating in the Editor's proclamation that the necessary restoration of India to its former "pristine condition" would leave the colonizers with only two options. Either they would come to understand the "truth" of his vision and therefore embrace his alternative civilizational framework, or they would have to withdraw from India as a result of their subjects' nonviolent noncooperation based on their superior ability to accept self-suffering. The message to the British was clear: become "Indianised" or find your occupation in India gone.[73] When the Reader suggests that many Indians consider it "impossible that Englishmen should ever become Indianised," the Editor condescendingly declares that even the British have humanity in them.[74] In other words, the terms "Indianising" and "humanizing" have become functional equivalents. If Gandhi's overall position was indeed to anchor his nonviolent philosophy in a politically effective moral universalism, why did he have to "Indianise" his vision?

George Fredrickson advances the same point when he writes that, "at times Gandhi's conception of who could and should undertake militant nonviolence was culturally specific to the point of chauvinism: in 1940 he suggested that the only nation with the capacity to create a nonviolent state was India."[75] Seemingly unaware of the conceptual violence at the heart of his process of collective identity formation, Gandhi focused on the task of bringing about the transformation of the violent Other through nonviolent means. Even if the latter would be possible (and the Editor spends much time making this case), he would still miss the main point of my critique, namely, that his construction of Indianness performed as a conceptual act of rupture, resentment, and vilification already contains violence—long *before* he chooses "nonviolent" political means.[76] Linking nonviolence exclusively to the correct choice of political means (that is, nonviolent forms of direct action) toward the desired end (*swaraj*) would confine *ahimsa* to the physical dimension of *satyagraha*—a practical method of securing political and economic rights. However, such a reductionistic understanding of nonviolence would run counter to Gandhi's broad definition of violence, which obliged him to consider its conceptual and psychological dimensions as well.

SOME IMPLICATIONS FOR GANDHI'S DILEMMA

Gandhi's inability to construct his nationalist vision without relying on pervasive forms of conceptual violence has significant ramifications for the possible reconciliation of nonviolent principles and the quest for nationalist power. For one, as the above discussion has shown, his nonviolent principles become tainted as a result of their association with his nationalist discourse. Or, to put the matter in different terms, his moral universalism suffers from the conceptual violence inherent in his cultural chauvinism. Since it is therefore no longer possible to speak of *ahimsa* in Gandhi's broad sense of the term, his attempts to construct a "nonviolent nationalism" must be judged as failing even on a *theoretical level*. I discuss in the epilogue the more general question of whether *any possible construction of nationalism* requires a consistent recourse to forms of conceptual violence. Yet it is important to emphasize from this point on that the claim to "nonviolent" principles in Gandhi's vision can only be ascertained on the level of physical violence, that is, in his choice of ahimsic political means. As pointed out above, however, narrowing the meaning of nonviolence in this way implies a rather problematic separation of its physical dimension from its conceptual and psychological aspects, allowing for the possibility that Gandhi's conceptually violent style of collective identity formation may have little or no bearing on the ahimsic nature of his nationalist politics. It is important to note that the choice of political means and processes of identity formation are interconnected. After all, the question of what we do appears to be closely linked with a sense of who we are.

This performative dimension of identity formation features prominently in my investigation of Gandhi's claim that the nonviolent building of a moral nation and the shaping of one's body and soul are intrinsically related activities. "It is difficult to become a passive resister, unless the body is trained. As a rule, the mind, residing in a body that has become weakened by pampering, is also weak, and, where there is no strength of mind, there can be no strength of soul."[77] As Anthony Parel notes, one of the most radical claims advanced in *Hind Swaraj* "consists in arguing that there is a connection between the process by which the nation attains its independence and the process by which the self attains control over itself. . . . [S]elf-control and self-realization ought to lead simultaneously to the well-being of the nation as a whole."[78] In other words, the persistent performance of personal experiments with self-control according to Gandhi's instructions would result in the transformation of both the distorted individual body-mind and the modern *rashtra*. Thus, he projected nonviolent control over passions as the basis for India's *swaraj*. In order to probe the extent to which Gandhi's reliance on conceptual violence affected his larger dilemma of reconciling principles and power it is important to investigate the nature of the "experiments" he suggests are indispensable to creating Indian patriots.

5

PURIFYING SELF AND NATION

ॐ

Gandhi's Experiments with Self-Control

Let Indian youth treasure in their hearts the quotation . . . "The future is for the nations who are chaste."

—M. K. Gandhi[1]

Gandhi was interested in the success of his own experiments primarily to the extent that others might learn from them and subscribe to a regimen of self-discipline. He wanted to engage young Indians on a level that would lead to self-control rather than mandate institutional reform through policy. He wanted to persuade people to change their way of life in order to rebuild India.

—Joseph S. Alter[2]

Some people, believing that . . . virtue is a single one, push it to extremes. They fail to realize that a nose which deviates from the perfect straightness by being either hooked or snub is still a fine nose and looks good as well; but if the process is carried to excess, first it will lose the proportion which belongs to this part of the body, and finally it will not look like a nose at all, because of the extreme to which either the hook or the snub has been pushed at the expense of its opposite.

—Aristotle[3]

THE *SATYAGRAHI* AS MORAL HERO

I n his recent book on Hindu nationalism, Thomas Blom Hansen suggests that cultural nationalisms are generally projects of ideological control that seek to shape the always unfamiliar and unpredictable social forms generated by processes of modernization.

Famously manifested in nineteenth-century organizations like Turn-vater Jahn's German gymnasiums or Mazzini's Young Italy corps, such schemes of ideological control emphasize social discipline and individual self-control, particularly the ability to control one's desires and libido in order to sublimate these urges to unconditional dedication and service to the nationalist cause.[4] As a result, the cultural nationalists' demand for the moral regeneration of their nation becomes inseparably entangled with elaborate schemes for the purification of body and soul. Viewed as a microcosm of a new moral order to be generalized in society, the individual self is subjected to various experiments designed to render visible the "inner truth" of the moral nation.

Nationalist leaders often present themselves to their audiences as the living laboratory of their vision, endowing their practices of self-purification with an aura of heroism, moral strength, and self-sacrifice. Thus, they hope for their ideological project to take root in society, ultimately leading to the creation of devoted and efficient organizations guided by exemplary patriots who provide leadership for the masses. Indeed, the restoration of the nation to its imagined pristine condition requires the sustained production of loyal subjects whose new identity is maintained and solidified through engagement in a repetitive regimen of disciplinary exercises. Successful nationalist leaders usually manage to encourage scores of ordinary citizens to internalize their images of the pure nation and act out their patriotic scripts. Consequently, national identity emerges as a collective process of performing clearly defined ideological roles, or at least accepting authoritative norms of nationhood as "ours."[5] Hence, such projects of control represent much more than narcissistic exercises in spiritual self-transformation with only derivative political value.

Linking the collective task of achieving Indian *swaraj* to the personal duty of establishing moral self-rule, Gandhi self-consciously claimed for himself the dual Socratic role of the virtuous soul doctor and the wise lawgiver. As Leela Gandhi notes, "Gandhi's eclectic and ultimately appropriative catalogue of notable *satyagrahis* ["adherents to truth"] assimilates Socrates as an *exemplum* for the correct fulfillment of Indian nationalism, simultaneously transforming him into a critic of Western civilization."[6] Integral to his general conceptual framework of nonviolent nationalism, Gandhi designed his ascetic "experiments with truth" as rigorous exercises aimed at individual moral detoxification. Like Socrates, true *satyagrahis* were to be fearless and willing to give up their bodies in the service of truth and justice. Such a demanding program of self-discipline represented, therefore, the prescribed course of treatment for the sick nation: "India is today nothing but a dead mass. . . . Let her come alive by self-purification, i.e., self-restraint and self-denial."[7]

Gandhi's conviction that the success of moral reform on a national scale depended on the faithful execution of such "soul control" becomes even more apparent in a 1910 letter to his cousin Maganlal: "Nobility of the soul consists in realizing that you are yourself India. In your emancipation is the emancipation of India. All else is make-believe."[8] The message was clear: if Indians wanted to exert national self-rule, they had to engage in a life-long process of self-purification rooted in the wisdom of their ancestors that would generate a new sense of identity. Hence, the stage was set for the enactment of a heroic spiritual battle with the most formidable of all opponents: *kama,* the dark god of desire and "arch-enemy of man."[9] What was at stake in this interminable struggle was nothing less than the purity and health of the soul and nation.

By insisting that his demanding project of self-control generative of nonviolent soul-force constituted the *only way* to achieve "real home rule," Gandhi also implied the need for experienced leaders who were ready to lead the masses in the performance of patriotic exercises designed to awaken the nation. Indeed, his strong emphasis on moral leadership highlights the important task of cultural nationalists to provide their audience with a pantheon of exemplary heroes and villains who furnish a rich repertoire of positive and negative role models.[10] As Bhikhu Parekh points out, "Gandhi looked upon such a cadre of spiritual elite as his 'army for *swaraj,*' which was to settle in the remotest villages, educate and energise the masses and to create a nation of energetic, proud, public-spirited and spiritually disciplined citizens."[11] In *Hind Swaraj,* Gandhi appealed especially to the professional classes—the "educated," the "lawyers," the "doctors," and the "wealthy"—for this type of moral leadership, hoping to convince them to dedicate their lives to the attainment of personal and political self-rule. More than half of the nineteen nationalist demands listed in his booklet are explicitly addressed to the Indian professional classes. It was only upon his return to India that Gandhi gradually broadened his appeals in an attempt to mobilize the masses. By the 1920s, he was aiming for nothing less than an entire nation of sober celibates who would embody his new moral order, starting with the formation of a cadre of "great souls" who might inspire popular enthusiasm.[12]

Chapter XVII of *Hind Swaraj* offers a first glimpse of Gandhi's heroic vision. Seemingly fascinated by the Editor's romantic account of exemplary *satyagrahis* leading the nation toward self-rule, the Reader immediately pushes his nonviolent interlocutor to address the matter of leadership in more detail: "From what you say, then, it would appear that it is not a small thing to become a passive resister, and, if so, I would like you to explain how a man may become a passive resister." The Editor's response comes without hesitation: "To become a passive resister is easy enough, but it is also equally difficult. . . . After a great deal of experience, it seems to me that those who want to become passive resisters *for the service of the country* have to observe perfect chastity, adopt poverty, follow truth, and cultivate fearlessness."[13] The Editor's reply is followed by a short description of each of these four points, including a brief set of instructions on how to deal with some related practical difficulties. Indeed, these four requirements constitute the nucleus of Gandhi's elaborate program for the moral regeneration of self and nation.

In order to assess this program—particularly its injunctions to follow truth and observe perfect chastity—it is necessary to go beyond an analysis of *Hind Swaraj* by drawing on relevant passages scattered throughout Gandhi's entire oeuvre. Before embarking on this task, however, I would like to insert a preliminary note of caution. There have been a number of attempts to offer profound psychoanalytic and symbolic readings of Gandhi's experiments with self-control, particularly those involving his attitudes toward sexuality and his dietary habits.[14] Some of the insights that emerge from such interpretations are useful insofar as they contribute to a better understanding of some enigmatic aspects of Gandhi's personality. Yet, valuable as these psychological and sociopsychological accounts may be, I wish to reemphasize that the focus of this study is not Gandhi's sexuality or lack thereof, but his attempts to reconcile his nonviolent principles with his commitment to Indian nationalism. While it may neither be possible nor advisable to avoid psychological matters altogether, I am nonetheless more interested in exploring below the problematic connection between his experiments with self-control and his vision of the pure nation than in joining the clinical search for explanations of Gandhi's sexual preoccupations.[15]

FOLLOWING TRUTH

Gandhi held that it was impossible to achieve national and individual self-rule without following truth (*satya*), which he defined in metaphysical terms as the essential attribute of God and the ultimate source of all existence. Deriving his understanding of "truth" from the Sanskrit verb *sat* (to be, or to exist), he sought to convey that "Truth alone is real, and everything else is unreal." Hence, he emphasized time and again that "Truth itself is God, and non-violence is just a synonym for truth." The latter part of this statement was meant to underline his conviction that truth seekers were always obliged to employ means that corresponded to a truthful end: "And when you want to find Truth as God, the only inevitable means is love, nonviolence—and since I believe that ultimately means and ends are convertible terms I should not hesitate to say that God is love."[16]

Although he confidently posited "absolute truth" as a transcendental principle unconditioned by space and time, Gandhi also argued that it could never be grasped in its fullness by mortal human beings who lived in a material world characterized by what the followers of Jainism call *anekantavada*—the many-sidedness of all phenomena. Even one's most noble efforts to behold absolute truth yielded, therefore, only provisional insights or, as Gandhi put it, "relative truths."[17] Still, his original postulation of absolute truth from within a framework of relativity fraught with human inadequacies created a serious epistemological problem. After all, if "finite human beings shall never know in its fullness Truth and Love which is in itself infinite," how could he so confidently assert the existence of absolute *satya*? Rather than addressing this deep paradox, Gandhi chose the seemingly less problematic route of simply restating his unshakable faith in god as truth, and then proceeded to connect his metaphysics of truth with his conception of moral action:

> Devotion to this Truth is the sole justification for our existence. All our activities should be centred in Truth. Truth should be the very breath of our life. When once this stage in the pilgrim's progress is reached, all other rules of correct living will come without effort and obedience to them will be instinctive. But without Truth it is impossible to observe any principles or rules in life. . . . There should be Truth in thought, Truth in speech and Truth in action.[18]

Thus anchoring his awareness of absolute truth in faith or intuition, Gandhi confronted the related problem of identifying with certainty what sorts of behaviors constituted truthful, that is, moral, conduct. In other words, how was one to distinguish between truthful and corrupt actions, given that imperfect people perceived truth in different, often even contrary, ways? Given his own acknowledgment of the fallibility of all human truth claims, Gandhi's own credo of the universal truthfulness of *ahimsa* and the moral worth of nonviolent action might eventually turn out to be a mistaken assumption. His solution to this problem was to posit the individual's duty to search for more complete manifestations of the necessarily incomplete "relative truths" *in interaction with others*—letting go of one's original truth claim only if the opponent(s) offered a "better argument."[19] Unfortunately, however, reasonable people might disagree on what constitutes a better argument, thus raising the possibility that the resolution of social and political conflicts through rational debate could fail. This problem is compounded by Gandhi's own admission that some of the highest spiritual truths "are only known to oneself and one's Maker" and are therefore "clearly incommunicable."[20]

In my view, one can find the source of these theoretical difficulties in Gandhi's dualistic worldview, which, although affirming the oneness of being, nonetheless cast human existence as an eternal struggle of spirit versus matter and mind versus body. True moral progress in society was measured in the growing mastery of spirit over matter.[21] His image of such a divided world gave birth to a moral imperative pointing to an elusive end: although the inevitable physicality and corporeality of the human condition prevented people from realizing absolute truth, their spiritual nature imposed on them nothing less than the search for moral perfection.[22] Viewed from within Gandhi's own conceptual universe, this quest for truth was therefore an impossible possibility—the highest moral duty whose ultimate objective was nonetheless beyond human reach. On one hand, the Gandhian search for truth required the seeker's unreserved faith in the existence of absolute truth, while on the other, it also gave a strong nod of approval to the skeptic's position regarding the difficulty of ever grasping *satya* in its fullness. Hence, Gandhi built his moral practice on an interpretation of truth that was at once ontological and empirical, dogmatic and flexible, determinate yet adaptable, categorical as well as experimental.[23] But neither the transcendental nor the pragmatic dimension of truth could stand on its own, because the realization of one's spiritual quest required practical action, just as much as action was dependent on transcendental guidance. How, then, in this confusing world of relative truths, were potential truth-seekers to commence their quest?

As might be expected, Gandhi's response bears the imprints of his indeterminate stance with regard to the validity and status of reason, faith, and intuition and their relationship to each other. As the first step on the path of pursuing truth, he prescribed a long and severe regimen of self-purification in order to increase the chances of catching "faint glimpses of the Absolute Truth." Thus, it was imperative for the truth-seeker to learn to listen to the dictates of his or her own conscience, because truth was what the "voice within tells one."[24] As Raghavan Iyer points out, Gandhi's glorification of conscience is strongly reminiscent of Socrates's deification of the *daimon*—an authoritative "inner voice" that, remaining beyond one's conscious control or manipulation, represents a mysterious link between human subjectivity and the divine moral law.[25] Once the inner voice suggested a particular course of action, it was incumbent upon the truth-seeker to embark on a series of experiments designed to test the validity of its demands in a social and political world characterized by conflicting claims and shifting perspectives. This imposed on the seeker the duty to "insist on truth" as he saw it, while at the same time urging him to revise his beliefs if they were found wanting after being put to the test. Likening such "experiments with truth" to the scientific method, which dictates "an indispensable course common for all," Gandhi claimed that these tests could only be undertaken by those extraordinary *satyagrahis* who had "the will and the patience to acquire the necessary qualifications."[26]

According to Gandhi, such individuals were required to commence their quest with the solemn "vow of truth—speaking and thinking of truth, the vow of *brahmacharya* [sexual abstinence], of nonviolence, poverty and non-possession. If you do not take these five vows you may not embark on the experiment." The ultimate goal of this sacred commitment was to reduce the pernicious influence of material forces reflected in the lustful cravings of the body: "If you would swim on the bosom of the ocean of Truth, you must reduce yourself to a zero."[27] Gandhi not only considered the utter extinction of one's egoistic tendencies a sign of individual liberation (*moksha*), but he also found it indispensable in the creation of a selfless nation and the achievement of true *swaraj*. Since, for Gandhi, *swaraj* of a people meant the sum total of the *swaraj* of individuals, the achievement of a moral national identity depended on the individual performance of pure *satyagrahis*. The fulfillment of their highest religious aspirations therefore required their engagement in political and social experiments based on the performance of *tapas* (exercises in self-purification). "The hard dusty way toward perfection," Gandhi wrote admiringly, entails "ceaseless self-discipline and purification of the spirit through the fire of suffering. . . ."[28] In other words, as Iyer points out, "*Satya* then requires the *tapas* of *ahimsa* and this means self-suffering and self-sacrifice in the midst of society."[29]

Thus, Gandhi's lifelong experiments with self-control went beyond the religious whims of those Hindu ascetics whose gaze was fixed exclusively upon the beyond. His rigorous experiments with truth represent the crucial microphysics of self-discipline required for all future political reformers who, having turned their backs on the materialism of modern civilization, were working for independence on a national scale in accordance with these presumed principles of India's ancient civilization. Holding that the spheres of spirituality and politics were inextricably intertwined, Gandhi argued that individual self-purification and service to the nation were part of the same continuum: "The message is to spiritualize the political life and the political institutions of the country. We must immediately set about realizing its practice. The students cannot be away from politics. Politics is as essential to them as religion. Politics cannot be divorced from religion. Politics divorced from religion becomes debasing."[30]

Any artificial attempt to separate these interconnected levels of human existence would only serve the goals of an instrumental "power-politics," understood in Hobbesian terms as the pursuit of self-interests and physical self-preservation and the expense of moral goodness and altruism. Selfish cravings for material benefits would further strengthen one's appetites and desires, ultimately resulting in the thorough moral pollution of self and nation. According to Gandhi, such a corrupt state of affairs was reflected in the "soullessness" of modern civilization. Conversely, by following truth through the practice of self-restraint, the *satyagrahi* would refuse to resort to the power of brute force "generated by the stirring up in us of evil passions." Instead, he or she would choose the pure means of *ahimsa*—even at the cost of self-suffering to the point of death, thereby demonstrating the "irresistible power of the soul over the body." For Gandhi, such instances of moral heroism represented crucial victories of spirit over matter, pointing to the possibility of creating a pure Indian nation: "[L]et our lives bear witness to our past. . . . Ours will only then be a truly spiritual nation when we shall show more truth than gold, greater fearlessness than pomp of power and wealth, greater charity than love of self."[31]

To sum up: Gandhi argued that the moral regeneration of the nation depended on the purity of *satyagrahis* who, in their search for truth, strove for a detachment from physical desires by submitting to demanding exercises in self-control. Confronted with their example, modern Indians might discover the untruth of their adopted way of life and begin to reorient their souls toward the inner voice of truth. Carrying out its divine commands, the nation would gradually reform its political and social life and recapture the moral virtue of its ancient civilization, thus setting a lesson in spiritual heroism to the world. He emphasized that he wanted India to become strong in order that she might infect the other nations also with her strength. Presenting this vision in the Hindu idiom as *ramrajya,* the righteous rule of Rama, Gandhi looked forward to the rule of truth and justice over all Indians. Indeed, he considered his ashrams in South Africa and India as the seeds of the coming all-Indian *ramrajya,* proudly referring to them as the perfect training ground for "right men" and "right Indians."[32]

GOD'S EUNUCH:
THE OBSERVANCE OF PERFECT CHASTITY

It would be a grave mistake to separate Gandhi's political thought from his concern with sexual abstinence and public health, since he left no doubt that *brahmacharya*—broadly conceived as the search after the divine (Brahma) through saintly conduct—constituted the centerpiece of his ambitious program of purifying self and nation. "Brahmacharya signifies the control of all the senses at all times and at all places in thought, word and deed. Perfect Brahmacharis, men or women, are perfectly sinless. They are therefore near to God, they are like God. I have no doubt that such perfect observance of Brahmacharya is possible."[33] In *Hind Swaraj,* considerations of space

forced Gandhi to limit his discussion of the subject to a short para-
graph in which he indicated that the perfect observance of chastity
was the key to self-control and represented "one of the greatest dis-
ciplines without which the mind cannot attain requisite firmness."[34]
Over the next two decades, however, he treated this topic at great
length, arguing that sexual abstinence ought to be an integral part of
Indian national reform. In 1928, he reissued his main articles and letters on issues of sexuality in a collection titled *Self-Restraint versus
Self-Indulgence.* The book was wildly successful with his Indian audience and quickly went through three editions and several additional
printings. In 1939, a second volume was added to the original.

The collection opens with Gandhi's extended and admiring review of Paul Bureau's austere *L'indiscipline des moeurs* (1920), a book
translated by Mary Scharlieb, five years after it appeared in French,
as *Towards Moral Bankruptcy.* Bureau's reflections on morality link his
advocacy of sexual restraint to his appeal for a French moral nationalism. The appendix of Gandhi's collection also contains a short
piece on chastity and sensuality authored by the American transcen-
dentalist Henry David Thoreau.[35] In addition, *Self-Restraint versus
Self-Indulgence* features a reprint of William Loftus Hare's pseudosci-
entific treatise, titled "Generation and Regeneration" (1926), in
which the author discusses the "enervating psychological effects" of
sex. Gandhi's fondness for such biologically based theories of morality is significant for two reasons. First, it confirms his lifelong pattern
of using European countercultural writings as authoritative sources
for his own radical ideas on health and sexuality. In this respect, his
intellectual debt to Henry Salt's *A Plea for Vegetarianism* or John
Ruskin's *Unto This Last* has already been pointed out in previous
chapters. Second, it betrays Gandhi's willingness to accept at least to
some extent the Western discourse of science. At various points in
the collection, he proudly refers to *brahmacharya* as the "science of
self-control."[36] To be sure, this attitude stands in stark contrast to his
vision of the ruin of any civilization built on the utilitarian foundations of science and technology.[37] This problem also applies to his
idea of a "science of food," which will be discussed in more detail
toward the end of this chapter.

Although he is reluctant to confine his understanding of *brahmacharya* solely to the sexual dimension, Gandhi nonetheless spends
much time propagating his puritanical views on birth control, procreation, celibacy, sexual passion, and such "sexual pervasions" as

masturbation and homosexuality. From the outset, the reader is confronted with the dogmatic position that the sole object of sexual intercourse should be one's desire for progeny rather than the gratification of one's "animalistic sexual instinct." Gandhi categorically rejects all artificial methods of birth-control and instead insists on total sexual abstinence as the only moral and sensible course of action. In his view, sexual union for any purpose other than procreation constitutes nothing but a "criminal waste of the vital fluid." Likewise, the "consequent [sexual] excitement caused to man and woman" represents "an equally criminal waste of precious energy." Invoking the authority of unnamed Indian "scientists of old," Gandhi expounds on the great value of conserving "vital fluids" for the purpose of transmuting their "animal energy" into "the highest form of energy for the benefit of society." Such a successful process of "purifying" sexual energy would lead to the "mastery of the Science of Life."[38]

Sexual abstinence represents for Gandhi the most potent medicine in the struggle to cure the nation of its materialist disease. In order to become a "living specimen" of the "giant Brahmacharis of old," one has to follow the national doctor's advice and discipline one's body and mind through the performance of rigid experiments of sexual self-control, including such controversial "experiments" as sleeping naked next to young women in order to test one's ability to resist sexual "temptation."[39] The successful conquest of sexual passions under such extreme conditions would prove to the nation and the world that *hind swaraj* in its fullest manifestation was indeed within the realm of human possibility: "One who has acquired a perfect control over his or her sexual energy strengthens the whole being, physical, mental and spiritual, and attains powers unattainable by any other means."[40] At its core, then, Gandhi's theory of *brahmacharya* postulates a strong link between the individual's commitment to sexual abstinence and the creation of a nonviolent national identity: "Let young men and women for whose sake *Young India* is written from week to week know that is their duty, if they would purify the atmosphere about them and shed their weakness, to be and remain chaste and know too that it is not so difficult as they may have been taught to imagine."[41]

This passage also conveys Gandhi's hope that the Indians' patriotic duty of "purifying the atmosphere" was not reserved only for the select few, but would eventually be accepted by young people and ordinary married couples as well. For the sake of the moral health of the nation, brahmacharic couples would voluntarily agree on having sex only for the purpose of reproduction or, better yet, they would abstain from sex altogether: "I have not the shadow of a doubt that married people, if they wished well of the country and wanted to see India become a nation of strong and handsome well-formed men and women, would practice self-restraint and cease to procreate for the time being. . . . it is our duty for the present moment to suspend bringing forth heirs to our slavery." Couples who were unable to live up to the vow of celibacy should at least limit their sexual activity to the procreation of a single child. Once it was born, sexual intercourse should cease in favor of a purely Platonic relationship which, in Gandhi's opinion, was much better suited for the spiritual development of both partners.[42]

At several points in the collection, he eagerly provides his readership with his list of moral priorities for an ideal marriage: "[S]piritual development ought to be given the first place in the choice for marriage. Service should come next, family considerations and the interest of the social order should have the third place, and mutual attraction or 'love' the fourth and last place."[43] This means not only that deeply ingrained traditions such as child marriage should be abolished, but also that all adult Indians have the moral duty to provide their offspring with the virtuous example of living in a spiritual union based on sexual abstinence. Such a strict program of *brahmacharya* would give a moral compass to India's struggle for *swaraj*. Its execution requires the cultivation of fearlessness on the part of the *satyagrahi,* because the unwillingness to practice sexual self-restraint represents a sign of cowardice: "A man who is unchaste loses stamina, becoming emasculated and cowardly. He whose mind is given over to animal passions is not capable of any great effort. This can be proven by innumerable instances."[44] Without the widespread practice of sexual abstinence, Indians would never acquire the purity and inner courage required for the practice of nonviolence. As a result, the country would remain but another "Englistan," beholden to a "highly artificial" European system of education. The imitation of the Western paradigm would result in the adoption of its loose sexual mores and "rob the nation's youth of physical and mental vigour."[45] Like their British masters, modern Indians, too, had to be properly "Indianised." Hence, in spite of his support of cultural and religious pluralism, Gandhi was clearly engaged in a process of moral homogenization: "We are trying to produce a homogenous nation."[46]

In Gandhi's view, an entire generation of nonviolent Indian nationalists bore the dual burden of first "building up the body and mind to the required standard" and then training the next generation in the "true science" of sex control: "The nation, God willing, can follow the godly way if only the parents prepare an atmosphere favourable to the observance of Brahmacharya on the part of the rising generation." Only those who had acquired a high degree of "mastery over the self" were equipped to impart to the nation's youth a proper sex education that "has for its object the conquest and sublimation of the sex passion."[47] Once again, Gandhi's vision contains an appeal to exemplary moral heroes to take the lead in this difficult task:

> Even if there are a handful of teachers endowed with practical experience, who accept the ideal of attaining self-control as the highest duty of man, and are fired by a genuine and undying faith in their mission, and are sleeplessly vigilant and active, their labor will light the path of the children of Gujarat, save the unwary from falling into the mire of sexuality, and rescue those who might be already engulfed in it.[48]

Gandhi's allusion to "the mire of sexuality" reflects his strong view that sexual pleasure in itself was evil and that human sexual urges were on a par with other "animalistic" tendencies, resulting in various manifestations of violence, hatred, and anger. He considered "incontinence" and the "madness" of sexual passion the "root cause of evil in the world," leading to moral and physical degeneration: "I can affirm, without the slightest hesitation, from my own experience as well as that of others, that sexual enjoyment is not only not necessary for, but is positively injurious to health."[49] Indeed, he even went so far as to agree with Hare's extreme opinion that the sexual act was essentially "a movement towards death." Men, in particular, were susceptible to the siren call of *kama* because their biological sex drive was more strongly developed than that of women. The best technique in dealing with this biological disadvantage, Gandhi asserts, is for a man to "look upon every woman as his mother, sister or daughter." This practice would eventually lead to the realization "that woman is his companion and helpmate in life and not a means of satisfying his carnal desire."[50] Thus, Gandhi writes that the accomplished *brahmachari* would not flee from the company of women, because biological sex differences had no longer any significance for him.

> What I mean to say is that, a man whose sexual desire has been burnt up ceases to make a distinction between men and women. It must be so. His conception of beauty alters. He will not look at the external form. There-fore, the sight of a woman called beautiful will not ruffle or excite him. Even his sex organs will look different. In other words, such a man has so controlled his sexual instinct that he never gets erections. He has not be-come impotent for the lack of the necessary secretions of sexual glands. But these secretions in his case are sublimated into a vital force pervading his whole being. . . . The cultivated impotency of the man, whose sexual desire has been burnt up and whose sexual secretions are being converted into vital force, is wholly different: It is to be desired by everybody.[51]

Recommending such experiments in sexual self-control to the members of his Indian *ashrams,* Gandhi made no secret of his aspi-ration to become not only the nation's *Bapu* (Father) but also its *Ba* (mother). In her short account of her life in Gandhi's *ashram,* enti-tled "Bapu—My Mother," Gandhi's grandniece Manu claims that her uncle encouraged her to relate to him as her mother. "Ever since then," she writes, "Bapu began to bring me up just as a mother would bring up her own daughter. . . ."[52] In much the same vein, Nirmal Kumar Bose, Gandhi's Bengali interpreter and biographer, reports that his boss publicly announced that he intended to con-quer his sexual urges by becoming a woman: "This *violent* reaction against any physical manifestation of sex and his psychological ef-fort to become as pure as his mother, led Gandhiji into a profoundly significant attitude in public life."[53] Praying to god for the eradica-tion of his male sexuality in addition to taking frigid hip-baths to cool down his lingering passions, Gandhi sought refuge in an ideal-ized view of feminine purity as well as in an even more radical vi-sion of complete sexlessness. Pushing beyond the limits of his religious hermaphrodism, he yearned to become "God's Eunuch," citing approvingly the Islamic belief that the prophet Mohammed looked kindly upon "those made eunuchs not through an operation but through prayer to Allah."[54] Just as eager as he was to sacrifice his male sexuality on the altar of spiritual purity, so he expected the Indian nation to be morally uplifted by a good dose of female virtue.

Feminizing the Nation

Gandhi held complex and, at times, even contradictory attitudes toward women. As Judith Brown notes, "He must have been deeply influenced at a conscious and unconscious level by the ambiguities in Hindu perceptions of womanhood: the sense of woman as temptress and a source of mysterious power, as well as the vision of the self-sacrificing wife and mother."[55] It seems that these ambiguities indeed underlie his construction of two conflicting female ideals: woman as selfless mother and wife, and woman as desexualized servant of the nation fighting violence and injustice. Before exploring Gandhi's female ideals and their role in his broader vision of Indian nationhood, it is important to note that he encouraged the participation of women in some of his major *satyagraha* campaigns. In the existing literature on the subject, there is a general consensus on his pivotal role in helping to improve the political and social status of women in early twentieth-century India.[56] His mobilization of diverse female constituencies for a nationalist agenda served as a catalyst for the wider participation of Indian women in public affairs, thus leaving an important legacy for contemporary Indian politics.

The first of Gandhi's two female ideals—woman as self-sacrificing wife and mother—is deeply embedded in a patriarchal desire to secure women's obedience and protect their moral purity. As Sujata Patel points out, Gandhi's construct is drawn from a space inhabited by an "urbanised middle-class upper-caste Hindu male's perception of what a woman should be. In a significant way, there is a sense of continuity in Gandhian ideas on woman and those formulated by the reformers of the late nineteenth century."[57] Though he affirmed the existence of formal equality between the sexes, Gandhi nonetheless subscribed to the view that men and women had distinct moral qualities and psychological attributes based on fixed biological differences. He considered these "innate" traits to be responsible for the existence of separate social spheres in which men and women were supposed to play distinct but complementary roles.

> Men and women are of equal rank, but they are not identical. They are a peerless pair, being supplementary to one another. . . . Man is supreme in the outward activities of a married pair and, therefore, it is in the fitness of things that he should have greater knowledge thereof. On the other hand, home life is entirely the sphere of women, and, therefore, in

domestic affairs, in the upbringing and education of children, women ought to have more knowledge.[58]

Hence, Gandhi's ideal of the selfless wife and mother reflected the confining structures of a pre-existing patriarchal gender system in which family and home served as the natural training ground for women who were encouraged to perfect their feminine qualities. Ketu Katrak emphasizes that Gandhi echoed this traditional idea of domestic femininity through essentialist "appeals to the 'female' virtues: chastity, purity, self-sacrifice, suffering."[59] Sujata Patel agrees, adding that one of the various forms in which patriarchy presented itself in early twentieth-century India was through the formulation of a "morally superior ideal woman, who was the embodiment of all the best and goodness of human life and the world, the conscience of the male and the society. Gandhi not only accepted these assumptions, but he extended them to fit his own perspective relating to the participation of women in politics."[60] Gandhi's extension involved, first and foremost, the linking of domesticity to his nonviolent nationalism, thereby enlarging the meaning and function of both arenas. By bringing nationalist politics to the home, he was able to bestow upon ordinary women the title of "defenders of the nation's purity" without demolishing the patriarchal "separate spheres" doctrine based on the "givenness" of biological differences. Thus, he created a central political role for the married Indian woman in the household.[61]

The selfless female homemaker behind the spinning wheel, in particular, emerged as a powerful symbol of the ideal Indian woman/nation. Gandhi's advocacy of spinning for the achievement of both personal and political *swaraj* transformed the stigma of "weakness" so often associated with female domesticity into a beacon of moral strength resulting from long years of self-discipline. Consequently, the female homemaker supplying the nation with *khadi* (home-spun cloth) assumed a prominent political role in Gandhi's famous *swadeshi* campaigns, which became an integral part of his *satyagraha* movement in India after 1918. "In spinning they [women] have a natural advantage over men . . . spinning is essentially a slow and comparatively silent process. Woman is the embodiment of sacrifice and nonviolence."[62] In order to amplify this message, Gandhi employed ahistorical representations of women and female sexuality drawn from popular Hindu myths and epics. For example, he frequently invoked the figure of the legendary Sita, the virtuous wife of King Rama, as the highest personification of *swadeshi,* purity, chastity, and self-sacrifice.[63] Wearing only simple garments made of *khadi,* Gandhi's Sita served as a powerful symbol of India's women, reminding them that the regeneration of "Mother India" depended upon their ability to emulate Sita's virtues in the epic struggle against the European colonizer. Sujata Patel puts it well:

> In Gandhi, the spinning of khadi was turned into a political message which was reposed onto the morally superior woman, who in turn became the symbol and conscience of the new nation-in-the-making. The woman as "mother" who had "innate," "natural" capacities for "wiseness," "strength," "courage," "patience" and "intuition" now becomes the symbol of the new political message and its strategy of non-violence. Only her involvement could free the nation from the clutches of the colonial power.[64]

In fact, Gandhi did not hesitate to apply the ideal of the self-sacrificing wife/mother to men as well. He elevated "female" activities like spinning, nursing, and cooking to the exalted status of "patriotic duties" to be carried out by all Indians regardless of their sex: "Whilst women naturally cook for the household, organized cooking on a large scale is universally done by men throughout the world." Through such attempts to feminize the entire nation, Gandhi gradually liberated notions of political activism and the performance of great deeds from their association with masculine aggressiveness and the glorification of male warrior violence.[65] Suggesting that all participants of India's nonviolent struggle for *swaraj* would be wise to emulate women's "infinite capacity for suffering," Gandhi dismissed the notion that women represented the "weaker sex," arguing instead that, "Woman is more fitted than man to make explorations and take action in ahimsa. For the courage of self-sacrifice woman is any day superior to man as I believe man is to woman for the courage of the brute."[66] More than anything, it is this assumption of women's superior capacity for self-suffering and ahimsic action that connects Gandhi's project of feminizing the nation to his vision of a nonviolent India.

If the spinning of *khadi* represented self-sacrifice and such patriotic women served as Gandhi's symbol for the pure nation-in-the-making, then the neglect of such activities by disobedient women could only signify their lack of love of country, the result of their lustful indulgence: "The spinning wheel is the symbol of chastity of womanhood of India. In the absence of the spinning wheel, I give you my testimony, that thousands of our poor sisters are giving themselves to a life of shame and degradation."[67] This passage confirms Judith Brown's suspicion about existing ambiguities in Gandhi's conception of womanhood, for his praise of female virtue rings with a patriarchal fear of uncontrolled female sexual power. Apparently, the tireless routine of spinning and mothering was not only necessary to safeguard India's indigenous wealth and well-being, but also to "protect" women from their own sexual desires.[68] Thus, the function of Gandhi's *swadeshi* campaigns seems to go deeper than just the employment of ahimsic strategies of political resistance directed against the British. *Swadeshi* also constituted a patriarchal-brahmacharic technique for "transforming" dangerous female sexual energy into the positive energy required for safeguarding the honor and purity of the woman-nation.

Apparently doubting that the ideal of the self-sacrificing wife/mother and the politicization of the home would be sufficient to control the transgressive sexual desires of those women who rejected even his politicized notion of domesticity, Gandhi introduced the more ascetic ideal of the desexualized woman selflessly supporting the nation outside the household. In order to overcome the conflicting messages contained in these respective ideals, he fell back on his advice to married women to consider giving up sex altogether. Married women who were prepared to take the vow of celibacy should therefore commence their experiments with self-control by resisting the sexual advances of their spouses. In short, they had to "learn to say 'no' to their husbands when they approach them carnally."[69] Unmarried or widowed women, on the other hand, best personified the ideal of the desexualized woman. Claiming that the Hindu widow embodied the highest virtues of self-control, Gandhi argued that a life of renunciation and self-denial had become "second nature" to her: "This is Hinduism at its best. I regard the widow's life as a reflection of Hinduism. When I see a widow, I instinctively bow my head in reverence. . . . A widow's blessing is to me a gift which I prize. I forget all my sorrows. Man is but a clod before her. A widow's patient suffering is impossible to rival."[70] While Gandhi strongly opposed *sati*—the Hindu custom of pressuring a widow into mounting her dead husband's funeral pyre—he nonetheless urged the widow to become an example of sexual restraint and to "strive to make her husband's ideals and virtues live again in her actions in this world."[71]

In addition to perpetuating powerful patriarchal stereotypes, Gandhi's elevation of Hindu widowhood spawned, once again, invidious comparisons on the basis of his affirmative orientalism, which presented Indian spirituality as a superior force of goodness in the world. Only a year before his death, Gandhi emphasized that "If women resolve to bring glory to the nation within a few months they can change the face of the country because the spiritual background of the Aryan women is totally different than the women of other countries."[72] As the repository of the spiritual strength of the nation, he expected the de-sexualized woman to curb male hypersexuality, police the desires of her sisters, and serve her country through her ability to become socially active outside the household. Indeed, Gandhi called especially on such women to spearhead his moral campaign to cure the nation of the evils of sexual indulgence, alcohol, tobacco, gambling, and other predominantly male vices. Arguing that the only jewels accepted by such female "personifications of renunciation" were chastity and honor, Gandhi urged all women to refrain from wearing lavish jewelry and using heavy perfumes. Likewise, he warned younger women against copying the "modern girl spirit" of dressing for the purpose of attracting sexual attention.[73] In addition to teaching men a valuable lesson in chastity, such demonstrations of female virtue would generate a moral climate favorable to the voluntary adoption of poverty and the cultivation of fearlessness—two other requirements needed for the successful moral regeneration of self and nation. Overall, then, Gandhi glorified the sacrifice of women's reproductive aspects and their family life to the service of the nation. Such a woman-renunciator, he emphasized, not only adorned "her sex and the nation," but also protected the precious legacy of ancient Indian civilization by the "sheer force of her purity."[74]

Conversely, Gandhi had very harsh words for those women who failed to structure their lives according to his two ideals. For example, he insisted that a pure woman would never sink to the level of a sex worker, for such sexual transgressions imperiled Indian womanhood. Although he conceded that prostitutes were "victims of man's lust," he also argued that women "like this" should not get married lest the existing system of marriage become impure.[75] In the 1920s, he objected vehemently to allowing some "dancing girls" from the city of Barisal to become Congress officials. Arguing that their professional and moral status had violated the ethical standards of Indian society, he demanded that Congress never incorporate sinful women who "are more dangerous than thieves," because "the latter steal material possessions, the former steal virtue." Although he admitted that there was no legal bar to their entry, he still insisted that public opinion should have kept them out. It was the duty of all true patriots to make sure that only those with pure hands and pure hearts could officiate at the altar of *swaraj:* "The movement of non-cooperation is nothing, if it does not purify us and restrain our evil passions."[76]

KEYS TO HEALTH

Gandhi's "science of *brahmacharya*" and his project of feminizing the nation were tightly linked to his conception of moral and physical health. In his view, the human body constituted merely an external shell housing the divine spirit. It represented, therefore, both a useful instrument in the search for truth and an insatiable lump of sensual matter standing in the way of moral perfection: "The body may either be a play-ground of passion, or a temple of self-realisation. . . . The spirit must curb the flesh every moment."[77] As Joseph Alter notes, Gandhi never regarded the human body as an object of beauty or something upon which to place any intrinsic moral value.[78] While he conceded that the body was an impressive "reflection of the universe," it amounted nonetheless to little more than a complex "human machine"—a valuable tool that was to be put to use for the achievement of greater ethical and spiritual objectives.[79] Apart from its subordinate function to serve the spirit, the body was merely "a bag of filth" and an "incarnation of hell," reflecting the "undeniable fact" that, on a purely physical level, the human being was "a contemptible worm."[80] Just as tons of dirt and stone separated the miner of precious stones from his desired objects, so stood the physical body between the *satyagrahi* and the divine spirit. To break through this layer of physicality and catch a glimpse of absolute truth, humans had the sacred duty to cleanse their "mine of dirt." "In order to get to what lies in those mines," Gandhi lectured, "we cannot take too much pains [*sic*] over keeping in a fit condition the temple of the spirit."[81]

Hence, the body constituted, at best, a natural testing ground for the will to truth and purity. Lasting moral results could only be produced through a comprehensive program of physical discipline, which included a vegetarian diet and regular periods of fasting, public health and hygiene, *pranayama* (mechanics of breathing fresh air), sleeping outdoors, strict regimens of hydrotherapy and naturopathy, walking, and, most importantly, sexual abstinence. A result of these persistent acts of personal self-control, good health was therefore the necessary condition for the nonviolent regeneration of the nation. Since "strong and vigorous bodies" were better equipped to endure the hardships of self-suffering, well-conditioned *satyagrahis* would greatly enhance the efficacy of nonviolent direct action, thereby moving the nation ever closer to *swaraj*. In short, "feeble physiques" reflecting modern forms of indulgence had to be replaced with healthy "bodies of steel." To that end, Gandhi encouraged all Indians to participate in physical education programs taught in regional gymnasiums under the stalwart image of the Hindu god Hanuman, whose physical strength derived from his deep devotion to Ram and his exemplary sexual self-control: "May you therefore be like [Hanuman] of matchless valour born out of your *brahmacharya* and may that valour be dedicated to the service of the Mother Land."[82]

Thus, Gandhi enshrined the individual's task of disciplining the body in what Joseph Alter calls "a sociology of individual increments, and elemental configurations, in which the geopolitical state of the nation gets reimagined one patient at a time."[83] In other words, the disease of modern civilization afflicting both individual bodies and the body politic was most effectively treated on the micro level. Gandhi's thin booklet, *Guide to Health,* the most popular of all his writings, pays particular attention to the connection between food and sex, emphasizing that the restoration of a chaste body (politic) was impossible without the individual's willingness to practice the control of the palate.

> A glutton who exercises no restraint in eating is a slave to his animal passions. One who has not been able to control his palate, will never be able to control the other senses. If this is true, it is clear that one should take just enough food for the requirements of the body and no more. The body was never meant to be treated as a refuse bin holding the foods that the palate demands. Food is meant to sustain the body. His body has been given to man as a means of self-realization. Self-realization means realization of

God. A person who has made this realization the object of his or her life, will never become a slave to the animal passion.[84]

Gandhi goes so far as to make control of the palate the "first essential" in the observance of the *brahmacharya* vow. Reflecting the truth-seeker's detached attitude from material pleasures, his diet should be "limited, simple, spiceless, and, if possible, uncooked." Invoking the authority of his own lifelong experiments with food, Gandhi assured his readers that the *brahmachari*'s ideal food should consist of nothing but fresh fruit and nuts. He emphasized that the immunity from passion that he enjoyed when he lived on this food was extraordinary.[85]

As in the case of women who failed to live up to his ideals of purity, Gandhi did not hesitate to exhort those who violated or ignored his dietary instructions. Rejecting tea, coffee, and cocoa as "substances harmful to the body," he reserved his sharpest criticism for the consumers of liquor, tobacco, and drugs. Advocating "prohibition at any cost," he declared alcoholic beverages an "invention of the devil" that destroyed the possibility of achieving true *swaraj* for nation, body, and soul: "I hold drinking spirituous liquors in India to be more criminal than petty thefts. . . . I must advocate the summary punishment of those who manufacture the fiery liquid and those even who will persist in drinking it notwithstanding repeated warnings." Informing his readers of his determination to end the production and consumption of alcohol, Gandhi declared, "If I was appointed dictator for one hour for all India, the first thing I would do would be to close without compensation all the liquor shops. . . ."[86] In short, he envisioned a pure India as a nation of teetotalers, emphasizing that the total prohibition of all "intoxicants" would be the clearest sign of the country's great moral awakening.

In addition to suggesting legal remedies for the problem, Gandhi once again urged women to make it their "sacred duty" to carry on a "whirlwind campaign for total prohibition." He envisioned "thousands of India's sisters" standing at the helm of nationwide picketing campaigns, surrounding drink shops and shaming both sellers and consumers into giving up their evil activities. Acting as fearless patriots, these women would be prepared to endure the abuses and assaults of these "addicts" in order to restore the health of the nation. Gandhi was confident that they would succeed in converting their fallen brothers through their loving appeals to the best in man.[87]

Gandhi's reliance on the purifying power of female virtue underlines his belief in the existence of a strong link between the consumption of alcohol, tobacco, and drugs and the rise of public immorality, particularly acts of sexual indulgence: "Those who are at present opposed to prohibition do not seem to realize the sex excesses drink leads one to. Sex excesses increase venereal disease. The loss of national wealth in the form of ill-health, loss of vitality, and loss of productive labor need better be imagined than figured out." When the Working Committee of the Indian National Congress passed a resolution in favor of total prohibition, Gandhi praised the action as the institution's "greatest achievement."[88]

Searching for a reformed national diet that would help decolonize Indian bodies and minds, Gandhi paradoxically embraced the discourse of modern science. He was convinced that only a detached, objective course of self-experimentation provided the most appropriate means by which to move closer to truth: "If those who have independent experience and have some scientific training would conduct experiments in order to find physical and spiritual values of different fruits, they would no doubt render service in a field which is capable of limitless exploration."[89] Although he rejected both modern Western medicine and traditional Hindu *ayurveda* (life knowledge), his own methods nonetheless reflected his fascination with Occidental "scientific theories of healing" such as Juste's naturopathy and Kuhne's hydrotherapy. Hence, as David Arnold notes in his seminal book on medicine in nineteenth-century India, Gandhi's views on health were a "demonstration of the hold which Western medical ideas and practices had begun to exert on Indian society and the extent to which what had once been the hallmark of an alien presence was fast becoming part of India's own ideology and leadership."[90] Once serving as a means of colonial hegemony, the scientifically-based discourse of national health emerged in the hands of Gandhi as a formidable threat to the empire. Assuming the mantle of India's "national physician," who viewed the body as a scientific site of medical facts and tactics, he linked health to nationhood, seemingly unaware of his reliance on the epistemological paradigm of the colonizer. As Joseph Alter notes perceptively,

With only a slight shift in perspective one might rightly conclude that Gandhi was not so much obsessed by sex and food as by a discourse of science which allowed sex and food to become social, moral, and political facts of life, as well as biological ones. . . . Looking toward the future of India, Gandhi escaped from the iron cage of rationality and blind faith into a science of his own creation which held out the possibility, at least, for public health to have a cumulative effect. . . .[91]

THE VIOLENCE OF GANDHI'S
EXPERIMENTS WITH SELF-CONTROL

While the rhetorical power of Gandhi's ideological project of self-control may constitute a striking achievement, the allegedly nonviolent character of his experiments is quite a different matter. There are strong indications that his elaborate schemes of self-control involved forms of conceptual violence. For example, he conveyed his struggle against physical desires in a language rife with violent images and metaphors of warfare. The body and its passions represented an "insidious enemy," comparable to "snakes" and "scorpions" eager to poison their innocent victims. He described his purification schemes as "war against desire" culminating in the interminable battle against the "lower part" of the self—a pernicious Other whose "destruction" and "annihilation" represented the supreme end of the spiritual quest for absolute truth. As Sudhir Kakar emphasizes, by casting physical desire and sensual pleasure in the role of vicious "opponents," Gandhi failed to engage them in a nonviolent fashion: "[T]he god of desire was the only antagonist with whom Gandhi could not compromise and whose humanity (not to speak of his divinity) he always denied."[92]

In my view, Gandhi's violent language of "subduing vile passions" arose from his belief that true moral heroes were obliged to transcend the adversities and vulnerabilities of the human condition. Representing an excessive program of renunciation, his ascetic-ethical practices sought to banish all forms of contingency from human life "by placing the most important things, things such as personal achievement, politics, and love, under our control."[93] The complete mastery of the self became the *summum bonum* of a Gandhian ethic of perfection that pitted the purported goodness and permanence of a disembodied moral order against the changing, messy conditions of the phenomenal world. Polluted by its unruly passions, the sensuous self constituted the target of his invariable will to truth that was intent on controlling all dimensions of human existence—even to the point of endorsing self-suffering unto death. Hailed as serving the imperatives of universal love, Gandhi's experiments with self-control relentlessly assailed the materiality of human life. Ironically, his vision of a "nonviolent" regeneration of self and nation seemed to suggest that all morally pure efforts aimed at reducing human suffering and political violence required the infliction of suffering on the body. Leela Gandhi puts her finger on this paradox when she writes, "While *ahimsa* seeks its utopian resolution in the end of suffering, it authenticates its [nonviolent] morality through a doctrinal commitment to suffering."[94]

By portraying women as the highest embodiment of self-suffering and *ahimsa,* Gandhi assigned to them the heavy burden of suppressing all "impure" thoughts as well as acts of sensual pleasure. After all, female moral goodness revealed itself in its fullness only in a woman's renunciation of her physical needs and her willingness to perpetually police both male and female sexuality. Thus, in the name of protecting moral purity, Gandhi allowed insidious forms of self-coercion—arising from a patriarchal imagination—to become constitutive elements of his supposedly nonviolent female ideal. By extension, then, his vision of a feminized Indian nation was also predicated upon the violent repulsion of so-called "animalistic" biological urges. What was presented as a "nonviolent" transformation of impure desires merely shored up Gandhi's nationalist-patriarchal impulse to produce obedient subjects.

Confronted with Gandhi's experiments of self-control, one is tempted to raise the fundamental question of whether all ascetic practices aimed at the suppression of passion are ipso facto violent. This theme has received much consideration by twentieth-century thinkers, perhaps most prominently in Sigmund Freud's thesis that "civilization" is only made possible by individual renunciation. Indeed, in *Civilization and Its Discontents,* Freud argued that, given the aggressive and egotistic nature of humans' instinctive tendencies, civilization, based on the rule of reason over desires and a sense of moral guilt, is designed to curb and prohibit instinctual drives. In my view, one need not subscribe to the rather totalistic view that all forms of "disciplining the passions" are inherently violent in order to criticize Gandhi's extreme experiments. After all, his grim battle against the physicality of human existence and the vulnerability of the human condition went far beyond any moderate suggestion to curtail the potentially destructive pull of physical desire.

In this context, it is useful to recall Michel Foucault's important discussion of the workings of disciplinary power. While pointing to the normalizing forms of (self)-coercion hidden in social networks that produce "docile bodies" at the expense of alterity and sensuous pleasure, the French philosopher spent much time fighting totalistic conclusions. Still, read through Foucauldian lenses, Gandhi's relentless regimen of self-discipline might be reinterpreted more soberly as the coercive construction of a particular "regime of truth" sustained by extreme narratives and practices that—his claims to remain within the parameters of nonviolence notwithstanding—ended up "doing violence to things."[95]

On this point, Gandhi's discourse of self-control is also reminiscent of Plato's critique of the ruthless world of power politics and its manifestations of violence, greed, and moral corruption. Dissatisfied with the irreducible plurality and contingency of the political realm, both Plato and Gandhi turned their political philosophy into a search for metaphysical unity and security, guided by their dogmatic vision of how the world ought to be. Pursuing ethical inquiries into the nature of "truth," they posited a transcendental realm of immutable ideas that provide uniform ethical standards and norms for individual behavior. For both men, to be spiritual meant not only to know the idea of the good, but also to infuse political action with contemplative ideals of unity, harmony, and divine reason. In other words, they demanded that politics rise to the level of soulcraft that involved the strengthening of the rational part of the soul through rigorous mental and physical exercises. Thus, both Gandhi and Plato advocated an educational program of self-purification designed to control the physical body and its "impure" desires for power and pleasure. Transcendental truth became the master of the body, shaping the individual's character according to its ascetic regimen of self-discipline.

This Platonic conception of spirituality encompassed, therefore, both a yearning to break free from the chains of physical attachment and a moral duty to return to the "cave" and reform the corrupted realm of politics. These imperatives reverberate throughout all of Gandhi's writings. Considering himself a "politician trying his hardest to be a saint," he wanted to be the ahimsic midwife of a moral nation comprised of exemplary human beings who confronted their cravings for sensual pleasure and worldly power by sacrificing their lesser human bodies for a greater spiritual purpose. For someone who dreamed of resurrecting the moral greatness of ancient Indian civilization, Gandhi articulated his vision in a decidedly Platonic-Christian idiom, perhaps best expressed in St. Augustine's declaration that, "[A]ll earthly activities have their value only in the service of God. Human life, including the state, has no value save for preparation. The 'heavenly home' is the goal."[96]

At the same time, the existing tension between the world-renouncing and the world-reforming tendencies inherent in this vision represents both the theoretical and practical source of the complex constellation of countervailing forces that I have termed "Gandhi's dilemma." As discussed in the previous chapter, Gandhi's theoretical attempt to construct a nonviolent nation suffers from forms of conceptual violence imported through a nationalist discourse that merely reverses liberalism's claim to moral superiority. On the practical level, Gandhi's comprehensive program of national reform, based on a strict regimen of self-control, relies on the employment of conceptually—and perhaps even physically—violent methods of "discipline." In other words, the production of the moral self occurs simultaneously with infliction of pain and hardship on the recalcitrant, pleasure-seeking body.

If it is reasonable to assume that any political order must address the issue of physical safety, that is, the preservation of physical bodies, then Gandhi's vision surely fails to do full justice to this vital aspect of politics. In a sense, the imperative to protect the body constitutes the most difficult problem in any formulation of "spiritual politics," because the latter must ultimately refuse to acknowledge the realm of material existence as the primary source of human happiness. By preaching the duty to maintain the purity of the soul over the imperative to preserve the body, Gandhi already seems to have made his choice in favor of putting principles before power. However, such a move would destroy the possibility of resolving his dilemma of nonviolent principles and nationalist power.

Moreover, the assumed priority of moral purity implies that Gandhi considered the nation primarily a spiritual community held together by the fine threads of ancient *dharma* and updated to suit a New Age. The protection of the nation's virtue was more important than its mere material existence as a modern nation-state. Gandhi's focus on *ahimsa* and absolute truth thus undermined the political nationalists' emphasis on the nation-state as a material phenomenon, leaving the Mahatma and his vision more and more marginalized.

Indeed, it was precisely on this issue that Gandhi's vision of nonviolent nationalism clashed with the aspiration of political nationalists to create their own nation-state as the only thinkable framework for collective material well-being. Focusing on the task of wresting political power from the hands of the British, political nationalists like Jawaharlal Nehru and M. N. Roy frequently considered Gandhi's "insistence on truth" as an impediment to their quest for *swaraj*. They felt that the Mahatma was pushing his moral idealism in politics far beyond the limits of the "possible" in that his calls for virtue conflicted with any "realistic" agenda for a future Indian nation-state: "He [Gandhi] was a very difficult person to understand, sometimes his language was almost incomprehensible to an average modern. . . . Often we discussed his fads and peculiarities among ourselves and said, half-humorously, that when *Swaraj* came these fads must not be encouraged."[97] For Nehru and his associates, Gandhi's moral purism seemed to be woefully out of step with modernity, thus making his ideas irreconcilable with the necessary task of state formation.[98]

For Gandhi, of course, the whole point of his ambitious vision of nonviolent nationalism was to solve the dilemma of principles and power through the regeneration of self and nation, based on the ideals of an imagined ancient Indian civilization. This meant that he did not want the feasibility of his program to be judged according to the corrupt standards of modernity. The solution of the dilemma was to transform modern civilization and thereby reconstruct the modern subject. As he put it,

> The theory is there: our practice will have to approach it as much as possible. . . . If you agree with me, it will be your duty to tell the [Indian] revolutionaries and everybody else that the freedom they want, or they think they want, is not to be obtained by killing people or doing violence, but by setting themselves right, and by becoming and remaining truly Indian. . . . The future, therefore, lies not with the British race, but with the Indians themselves, and if they have sufficient self-abnegation and abstemiousness, they can make themselves free this very moment. . . . [99]

Hence, the successful resolution of Gandhi's dilemma required that he succeed in persuading the Congress leadership and the Indian masses to pursue *swaraj* strictly within the framework of his nonviolent nationalism. The practical implementation of his vision would therefore require the truly Herculean effort of inspiring millions of ordinary people to commit themselves, on a long-term basis, to the radical transformation of modern civilization. But what if they did not agree with his theory or failed in their efforts to "set themselves right"? What if nonviolent direct action, such as demonstrations, strikes, boycotts, and civil disobedience, did not force the British to hand over political power, and, as a result, a sizable portion of the Indian population resorted to physical violence? As the three case studies in the following chapter will show, Gandhi actually found himself in the situation of having to confront these questions on a practical level. This meant that even his flawed nonviolent principles (because they contained elements of conceptual violence inconsistent with his own broad definition of *ahimsa*) had not taken sufficient root in the populace. Why?

For one, Gandhi's ethical demands went far beyond what ordinary human beings were prepared to do and perhaps were even capable of doing. Thus, in spite of the widespread admiration his saintly conduct commanded, Gandhi and his vision ceased to be a model that people really could—and perhaps should—follow.[100] Second, he could not escape the structural constraints inherent in a historically specific project called nationalism. Gyan Prakash emphasizes that the state, as an expression of the collective life of the community, was immanent in the concept of the nation even as the association of modernity with colonialism demanded that the new Indian nation-state be different. Try as it might, not even Gandhi's powerful cultural nationalism could wish away the modern state. The fact that Gandhi's vision of a nonviolent India found itself increasingly sidelined by political nationalists and their focus on the nation-state and its program of modernization was not only due to the clever machinations of Nehru and his associates. Rather, Gandhi's "commitment to [cultural] nationalism left him with no ideological resources to contest what he opposed but had in fact helped to bring about. He was fated by his own ideological discourse of the modern nation to cut a tragic figure."[101]

Hence, nonviolent nationalism—Gandhi's proposed solution to the dilemma of balancing nonviolent principles and nationalist power—never escaped the status of an unfulfilled ideal. Facing the recalcitrant arena of modern politics and unable to extricate himself from the force field of modernity, the Mahatma was compelled to do what he had so fervently sought to avoid: choose between the dilution of his moral principles or political impotence.

6

Reconciling Nonviolent Principles with Nationalist Power?

੨੦

Three Cases

A great many men have imagined states and princedoms such as nobody ever saw or knew in the real world, and there's such a difference between the way we really live and the way we ought to live that the man who neglects the real to study the ideal will learn how to accomplish his ruin, not his salvation. Any man who tries to be good all the time is bound to come to ruin among the great number who are not good. Hence a prince who wants to keep his authority must learn how not be good, and use that knowledge, or refrain from using it, as necessity requires.

—Niccolo Machiavelli[1]

Within the Gandhi-Event a running discourse on renunciation and moral regeneration is carried on with another, of ruthless pursuit of monopoly, political power. . . . Gandhi himself seems to carry this seed of contradiction within his person. . . .

—G. Aloysius[2]

[I]f I seem to take part in politics, it is only because politics encircle us today like the coil of a snake from which one cannot get out, no matter how much one tries. I wish therefore to wrestle with the snake. . . .

—M. K. Gandhi[3]

Nonviolence and War: The Great War, 1914–18

Both the active and passive support of war constitute a serious violation of the moral principles of the pacifist, let alone those of the committed adherent to a philosophy of nonviolence.

Thriving on accentuated differences and hard boundaries that pit an idealized "us" against a demonized "them," wars have always caused incalculable human suffering culminating in the irreparable loss of life. They have left in their wake lasting psychological scars for the victor and the vanquished alike. Since war, by its nature, represents a highly institutionalized form of conceptual and physical violence, various religious groups wedded to a strong pacifist-nonviolent position have long maintained an unequivocal opposition to war. Some Christian-pacifist denominations such as the Society of Friends hold that participation in even so-called just wars—those fought against external aggression within certain ethical limits—cannot be morally justified. Given Gandhi's own broad definition of *ahimsa,* one would expect him to hold similar views on the moral illegitimacy of all wars. At a minimum, one would assume that he would not allow his principles of nonviolence to be compromised by adding his influential voice to those calling for belligerent resolutions of social conflicts.

Yet, during World War I, Gandhi actively supported the British war effort. Telling scores of ordinary Indians that it was their duty to enlist, he even agreed to serve as the Indian recruiter-in-chief for the British army. As his passionate belief in truth and nonviolence clashed with his recognition of possible political advantages arising from his endorsement of the British war effort, he oscillated between the extreme positions of unqualified pacifism and nationalist realism. In order to appreciate the full extent of Gandhi's dilemma in World War I, it is important to first consider his involvement in the Boer War and the Zulu Rebellion in South Africa. After all, these events deeply influenced Gandhi's attitude toward war in general.

In October 1899, when lingering hostilities between the Dutch settlers and their British counterparts broke out in the open in the Boer War, Gandhi called upon the Indian community in South Africa to demonstrate its loyalty to the British empire. This was a difficult decision for Gandhi to make because his sympathies rested with the Boers. Admiring their respect for tradition and their simple lifestyle, he was also impressed with their "discipline and courageous fighting spirit." Moreover, he realized that the Dutch settlers, too, had been the victims of British oppression. On the other hand, he was keenly aware of the Boers' racist attitudes toward the Indian population. Most importantly, however, Gandhi felt that the Indians' claim to full citizenship status required that they accept their obligation to lend "unreserved" and "unconditional" support to the empire in a time of crisis: "It would be unbecoming to our dignity as a nation to look on with folded hands at a time when ruin stared the British in the face as well as ourselves, simply because they ill-treat us here [in South Africa]."[4]

Although he emphasized that most Indians did not know how to handle arms, Gandhi assured the British Colonial Secretary in Maritzburg of his community's "unflinching devotion to duty and extreme eagerness to serve our Sovereign," leaving it up to the colonial authorities to decide whether they wanted to deploy Indians in the "field of battle" or in the "field hospitals or the commissariat."[5] Initially, the Colonial Secretary rejected his offer, but after British casualties began to mount, Gandhi was permitted to spearhead the organization of an ambulance corps made up of nearly eleven hundred Indian recruits. Gandhi himself served as a platoon leader with distinction, proudly observing that his countrymen's exhibited loyalty and their "valiant self-sacrifice" disproved racist allegations frequently made by Europeans that Indians were cowards. He also reported with much satisfaction on a general "spirit of brotherhood" that prevailed in the field "irrespective of people's color and creed."[6]

While Gandhi had not yet arrived at a polished formulation of his philosophy of nonviolence, he had nonetheless expressed the moral core of his *satyagraha* method as early as 1896: "Our method in South Africa is to conquer this hatred by love. At any rate, that is our goal. We would often fall short of that ideal, but we can adduce innumerable instances to show that we have acted in that spirit. We do not attempt to have individuals punished but, as a rule, patiently suffer wrongs at their hands."[7] Hence, he admitted that his decision to participate in the Boer War was precipitated by a painful "inner struggle"—another indication that he was fully aware of the existing tension between his willingness to support the British war effort and his moral principles. Still, at the time, he believed that he had no right to enforce his individual convictions during a national crisis:

> As a Hindu, I do not believe in war, but if anything can even partially reconcile me to it, it was the rich experience we gained at the front. It was certainly not the thirst for blood that took thousands of men to the battlefield. If I may use a most holy name without doing any violence to our feelings, like Arjun[a], they went to the battlefield, because it was their duty. And how many proud, rude, savage spirits has it not broken into gentle creatures of God?[8]

Thus, at the dawning of the new century, Gandhi offered two distinct rationales for his decision to support war. On a philosophical level, he argued that considerations of civic duty and patriotic loyalty outweighed moral concerns about the violence employed in warfare. If one demanded the full rights of British citizenship, Gandhi reasoned, one had to be prepared to accept the corresponding obligation to defend the nation in a time of need. Even though he acknowledged that justice seemed to be on the side of the Boers, he insisted that British subjects ought not disavow their patriotic duty and cut the ties of allegiance that bound them to the empire. In addition, Gandhi highlighted war's potential for bringing out positive qualities in humans, particularly the virtues of comradeship, heroism, courage, and "manhood." He did so not only to put to rest false rumors about Indian cowardice, but also to stress the importance of developing these virtues as the building blocks of a moral character. As Peter Brock notes, Gandhi's mature expression of *satyagraha* would ultimately champion a technique that sought to preserve the "good" virtues of the warrior—particularly courage and discipline—while eliminating the violent aspects of warfare.[9]

On a political level, Gandhi argued that the Boer War presented the Indian community with a "golden opportunity" to win full citizenship rights by proving their loyalty through acts of martial heroism. Choosing to remain aloof at such a time, he insisted, amounted to a case of "criminal inaction" that would only aggravate the Indians' present difficulties in South Africa: "If we missed this opportunity, which had come to us unsought, . . . we should stand self-condemned, and it would be no matter for surprise if then the English treated us worse than before and sneered at us more than ever."[10] Reflecting on his involvement in the Boer War a quarter of a century later, Gandhi admitted that he had since been confronted with harsh moral objections to his pro-war stance. Still, he found no reason to change his views. After all, this was how truth appeared to him in 1899, and the conscientious adherent to truth was obliged to follow *satya* as it presented itself at the moment.[11] Although Gandhi's feelings of loyalty to the British empire were greatly diminished by the 1920s, he continued to state that if it were still possible "to achieve freedom under its [the empire's] aegis, I would advance the same arguments, word for word, in South Africa, and, in similar circumstances, even in India."[12]

Gandhi's actions during the 1906 "Zulu Rebellion" in Natal almost mirrored the sequence of events that had transpired seven years earlier. Once again seizing upon the violent outbreak of hostilities to demonstrate the Indian community's loyalty to the Crown, he urged his compatriots to fight on the side of the British: "Indians have now a splendid opportunity for showing that they are capable of appreciating the duties of citizenship. . . . And if Indians come successfully through the ordeal, the possibilities for the future are very great."[13] Appealing to the readers of *Indian Opinion* to follow the example of many white South Africans who had volunteered for the war, he admonished his audience to put aside their reservations and instead "steel their hearts" and "take courage."[14] This time, his offer to the colonial authorities to raise an Indian ambulance corps was promptly accepted, and his small unit eventually consisted of twenty-four stretcher-bearers. Quickly promoted to the rank of sergeant-major, Gandhi embarked on the campaign only to discover that what had been advertised as a punitive expedition against "vicious Kaffir rebels" amounted in reality to nothing but a cruel manhunt against a largely unarmed people. The Zulu territory had been annexed by the British in 1887, and the current conflict had emerged because the Zulu farmers had refused to pay a new tax imposed on them by their conquerors. During the entire campaign, the British troops showed little discipline, and their martial "heroism" consisted mostly of leading disorganized raids into Zulu territory. After giving orders to set defenseless villages on fire, the British commanding officers would proceed to have the suspected leaders of the tax rebellion publicly flogged or hanged.[15]

Appalled by the callousness of these actions, Gandhi's sympathy rapidly shifted to the Zulus. Unlike in the Boer War, where his platoon had seen very little action, he was now confronted with the unspeakable horrors of battle. Scores of wounded Zulus were left to their own devices as white nurses refused to treat the often life-threatening injuries of "bloody Kaffirs." After encountering initial resistance, Gandhi finally managed to persuade his commanding officers to allow his ambulance unit to attend to these unfortunate casualties. For the next few weeks, he and his comrades sought to alleviate their guilty consciences by giving their utmost medical attention to the festering wounds of the Zulus.[16] Although the raids continued and Gandhi had to witness more British atrocities, he resolved to "swallow the bitter draught" and fulfill his patriotic duty.

However, the horrific events and images of war burned themselves deeply into his psyche. He later admitted that his participation in the Zulu Rebellion triggered not only his decision to take his final vow of *brahmacharya,* but that it also led to his renewed commitment to the method of nonviolence, culminating a few months later in the birth of the *satyagraha* movement in South Africa.

And yet, at the outbreak of the Great War in 1914, Gandhi again rushed to the defense of the empire, making the same old arguments in support of the British cause. Having just left South Africa after eight years of leading highly publicized *satyagraha* campaigns on behalf of his Indian constituencies, he decided to stop over in London on his way back home to India in order to meet with his political guru Gokhale, who was then touring Europe. In his London reception speech given a few days after the British declaration of war, Gandhi emphasized once again the importance of remaining loyal to the empire, telling his mostly Indian audience that their support for the British war effort constituted "a sacred matter of duty." In a letter of support that bore the signatures of over fifty prominent Indians residing in London, Gandhi assured the Undersecretary of State for India that, "We, the undersigned have, after mature deliberation, decided for the sake of the Motherland and the Empire to place our services unconditionally, during this crisis, at the disposal of the authorities. We advisedly use the word 'unconditionally' as we believe that, in a moment like this, no service that can be assigned to us can be considered to be beneath our dignity or inconsistent with our self-respect."[17]

In the following weeks, Gandhi organized an Indian Field Ambulance Corps destined to work with the Red Cross alongside Indian combatant troops on the European front. Most of the recruits were college students from the Indian community in England who were required to participate in military training sessions given under the auspices of the British War Office.[18] As James Hunt notes, it was truly remarkable that a man of nonviolence, an avid follower of Tolstoy, and a committed pioneer of *satyagraha,* should be moved by the spectacle of devoted war service more than by the terrible carnage that was already being unleashed on the continent. Indeed, throughout the few months of his London visit, Gandhi never uttered a word condemning the horrors of war or exposing the folly of the European nations as they were descending into an imperialistic war of unimaginable magnitude.[19] Instead, he spent most of his time protesting discriminatory appointments that unfairly privileged

British Oxford students to serve as section leaders of the all-Indian medical corps.

Yet within a few weeks, Gandhi found himself inundated with passionate objections to his military venture. The protests were raised by some of his closest followers and friends in London and abroad who questioned the consistency of his actions with his profession of *ahimsa*. Deeply disappointed in his decision to support the war effort, Gandhi's critics had until then made the reasonable assumption that his views on the matter had undergone drastic change in the years following the Zulu rebellion. Hence, they struggled to make sense of the obvious rift between his theory of nonviolence and his opportunistic political practice. Indeed, by 1914, there was no doubt that Gandhi had long embraced nonviolence as a way of life.

Groping for a coherent response to his critics, Gandhi was forced to acknowledge the immorality of all wars. Yet, he quickly proceeded to point out that, by living in London, he was personally benefiting from the consequences of the British war effort. Since he accepted the empire's military protection, Gandhi reasoned, he was already indirectly participating in the war. After all, the fulfillment of the basic needs of British residents was made possible only through the protective actions of the British Navy. In addition, Gandhi pointed to his newly acquired status of "public figure" and its ensuing responsibilities, which did not allow him the luxury of retreating into the cozy realm of private opinions. As he saw it, there was no alternative to accepting the weighty obligation arising from his position of prominence and his status as a British citizen. The least violent option available to him, Gandhi insisted, was to contribute to the war effort by serving as a noncombatant nurse.[20]

But what about the possibility of announcing his opposition to the war and, in accordance with the moral principles of nonviolence, accepting possible self-suffering and boycotting the empire until it changed its militaristic posture or put him in jail? Gandhi explicitly acknowledged this option as the only path that would restore the consistency of nonviolent theory and political practice, but he admitted that he lacked the moral courage to live up to his principles: "As long as I have not developed absolute fearlessness, I cannot be a perfect satyagrahi. I am striving incessantly to achieve it, and I will continue to do so. Till I have succeeded, do all of you save me (from doing anything wrong) and put up with my cowardice. You should all keep struggling to make yourselves fearless."[21]

In his *Autobiography*, written a decade later, Gandhi expanded this defensive posture in a section appropriately entitled "A Spiritual Dilemma." Affirming that it had been quite clear to him that his participation in war could never be consistent with the principles of *ahimsa*, he now argued that humans were but "helpless mortals caught in the conflagration of *himsa*." Hence, one could not help but participate "in the *himsa* that the very existence of society involves." Reaffirming his own lack of "capacity and fitness" to protest the empire's war effort nonviolently, he nonetheless saw no reason to retract his earlier statement that noncombatant service in the war represented the next best course of action available under such trying conditions: "When two nations are fighting, the duty of a votary of *ahimsa* is to stop the war. He who is not equal to that duty, he who has no power of resisting the war, he who is not qualified to resist war, may take part in war, and yet whole-heartedly try to free himself, his nation and the world from war."[22]

There are at least three serious problems with this argument. Firstly, Gandhi's alternatives of either an all-out resistance to the war or its wholehearted support are extreme positions. Wasn't it possible to lay out a middle position that stopped short of supporting the war and offered at least some moderate forms of resistance? Secondly, Gandhi's position implicitly cast doubt on whether nonviolent direct action could actually live up to its claim of representing a "realistic" alternative to the violent method of "brute force" he so decried in *Hind Swaraj*. Indeed, one of the major strengths of Gandhi's method of *satyagraha* was its avowal toward achieving tangible results in the "real world" of politics. Throughout his life, he always stressed the unique ability of his militant method of nonviolence to maintain the connection between theory and practice: "Passive resistance is a great moral force meant for the weak, also for the strong. Soul-force depends on itself. Ideals must work in practice, otherwise they are not potential."[23]

Thirdly, one finds it hard to believe that the dedicated veteran of several *satyagraha* campaigns who had spent many months in the notorious prisons of South Africa was suddenly running out of moral courage. It seems more likely that his professed lack of courage to protest the war concealed a rather instrumental political motive. After all, supporting the British effort might result in an improved status for Indians after the war. In fact, Gandhi later acknowledged the central importance of this political factor.[24] In other words, professing moral cowardice in the Great War ultimately served his quest for nationalist power. However, since this position clearly undermined his nonviolent principles, Gandhi simultaneously advanced the above argument about the physicality of the human condition foreclosing the possibility of remaining "absolutely nonviolent." Rather than living up to his promise of reconciling the dilemma of nonviolent principles and nationalist power, Gandhi suffused his political motives with a moral defense that relied on often confusing and contradictory notions of civic duty, self-sacrifice, and courage.

Perhaps as a result of this exhausting struggle with his "spiritual dilemma," Gandhi experienced a dramatic deterioration of his physical health. Instead of joining the Indian ambulance corps on the Western front, he contracted a serious case of pleurisy that confined him to his sickbed for weeks. When his unorthodox healing methods failed to cure his illness, he resolved to follow the advice of Western doctors by bidding farewell to London's inhospitable winter and returning to the more conducive Indian climate. He arrived in Bombay in January 1915 and spent the next few months setting up his *ashram* near Ahmedabad, modeling it after the South African Phoenix Settlement. Honoring the wishes of his recently deceased mentor Gokhale, he did his best to keep out of Indian politics and instead toured the entire country. Paying very little attention to the war raging in Europe, he organized, between 1917 and 1918, three local *satyagraha* campaigns involving peasants against landlords in the Champaran district, farmers against revenue officials in the Kaira district, and mill workers against their employers in Ahmedabad. However, as the Western allies' war situation deteriorated in the spring of 1918 and the Great War moved into its final phase, Gandhi found himself once again in the throes of his old dilemma.

Having just two weeks before preached to Indian peasants that "non-violence is the supreme dharma [duty]," Gandhi now informed Lord Chelmsford, the Viceroy of India, that "in the hour of its danger, we must give . . . ungrudging and unequivocal support to the Empire, of which we aspire, in the near future, to be partners in the same sense as the Dominions overseas. But it is the simple truth that our response is due to the expectation that our goal will be reached all the more speedily on that account—even as the performance of a duty automatically confers a corresponding right."[25] Gandhi left no doubt of the political motives underlying his support: nothing less than a "definite vision of Home Rule realized in the shortest possible time" would satisfy the Indian people. In exchange for home rule, he was prepared to "make India offer all her able-bodied sons as a sacrifice to the Empire at its critical moment; and I know that India by this very act would become the most favoured partner in the Empire and racial distinctions would become a thing of the past."[26]

Gandhi's offer was not an exaggeration. In order to achieve his political objective, he was even willing to personally spearhead an ambitious recruiting campaign to enlist Indian volunteers for the British armed forces. His engagement, therefore, no longer represented a case of supporting noncombatant war service designed to save lives on the front. Instead, his new campaign explicitly sought to provide a new supply of Indian troops to replenish the depleted British army. Constituting a "strange phenomenon in one who preached non-violence," Gandhi's recruiting activities were once again greeted by a vociferous chorus of pacifist dissenters.[27] Much to their surprise, however, the Mahatma still maintained that he had remained committed to his philosophy of nonviolence. Arguing that he was not personally killing or injuring anyone—"friend or foe"— he pointed to the possibility of Indian soldiers practicing on the European front a "real *ahimsa*" that consisted of receiving rather than giving blows: "If our soldiers go and stand before them [Germans] weaponless and will not use explosives and say, 'We will die of your blows', then, I am sure our Government will win the war at once."[28] At the same time, he was well aware of the fact that such action was almost tantamount to suicide, leading either to the death of the Indian recruits serving in the British army at the hands of the Germans or to their certain British court martial for insubordination. Once again dressing up political motives in ethical garments, Gandhi had set himself the task of squaring the circle. As Peter Brock asks, "How was he ever to succeed in combining recruitment of his fellow countrymen for the most destructive war the world had so far seen with continued devotion to the doctrine of nonviolence?"[29]

In addition to giving questionable advice to Indian soldiers, Gandhi made another theoretical attempt to resolve his dilemma that relied heavily on his understanding of courage as a prerequisite to nonviolence. Emphasizing that he would have preferred to see India assemble a nonviolent peace army whose moral heroism "could defy the world to do its worst," he grudgingly acknowledged that most Indians—presumably including himself in this category as well—had not yet adopted unconditional *ahimsa*.[30] The reason for Indians' inability to embrace nonviolence as a way of life was their lack of courage, caused by modern civilization and its tendency to elevate physical pleasure and material possessions over spiritual principles. Revising his previous image of ancient India as the motherland of *ahimsa,* he now pictured the "ancients in India" as experts in "the art of warfare—the art of killing" who chose to "reduce this activity to a minimum." Conversely, modern Indians were "timid" and "effeminate," afraid to harm their physical bodies or, even worse, lose their lives. Venting his frustration about the profound skepticism on the part of ordinary Indians he encountered in his recruiting campaigns, Gandhi wrote to his friend Charlie Andrews, "I find great difficulties in recruiting, but do you know that not one man has yet objected because he would not kill. They object because they fear to die. This unnatural fear of death is ruining the nation."[31] Since his countrymen apparently possessed "not a particle of the courage [they] should have," Gandhi concluded that they were in no position to defend their lives, their women and children, their cattle, and their lands. "How can a nation whose citizens are incapable of self-defense ever expect to achieve *swaraj?,*" he wondered despairingly.[32]

In Gandhi's opinion, participation in the Great War offered Indians the opportunity to regain the valor of their ancestors and thus build the foundation for their country's *swaraj.* Reporting to his cousin that he was in the process of developing a "new view of *ahimsa,*" Gandhi suggested that the cultivation of moral courage was greatly facilitated by martial valor. In fact, the successful practice of nonviolence might even have to be predicated upon the act of killing, especially for a nation that had lost its courage: "It is clear that he who has lost the power to kill cannot practice non-killing. Ahimsa is a renunciation of the highest type. A weak and effeminate nation cannot perform this grand act of renunciation, even as a mouse cannot be properly said to renounce the power of killing a cat."[33] Vowing to spread "the gospel of ahimsa, or satyagraha, by asking *himsak* [militant] men to work out their *himsa* in the least offensive manner," Gandhi indicated that he was personally willing to teach the use of force to people who were seeking to restore their courage through military training: "But he cannot be a satyagrahi who is afraid of death. The ability to use physical force is necessary for a true appreciation of satyagraha. He alone can practice ahimsa who knows how to kill, i.e., knows what *himsa* is." Exhorting Indian women not to worry their husbands, brothers, and sons with their selfish objections, Gandhi thundered: "If you want them to be true men, send them to the army with your blessings. Don't be anxious about what may happen to them on the battle-field. Your piety will watch over them there. And if they fall, console yourself with the thought that they have fallen in the discharge of their duty and that they will be yours in your next incarnation."[34]

There is, of course, a serious flaw in Gandhi's argument that Indians first had to regain the martial valor of their ancestors in order to acquire the moral courage necessary to become true disciples of nonviolence. For one, as Peter Brock points out, such a rhetoric of courage increasingly merged *ahimsa* and *himsa* to the point where these concepts no longer possessed any distinct analytic value. This unfortunate tendency is especially apparent in Gandhi's concession that through his recruiting activities he had come to understand what he had not so clearly seen before, namely that, "there is non-violence in violence."[35] Second, and most importantly, by making the practice of *satyagraha* dependent on previous performances of martial valor, Gandhi set up a hierarchy of moral values that placed nonviolence below courage. In other words, he subordinated his philosophy of nonviolence to a theory of courage. If the capacity to engage in ahimsic action indeed derived from the moral courage of resisting evil—to be cultivated in an "effeminate" nation through its citizens' participation in martial practices—then nonviolence was no longer the *summum bonum* of Gandhi's moral universe. Perhaps this surprising inference explains his lifelong admiration for "soldierly courage" as well as his widely debated admonition to his son Harilal that it was better any day to use brute force than to betray cowardice.[36] According to his new emphasis on valor, Gandhi's insistence on nonviolence as the only way to truth would have to be revised in favor of courage. And, as his involvement in the Great War clearly shows, the cultivation of valor was not always a nonviolent affair.

Hence, rather than resolving his dilemma, Gandhi's emphasis on courage had weakened his principles of nonviolence. But there was more to his revision than his surprising theoretical emphasis on the primary role of courage. One can detect a potent streak of nationalist realism in Gandhi's open admission that cooperation with the British in the war might result in the attainment of Indian home rule. Even if the Crown were to withhold *swaraj* from its colony after the successful conclusion of the Great War, India's participation in the war still contained an important pragmatic value—albeit one inconsistent with Gandhi's nonviolent principles: scores of ordinary Indians would have gained valuable experience in handling weapons, allowing them to make a serious attempt to extract independence from their European colonizers by violent means.

> With that [military] strength, we may even fight the Empire, should it play foul with us. . . . By raising an army now, we shall be insuring against future eventualities. If the British people have the ability to rule, they do not owe it merely to their physical strength. The have the art (of government), they have skill and foresight, shrewdness and wisdom. They know how to deal with people according to their deserts. They know that, if we help, it will be in expectation of getting swaraj. . . . They invite us to examine their history. The Boers got swaraj because they could fight the British. When we can do so, they say, we too shall have swaraj. We can only count on our own military strength. . . . If we, who would have swaraj, can train ourselves to be their equal as soldiers, if we renounce fear of death, we shall be soldiers in a national army.[37]

Gandhi had once boasted that if the Viceroy would appoint him recruiter-in-chief, he would soon "rain men on the British." Yet, his political and theoretical arguments failed to convince most of his countrymen. Greeted with a mixture of stunning incomprehension and open hostility by the same villagers who had only recently rallied around their nonviolent saint in regional *satyagraha* campaigns, Gandhi managed to raise less than 200 recruits by early August 1918. As Judith Brown comments, "It was hardly surprising that people were reluctant to become cannon fodder in the service of a government which Gandhi himself had taught them to resist."[38] The unrelenting psychological pressure of meeting British expectations while assuaging the fears of his countrymen brought him a bout with serious illness. Confined to his bed, Gandhi received the news that the Western allies were making progress in the war. Although he warned his friends against drawing the premature conclusion that the need for Indians joining the army had finally come to an end, his struggle with his emaciated body seemed to cause him to reconsider some of his former arguments: "One need not assume that heroism is to be acquired only by fighting in a war. One can do so even while keeping out of it. War is a powerful means, among many others. But if it is a powerful means, it is also an evil one. We can cultivate manliness in a blameless way." In other words, while war was still a useful catalyst for courage, the benefits of war-fare could be acquired by battling one's own body: "If, through the fight we are carrying with the body, we can develop the strength for the war which the *atman* [self] must wage against the *anatman* [no-self], we shall have acquired manliness."[39] Refusing to repudiate the motives underlying his recruitment campaign, Gandhi nonetheless greeted the news of the November 1918 Armistice with a sense of great relief.

In summing up, it is important to briefly consider three main arguments advanced by students of Gandhi's life and thought in defense of his wartime activities. First, there is the claim that his position in the Great War represented merely a "flexible adjustment of his idealism to the demands of his nationalism."[40] The underlying message here seems to be one of tacit approval or even admiration of Gandhi's willingness to heed the political imperative. Regardless of one's assessment of the value of Gandhi's political realism, however, one must concede the following point: by choosing nationalist power at the expense of his nonviolent principles, Gandhi failed to resolve his dilemma according to his own standards. Second, there is the argument that Gandhi never claimed to be a pure pacifist—an important fact missed by contemporary European pacifists who criticized his wartime activities.[41] Yet, even if one is prepared to accept this objection, this still does not let Gandhi off the hook on the issue of nonviolence. As soon as the definition of pacifism is expanded to allow for conditional forms of pacifism such as "war-pacifism," violence has become, under certain conditions, a morally permissible means.[42] This move, therefore, would turn Gandhi's nationalist doctrine from a "nonviolent" vision into merely a "less violent" one. Third, there is the claim that his attitude toward the Great War should be considered within a theoretical framework that is more sensitive to the evolutionary nature of his political thought.[43] While it is true that Gandhi's commitment to nonviolence firmed during World War II to the point where he sometimes spoke of his total opposition to the war, one can also find in his later writing several passages that indicate his "unconditional support" for the Allies' war effort. Some of these arguments will be discussed in more detail below. Moreover, when a territorial dispute between India and Pakistan broke out in the fall of 1947, Gandhi argued that if Pakistan was not willing to reconsider its "unjust position" on Kashmir, war would be the only alternative left to the government of India.[44]

Hence, none of these three arguments manages to invalidate my main claim: namely, that Gandhi decided to opt for political "flexibility" (or expediency) during the Great War in order to hasten the arrival of Indian home rule, and that this decision came at the price of diluting his nonviolent principles. As soon as he chose to involve himself more deeply in the political battle for India's *swaraj,* Gandhi's actions became inextricably entangled with the instrumental logic of political nationalism. Struggling to translate the communitarian platform of his cultural nationalism into a workable political program, he found himself subject to the imperatives of the very modernity he had so vehemently rejected in *Hind Swaraj.* Thus, it was one thing to criticize the processes of modernization as morally corrupt, but it was quite another to escape their structural pressures. The unavoidable historicity and situatedness of Gandhi's nationalism in the conditions of the early twentieth century made the desired reconciliation of his nonviolent principles with the pursuit of political power an extraordinarily difficult, if not impossible, project.

THE INDIAN NONCOOPERATION CAMPAIGN, 1920–22

On August 1, 1920, Gandhi called upon his followers to engage in a nationwide noncooperation campaign against the British. Emerging as the principal leader of an increasingly united Indian nationalist movement, he felt so confident in his new position of power that he announced the start of the campaign several months before he secured the official endorsement from the Indian National Congress. As Judith Brown points out, before 1919, Gandhi was only a peripheral figure in the politics of Indian nationalism. He ventured into that realm only when he felt he had to advance the causes that were his life's work—the immediate service to his people by righting the "wrongs" inflicted on them—and the "wider service of his country by promoting the ideals of true Swaraj, when Hindus and Muslims, the high and low castes would live together in harmony, where the corruptions of modern civilization would have been purged out of society, and where the relationship of British and Indian would be one of partnership rather than subjugation."[45] By mid-1919, however, Gandhi was breaking out of these limits, thereby consciously joining the ranks of the politicians and challenging their leadership in Congress—their citadel of power.

Two initiatives, in particular, contributed to Gandhi's rising political stature. First, he supported the "Khilafat movement," formed by Indian Muslims to defend the Caliphate after the Turkish defeat in the Great War. British anti-Turkish policies and the harsh terms of the 1920 Peace Treaty of Sèvres were threatening the dissolution of the Ottoman Empire and the removal of the Turkish sultan. In addition to being a temporal ruler, the latter bore the title of Caliph and was widely considered the religious leader of all Islam. Sidestepping a potentially contentious debate with regard to the exclusivist tendencies inherent in the Khilafat and the Pan-Islamic movement, Gandhi seized on this issue as "a golden opportunity" to forge a lasting alliance between Hindus and Muslims in India. He established important political connections to Muslim leaders and organized mass movements of political protest, which allowed him to extend his range of support to areas and groups previously unconcerned with institutional politics. In short, Gandhi was able "to bring their influence to play at the level of institutional politics and so acquire personal influence at that level, because he was the crucial link between two communities whose leaders both needed and feared each other."[46]

Second, Gandhi organized a mass *satyagraha* campaign against the 1919 Rowlatt Bill—a piece of legislation that gave the British raj emergency powers to effectively combat "political subversives." The bill included the power to try seditious crimes without a jury, to demand security from suspects, to restrict places of residence, to require abstention from certain activities, and to arrest and imprison suspects in nonpenal custody. Realizing that his loyal recruitment efforts during the Great War had not changed British policies toward India, a disappointed Gandhi argued that the bill violated the "principle of liberty of the subject" by destroying "the elementary rights of the individual." Hence, he concluded that the Rowlatt Bill represented "an unmistakable symptom of a deep-seated disease in the governing body."[47] He called on the entire country to observe a day-long, nonviolent *hartal* (a religiously-based strike traditionally used to indicate mourning or protest) that was observed with mixed success in various regions. Contrary to Gandhi's expectations, the strike led to some incidences of violence on both sides, prompting him to confess that he had made a "Himalayan miscalculation" in prematurely calling upon the Indian masses to engage in civil disobedience without assuring their proper training. As a result of the violence committed by Indians, he called off the entire *Satyagraha* campaign and imposed upon himself a penitential fast for three days. Still, from a political perspective, Gandhi's agitation against the Rowlatt Bill represented a sound success because it had showcased his ability to mobilize the masses, which, in turn, enhanced his growing reputation as India's rising nationalist leader.

However, only a few days after the April *hartal,* British troops under the command of Brigadier General Reginald Dyer opened fire on peaceful demonstrators in the city of Amritsar, killing 379 persons and wounding 1,137—many of them children and women.[48] In the wake of the massacre, martial law was declared in large sections of the Punjab, which allowed Dyer's troops to inflict public floggings and other forms of cruel and humiliating punishment on suspected "subversives." As a result of the tight censorship imposed, Gandhi and most Indians did not become aware of the extent of the tragedy until June 1919. Although the Amritsar massacre outraged Congress leaders and radicalized Indian opinion, the raj did not initiate an official inquiry into the events until late summer. Headed by Lord Hunter, a senior judge of the College of Justice of Scotland, a commission consisting of seven members—four British and three Indian—was appointed to investigate the events in the Punjab. Two months before the May 28, 1920, publication of the committee's final report, the Indian National Congress put forward its own views in order to pave the way for a probable dissenting minority report by the Indian members of the Hunter Committee.[49] In addition to criticizing Dyer's shooting orders, the Congress report championed the view that there had been no justification for the introduction of martial law.

The Hunter Report saw things differently. While it condemned most of Dyer's decisions relating to the massacre—especially his order to fire on the crowd indiscriminately and without prior warning—the report agreed with the imposition of martial law and criticized Gandhi's method of *satyagraha* as being partially responsible for undermining law and order. Predictably, the report was divided along racial lines, with the Indian minority issuing an unequivocal condemnation of the events. Acting on the recommendations of the Hunter Committee, the British government censured Dyer's actions relating to the massacre and subsequently relieved him of his command. Yet it concurred with the opinion of the majority report with regard to the unlawfulness of various *satyagraha* campaigns, therefore affirming the correctness of the decision to impose martial law.

Incensed, Gandhi returned his two South African war medals and his Kaiser-I-Hind gold medal for humanitarian work in South Africa, announcing that the time had come when such "blatant expressions of injustice" could no longer be remedied through conventional political channels. Referring to the Punjab events and the Khilafat grievances as the "twin humiliating signs that Indian feelings counted for little in the British empire," the Mahatma suggested that the organization of a nationwide noncooperation campaign with the goal of attaining complete *swaraj* was the only option left for Indian nationalists:

> India has the choice before her now. If then the acts of the Punjab Government be an insufferable wrong, if the report of Lord Hunter's Committee and the two dispatches be a greater wrong by reason of their grievous condonation of these acts, it is clear that we must refuse to submit to this official violence. Appeal to the Parliament by all means if necessary, but if the Parliament fails us and if we are worthy to call ourselves a nation, we must refuse to uphold the Government by withdrawing co-operation from it.[50]

After securing the endorsement of the major Muslim organizations as well as receiving belated approval from the Congress, Gandhi assumed overall command of the nationalist agitation. This was particularly highlighted by the fact that the delegates of the 1920 Nagpur Congress session overwhelmingly adopted Gandhi's newly drafted constitution for the Indian National Congress. In addition to formally embracing the principle of nonviolence, the new document transformed the institution from an upper-middle-class debating society into a closely knit and effective political organization with a fifteen-member Working Committee, an All-India Committee, and provincial committees reaching down to districts, towns, and even villages.[51] Promising the attainment of "*swaraj* within a year," Gandhi likened the emerging noncooperation campaign to an act of war: "Our struggle has all the attributes of war. The thing we want, namely swaraj, is not to be had without fighting and, therefore, all the means we employ must be those used in a war."[52] Announcing that he was prepared to "train a big [nonviolent] national army," he nonetheless emphasized that there remained one important difference between the methods of the noncooperation campaign and those of conventional warfare: the former was predicated upon nonviolence whereas the latter relied on the application of "brute force."

As the campaign heated up, however, Gandhi added a sharp tone of apocalyptic urgency to his public addresses and journal articles. Designed to rally the masses behind the nationalist cause, his speeches often surpassed even his most extreme statements in *Hind Swaraj*. For example, he told his audiences that they ought to consider the current struggle between the forces of "good" and "evil" as a moral challenge to all "true Indian patriots" to choose between "God" and "Satan." "The British Empire, today," he proclaimed, "represents Satanism and they who love God can afford to have no love for Satan." Unless the representatives of the "oppressive, godless, and evil empire," apologized publicly for past injustices and changed Britain's current policies toward India, it was "the duty of every Indian to destroy it."[53] Incessantly labeling the British raj and its underlying civilization "satanic," some of the most extreme passages in Gandhi's angry speeches left the impression that the "devilish enemy" might not be worthy of love. Indeed, his generous use of pejorative epithets throughout the entire duration of the noncooperation movement represents a clear-cut case of conceptual violence that infringed upon his self-imposed ahimsic standards.

There is evidence that the Mahatma continued to be aware of the moral importance of these standards, although he himself chose to violate them. For example, he scolded Indian demonstrators for using the terms "donkeys" and "monkeys" to describe their opponents: "[T]hose who used such terms were clearly guilty of violence in speech; they abused others, showed their anger and violated the pledge which they have taken. They forsook civilized manners. We should never use such terms to describe our rivals or opponents. Our language should always breathe the spirit of peace."[54] Yet the labeling of the opponent's civilization as "satanic" appears to be a much stronger case for "violence in speech" than the use of the word "donkey." In fact, the conceptual violence contained in his harsh language during the 1920–22 noncooperation campaign casts severe doubt on the validity of an influential argument made by some contemporary Gandhi scholars that, within ten years of the publication of *Hind Swaraj,* "Gandhi's exclusivist attitudes would evolve into an inclusivist approach."[55]

At the time, some of Gandhi's closest followers maintained that he deliberately employed such Manichean language in order to achieve the political objective of mobilizing the Indian masses for the noncooperation movement: "Gandhi knocked the bottom out of that overwhelming prestige of the mighty British Empire by one single word 'Satan.' How could people, after this telling epithet, retain any respect or awe or fear of Government officers?"[56] At the same time, however, by designating as "satanic" any action he considered to be outside of his own conception of truth, Gandhi also put political pressure on a number of Indian nationalists who were reluctant to embrace his vision. For example, he emphasized the importance of *brahmacharya* for all Indian patriots, calling the struggle for self-purification "the battle with the Satan within." This implied that the rejection of his idiosyncratic project of self-control would amount to the denial of God. Likewise, he considered any criticism of his efforts to bring about his own version of Hindu-Muslim unity as expressions of the "Satanic way." Finally, he viewed Hindu traditions that sanctioned untouchability as practices defending and sharing "Satan's work."[57]

While he was careful not to refer to particular individuals as "satanic," Gandhi nonetheless often relied on invectives that depersonalized the "systems" he abhorred. In the end, his satanic language served both political and moral-disciplinary purposes as his crafty political instrumentalism coexisted with genuine moral appeals to his opponents. For example, in two open letters addressed "To Every Englishman in India," the Mahatma urged the British to "repent of the wrongs done to Indians" and lend their hand to the destruction of the "satanic system" that "has dragged both you and us down."[58] Hence, as William Emilsen notes, it was against what he considered to be a combination of "evil" forces—modern civilization, corrupt law-courts, government schools, symbols of colonialism, and so on—that Gandhi whipped up patriotic passion: "God (Truth) in his rhetoric, came to represent Indian civilization and the non-co-operationists; Satan became the symbol for British or Western rule locked into the demonism of power. The non-co-operation movement, as Gandhi gladly agreed . . . , was a struggle between religion and irreligion, the powers of light and the powers of darkness."[59]

From January 1921 to March 1922, Gandhi steered the noncooperation campaign through several phases in accordance with a hazy general plan that lacked a detailed conception of the tactics to be employed.[60] In the first few months of 1921, he urged Indians to renounce their British titles and decorations as well as engage in a boycott of regional elections and the British law courts. In addition, he encouraged Indian students to withdraw from government-sponsored schools. Thousands of professionals and students followed his call, abandoning their positions forever. Next, at the March 1921 meeting of the All-India Congress Committee, Gandhi introduced a number of resolutions—which were all passed—emphasizing the need to register more members in the Congress, to uphold the principle of nonviolence, and to introduce the *charkha* (spinning wheel) into the villages. In order to purchase two million spinning wheels, ten million rupees were collected by the end of June, thanks to the generous donations of several rich industrialists. Reinforcing his appeal to use the *charkha* as a means of political and spiritual liberation, Gandhi decided to simplify his own dress even further. He combined his dramatic adoption of the loin cloth with his call for the boycott of foreign cloth. In open letters to Indian mill owners and cloth merchants, he emphasized that the necessary abandonment of the "unholy trade in foreign cloth" represented an "enterprise worthy of your patriotism."[61]

Urging all Indians to crown the *swadeshi* campaign by publicly burning their foreign-made clothes, Gandhi spoke in glowing terms of the "inspiring sight" of large piles of garments going up in smoke: "And as the flames leapt up and enveloped the whole pyramid [of clothes], there was a shout of joy resounding through the air. It was as if our shackles had been broken asunder. A glow of freedom passed through the vast concourse. It was a noble act nobly performed."[62] Yet, the flames of *swadeshi* kindled by thousands of ordinary Indian also symbolized, like no other *satyagraha* action, the fundamental tension at the core of Gandhi's nonviolent nationalism. For the Mahatma, the burning clothes manufactured in England conveyed India's economic, political, and spiritual emancipation from the threads of oppression. He viewed these spectacles as symbols of the nonviolent purification of a corrupted civilization and its materialist culture, and, therefore, the purgation of a tainted Indian identity. For others—including some of Gandhi's closest associates and friends, like Charlie Andrews—the flames of *swadeshi* signified a rather violent act of self-definition that seemed to be an ominous sign of things to come: the obliteration of the Other by nationalist passions set ablaze.

Indeed, the first indication that Gandhi was incapable of controlling the nationalist passions of the masses set free during the noncooperation campaign came as early as April 1921, when a sub-inspector of police and four constables were killed in an act of mob violence provoked by the trial of Khilafat workers in the city of Malegaon. Gandhi chided the perpetrators for having "put back the hands of the clock of progress," and reminded them that, "Non-violence is the rock on which the whole structure of non-co-operation is built."[63] Yet another incident took place in Bombay on November 17, 1921, the day the Prince of Wales arrived there for an official visit. Violent attacks were launched by Hindu and Muslim noncooperators upon Parsi and Christian Indians who had voluntarily taken part in the Prince's welcome. The violence escalated as many noncooperators looted shops and burned clothes. Soon these actions expanded to the torching of entire buildings and the beating of government officials, ultimately leading to the deaths of several policemen and demonstrators. When, after three days of violence, the passions had finally cooled down, fifty-eight Bombay citizens had been killed and nearly four hundred had been injured.[64]

Gandhi accepted personal responsibility for these atrocities, declaring that he had been "more instrumental than any other in bringing into being the spirit of [violent] revolt." Confessing that he had been incapable of maintaining "sufficient control over the people to keep their violence under check," he vowed to observe henceforth every Monday a twenty-four-hour penitential fast until *swaraj* was attained. Reflecting on the events in Bombay, he recognized the magnitude of his dilemma: "If I can have nothing to do with the organized violence of the Government, I can have less to do with the unorganized violence of the people. I would prefer to be crushed between the two."[65] Indeed, it began to dawn on him that, instead of embracing his idea of *swaraj* as a process of moral regeneration involving both self and nation, the masses seemed to be much more excited about the prospect of expelling the British from Indian soil by any means necessary. Although Gandhi had always insisted on maintaining the nonviolent character of the noncooperation campaign, his own instrumentalist tendencies, together with his apocalyptic language, had sowed some of the very seeds that bloomed into the masses' limited and woefully inadequate interpretation of the movement's primary objective.[66] As Nehru put it years later, "Gandhiji was delightfully vague on the subject [of *swaraj*], and he did not encourage clear thinking about it either."[67]

In spite of the deadly display of violence in Bombay, Gandhi eventually decided to press ahead with the noncooperation campaign. After all, the end of the year in which *swaraj* was supposed to be achieved was approaching fast. Moreover, the movement seemed to catch on in some regions that had previously remained rather detached. Nearly thirty thousand political prisoners filled the jails of the raj, and the government was beginning to tremble at the prospect of millions of rioting Indian peasants. In November 1921, the All-India Congress Committee authorized every province to make its own autonomous decisions regarding when to undertake *satyagraha* actions. A month later, the Ahmedabad session of Congress resolved to continue the noncooperation campaign "until *swaraj* was established and the control of the government of India passes into the hands of the people." Calling upon all Indians over eighteen years of age to join the National Volunteers (a group outlawed under British rule), and pledging "to concentrate attention upon civil disobedience, whether mass or individual, whether of an offensive or defensive character," Congress placed full powers for this purpose in the hands of "Mahatma Gandhi, the sole executive authority of the Congress."[68]

In early February 1922, Gandhi was preparing a massive civil disobedience campaign in the district of Bardoli when bad news caught up with him. In the small village of Chauri Chaura, some eight hundred miles from Bardoli, a group of noncooperators had responded to ugly taunts and provocations by the local police with violence, beating and hacking to death twenty-three constables after setting the police station on fire. Struck by grief and remorse, Gandhi summoned the members of the Congress Working Committee and informed them that he now advocated the complete suspension of the entire noncooperation campaign. The members eventually yielded to his arguments, but the Mahatma's decision proved to be extremely controversial with imprisoned Congress leaders like Motilal Nehru, Lajpat Rai, C. R. Das, and Subhas Chandra Bose, who all bombarded him with long and indignant letters. Jawaharlal Nehru best expressed the reasons behind the outrage of these political nationalists:

> We were angry when we learned of this stoppage of our struggle at a time when we seemed to be consolidating our position and advance on all fronts. . . . Chauri Chaura may have been and was a deplorable occurrence and wholly opposite to the spirit of the non-violent movement; but were a remote village and a mob of excited peasants in an out-of-the way place going to put an end, for some time at least, to our national struggle for freedom? If this was the inevitable consequence of a sporadic act of violence,

then surely there was something lacking in the philosophy and technique of a non-violent struggle. For it seemed to us to be impossible to guarantee against the occurrence of some such untoward incident. Must we train the three hundred odd millions of India in the theory and practice of nonviolent action before we could go forward? And, even so, how many of us could say that under extreme provocation from the police we would be able to remain perfectly peaceful? But even if we succeed, what of the numerous *agents provocateurs,* stool pigeons, and the like who crept into our movement and indulged in violence themselves or induced others to do so? If this was the sole condition of its function, then the non-violent method of resistance would always fail.[69]

Nehru's politically astute assessment of the role of nonviolence in a struggle for national liberation failed to sway Gandhi. His response was unambiguous: "I personally can never be a party to a movement half violent and half non-violent, even though it may result in the attainment of so-called swaraj, for it will not be real swaraj as I have conceived it." Elaborating on this argument, Gandhi stated: "I would decline to gain India's freedom at the cost of non-violence. . . . That I may be hopelessly wrong in holding the view is another matter, but such is my view and it is daily growing on me. . . . [W]hatever may be true of other countries, India's salvation lies only through the path of non-violence."[70] Lamenting that "the country at large has not at all accepted the teaching of non-violence," he assured his jailed correspondents that he was "standing firm" in his "dharma," and that he would not reconsider his decision to call off the campaign.[71]

Yet Gandhi's disappointment in the inability of the "Indian mass mind" to grasp the "necessity of non-violence as an integral, active, and chief part of mass civil disobedience" seems rather contradictory and hubristic. With regard to the former, Gandhi's criticism of the masses can hardly be reconciled with his self-image as a "practical idealist" who claimed that "The religion of nonviolence is not meant for the *rishis* and saints. It is meant for the common people as well."[72] As far as the latter is concerned, Gandhi's critique reveals his grandiose expectation that it was in his power to raise the collective moral consciousness of the nation in the short span of two years. As Paul Mundschenk notes,

There were some, of course, whose lives were to become reflections of the Gandhian spirit, but these would always be in a tiny minority. . . . Gandhi was able to bring the change in Indian thinking just so far; . . . a nation-wide conversion to Gandhian morality might conceivably be approximated to a small degree within a generation, say, but nothing substantial could possibly come to fruition in one year.[73]

The events of Chauri Chaura also exposed as a romantic illusion Gandhi's idyllic picture of an unadulterated Indian peasantry, one that he had held since the time of his study years in London. Although he was building his political career on the reputation of being a "champion of the toiling masses," the Mahatma was not one of them—neither by birth nor by temperament. Indeed, he never came to know them intimately, and on their terms. Granted, his *ashrams* were remarkably successful laboratories fueled by his affirmative orientalist vision and dedicated to the creation of the "new Indian" according to his moral ideals of ancient Indian civilization. But his *ashrams* were poor substitutes for real Indian villages populated by ordinary people. Perhaps Gandhi mistook the adulation he received from the peasants during his high-profile visits in their villages for their genuine approval of his vision of nonviolent nationalism.

His claim to speak for "the nation as a whole" was therefore only correct in the sense that he came to symbolize a popular religious ideal associated with Hindu sainthood and spiritual perfection. However, as far as his calls for moral self-discipline were concerned, the masses were eluding his grasp, for the immediate demands and structural pressures of their lives hardly resembled the atmosphere of moral discipline that prevailed in Gandhi's *ashrams.* In many cases, the villagers and city-dwellers were unable to escape situations in which violence had become inevitable for even a marginal amelioration of their conditions. Yet, the passions and energies released in the militant actions of the masses frightened Gandhi because they challenged the acceptable moral limits contained within his rational project of self-control. The boisterous, unruly behavior of the common folk he witnessed on many occasions led him to distrust them. Time and again, he warned his middle- and upper-class readership of the dangers of "mobocracy" and the "cruel" and "unreasonable" tendencies of a "mob without a mind." "The nation," he insisted, "must be disciplined to handle mass movements in a sober and methodical manner."[74]

When faced with the historic opportunity to realize his vision of nonviolent nationalism in the reconciliation of his nonviolent principles with the effective quest for nationalist power during the 1920–22 noncooperation campaign, Gandhi encountered once again the recalcitrance and contingency of the political arena. Reversing the decision he made during the Great War, he opted this time for moral purity. Whether it disclosed the depth of his ethical convictions or simply reflected a more sober political calculation, Gandhi's choice failed to resolve his dilemma, because it failed to turn his vision of nonviolent nationalism—his ideal of spiritual politics—into political reality. On one hand, Gandhi needed to mobilize the energy of the masses in order attain his political objective, while, on the other, their awakened passions proved to be too volatile and unpredictable to be harnessed to his Apollonian vision of the nonviolent nation. The very task of the political nationalist to kindle the enthusiasm of the masses for the purpose of achieving home rule turned out to be the most formidable enemy of the disciplined soul worker.

Paying the ultimate political price for his choice to honor his principles, Gandhi was forced to watch the noncooperation campaign crumble in the course of only a few weeks. The Khilafat movement did not fare much better as it collapsed in the aftermath of Chauri Chaura and the abolition of the Caliphate by the Turks themselves. Historically, Gandhi's dramatic suspension of the noncooperation campaign generated a new focus on schisms and differences between various factions of the Indian population.[75] As different groups promoted their own visions of communal reform and new national order, Gandhi's own vision of a united community, which had found its culmination in the Khilafat movement, was increasingly challenged by images of separatism championed by distinct Muslim and Hindu organizations.

Keenly aware of his political impotence following the collapse of the noncooperation campaign, the British arrested Gandhi and put him on trial for sedition. Pleading guilty to the charge, the Mahatma explained his dilemma in a dramatic performance in the courtroom:

> I wanted to avoid violence. Nonviolence is the first article of my faith. It is also the last article of my creed. But I had to make a choice. I had either to submit to a system which I considered had done irreparable harm to my country, or incur the mad fury of my people bursting forth when they understood the truth from my lips. I know that my people have

sometimes gone mad; I am deeply sorry for it. I am, therefore, here to submit not to light penalty but to the highest penalty.[76]

Moved by Gandhi's principled stance, the British judge sentenced Gandhi to only six years of imprisonment, adding that that if
his Majesty's government later deemed it fit to reduce his term, he
would have no objections. Lord Lloyd, the Governor of Bombay, as-
sessed the situation more soberly. In an interview with a British
journalist shortly after the trial, he made the following statement:

> He [Gandhi] gave us a scare. His program filled our jails. You can't go on
> arresting people forever, you know—not when there are 319,000,000 of
> them. And if they had taken his next step and refused to pay taxes! God
> knows where we should have been! Gandhi's was the most colossal exper-
> iment in world history; and he came within an inch of succeeding. But he
> couldn't control men's passions. They became violent and he called off his
> program. You know the rest. We jailed him.[77]

THE QUIT INDIA MOVEMENT, 1942

By 1942, World War II was fully underway, and Gandhi found himself once again in the thick of Indian nationalist politics. At the outbreak of the war in 1939, Lord Linlithgow, the new Viceroy of India,
proclaimed without consulting with Congress representatives that
India was at war with Germany. He knew that open discussions of
Indian involvement in an "imperialist war" would be contentious
and difficult, and he hoped that once London's unilateral decision
was announced, a majority of Congress members could eventually
be persuaded to accept it. Following his old pattern of supporting
the empire's war efforts, Gandhi assured the Viceroy that his personal
sympathies were with England and France, but he emphasized that
his unconditional moral support was not widely shared by other
members of the Congress Working Committee. Indeed, within days,
the latter adopted an instrumentalist resolution drafted by Nehru
stating that Congress would only support the war effort if Britain
immediately granted Indians the right to frame their own constitution through a constituent assembly. Linlithgow responded with a
vague statement, arguing that dominion status was indeed the goal
of British policy in India, but that the exact terms of this long-term
objective would have to be worked out after the end of the war. The

Working Committee promptly rejected the statement, affirming that the Congress would withhold its support of Great Britain's war effort. In a dramatic gesture, all of the Congress' provincial ministries resigned in the fall of 1939, leaving it to the British governors to deal with an increasingly volatile political situation.[78]

Torn between his previous announcement of unconditional support for the British cause and the antagonistic posture of the Congress, Gandhi decided to throw his weight behind the actions of the Working Committee. He defended his sudden turnabout by downplaying the "dogma" of adhering to a consistent political position: "My aim is not to be consistent with my previous statements on a given question, but to be consistent with truth as it may present itself to me at a given moment. The result has been that I have grown from truth to truth. . . . [F]riends who observe inconsistency will do well to take the meaning that my latest writing may yield unless, of course, they prefer the old."[79] Although, as Stanley Maron points out, devotion to principle was fundamental in Gandhi's activities, his defense of such "inconsistencies" often gives rise to "the feeling that Gandhi was not above using principle for political ends and even changing his principles where convenient."[80]

In the early months of 1940, the respective positions of Congress and the raj hardened as the latter issued an "Emergency Powers Ordinance" that made public anti-war agitation a crime punishable by imprisonment. The two old antagonists seemed to be on an inevitable path of collision—a development masterfully exploited by Mohammed Ali Jinnah, the head of the Muslim League. Gaining in importance after the resignation of the Congress ministries, Jinnah and the Muslim League pursued a policy of cooperation with the British government, hoping to gain political advantage in their efforts to carve out a separate Muslim state after the end of the war. In March 1940, the Muslim League voted overwhelmingly for the creation of the future state of Pakistan. Addressing a crowd of over one hundred thousand supporters, Jinnah attacked as illusion Gandhi's "dream" that Hindus and Muslims would ever evolve a common nationality: "The Hindus and Muslims have two different religious philosophies, social customs and literatures. They neither intermarry, nor interdine together, and indeed they belong to two different civilizations which are based mainly on conflicting ideas and conceptions."[81]

Declaring Jinnah's two-nation theory as "untruth," Gandhi soon discovered that his cherished vision of nonviolent nationalism had come under attack not only by Muslims but also by prominent Hindu congressmen who increasingly objected to the nonviolent character of resistance to the British. In June 1940, the Working Committee passed for the first time a resolution stating that it could not go "to the full length with Gandhiji" on his philosophy of non-violence. Subhas Chandra Bose, the immediate past president of the Congress, best personified this new militant outlook. Managing to escape from a British prison to Germany, he worked with the Axis powers against the Allies, making broadcasts from Berlin to India and raising armies from Indian prisoners of war in Germany and later in Singapore.[82] Yet, in spite of their critical attitude toward Gandhi's method of nonviolence, the members of the Working Committee never completely broke with their leader. Gandhi, too, did his best to ease existing tensions, accepting that, for many Congress members, *ahimsa* was at best an expedient means. When Linlithgow announced in August 1940 that the "Indian question" could not be solved at a moment when Great Britain was engaged in a bitter struggle for its very existence, the opportunity for a reconciliation between Gandhi and the Congress arose quite naturally. Congressmen who had so recently rejected Gandhi's philosophy now felt that they could ill afford to organize nationwide resistance without the Mahatma's guidance. A resolution adopted at the All-India Congress Committee meeting in Bombay thus affirmed the institution's allegiance to Gandhi, authorizing him to lead a nonviolent campaign of civil disobedience.[83]

Over the next year, the Mahatma guided a largely symbolic *satyagraha* campaign that was designed to put modest pressure on the British while simultaneously allowing sufficient time to build a national movement powerful enough to survive the possible imprisonment of its primary leaders.[84] Gandhi relied on a select group of leaders like Nehru and Vinoba Bhave to defy the official ban on propaganda against the war and thus court arrest. Gradually, more individuals were encouraged to do the same, and soon over twenty-thousand Indians filled British jails. Just as Gandhi was considering the escalation of his confrontation with the raj, news of the Japanese attack on Pearl Harbor reached India. Within the next few weeks, the Japanese managed to defeat the British in Singapore, Burma, and Malaya, raising the specter of an impending invasion of India. Deeply concerned with the possible loss of another crucial Allied base in the Pacific, British Prime Minister Winston Churchill dispatched Sir Stafford Cripps, the Labor leader of the House of Commons, on a conciliatory mission to New Delhi in March 1942. Unanimously approved by the War Cabinet, Cripps's plan offered full dominion status for an "Indian Union," including the right to "separate itself from the equal partnership of the British Commonwealth of Nations."[85] At the same time, however, the plan contained a number of oblique clauses and unacceptable conditions. For example, in addition to allowing for the possibility of partition through the nonaccession of some of the Muslim-majority provinces, the document affirmed British rule over India for the entire duration of the war, citing His Majesty's government's "responsibility to defend India during this critical period." After three weeks of intense negotiations with many Congress members, Cripps finally admitted the failure of his mission, leaving India depressed and empty-handed.

Deeply disappointed in London's stubborn unwillingness to recognize India's right to self-determination, an angry Gandhi publicly speculated that, "Nazi power had risen as a nemesis to punish Britain for her sins of exploitation and enslavement of the Asiatic and African races." Arguing that the United States of America and Great Britain "have no right to talk about protecting democracies and protecting civilization and human freedom, until the canker of white superiority is destroyed in its entirety,"[86] the Mahatma was now prepared to accept what he had rejected *in principle* two decades earlier: the possible descent of the *satyagraha* campaign into anarchy and mass violence. Since the following passage sheds much light on Gandhi's dilemma, it deserves to be cited at some length:

> I always thought that I would have to wait till the country was ready for a non-violent struggle. But my attitude has now undergone a change. I feel that if I continue to wait I might have to wait till doomsday. For the preparation that I have prayed for and worked for may never come, and in the mean time I may be enveloped and overwhelmed by the flames of violence that are spreading all around. I have noticed this shortcoming in my ahimsa. However, in spite of that, the result of the experiments I have conducted have always been good. I do not feel sorry for these. But today we have to go a step further. We have to take the risk of violence to shake off the great calamity of slavery. But even for resort to violence one requires the unflinching faith of a non-violent man. There cannot be any trace of violence in my plans or in my thoughts. A non-violent person has complete faith in God. My ahimsa was always imperfect and therefore it was ineffective to that extent. But I have faith in God. In this context I say

"Rama is the strength of the weak." There is no trace of violence in my consciousness or in the remotest corner of my being. My very being is full of consciousness. How can a man who has consciously pursued ahimsa for the last fifty years change all of a sudden? So it is not that I have become violent.

The people do not have my ahimsa. And therefore I have to take a risk, if I cannot curb their violence. I cannot remain inactive. I will certainly launch a non-violent movement. But if people do not understand it and there is violence, how can I stop it? I will prefer anarchy to the present system of administration because this ordered anarchy is worse than real anarchy. I am sure that the anarchy created by our efforts to mitigate this dangerous anarchy will be less dangerous. The violence extorted then would be just a trifle compared to the existing violence. Violence which is due to the weakness of human nature, is bound to be there. Crores [tens of millions] of people in the country have no weapons. Even if they indulge in violence among themselves how long can they do it? Ultimately they will have to listen to me even if some of them will die in mutual violence. We have to take the risk of anarchy if God wills it. However, we shall do our best to prevent violence. If in spite of that there is violence then it is His wish. I am not responsible for that. But if I enjoy my milk and remain inactive and unconcerned about the terrible violence that is going on in the name of resisting a possible foreign [Japanese] aggression and about the prevalent, dangerous, orderly anarchy in the name of administration, I will be proved guilty. My ahimsa will not be effective at all then. For me such a situation will be intolerable. I will be ashamed of such ahimsa. Ahimsa is not such a useless thing. I hope that pure ahimsa will arise out of such anarchy.[87]

Remarkably, Gandhi's rationalization for putting up with possible violent excesses associated with a new, nationwide noncooperation campaign sounded very similar to Nehru's realist assessment of the nonviolent method in the wake of the Chauri Chaura incident. While Gandhi continued to disavow the *active* employment of violent means, the above passage testifies to the Mahatma's virtual acceptance of Nehru's criticism. Like his pragmatic comrade, Gandhi was now extremely concerned with the "effectiveness" of his nonviolent method—that is, with its practical utility in the political process toward the ultimate power objective of the Indian nationalist movement: the complete and immediate cessation of British rule. In order to enhance its political potency, Gandhi seemed to be prepared to allow his *ahimsa* to co-exist with regrettable forms of *himsa*. Of course, such a concession soiled the purity of the nonviolent principle, turning Gandhi's ambitious vision of nonviolent nationalism into a moderate plea for a less violent nationalism. His hopes for a regenerated nation comprised of disciplined, nonviolent truth-seekers gave way to the recognition that India was still not ready to live up to his moral expectations. Unfortunately, the nation was not "sufficiently non-violent."[88] Once again caught on the horns of his dilemma, the Mahatma reluctantly embraced a political realism qualified by a sad note of fatalism as he attempted to transfer the responsibility for future acts of violence from his own person into the hands of God.

Responding to the frequently raised objection that a British relinquishment of power would only encourage the Japanese to invade India or, alternatively, that it might lead to a bloody Indian civil war between Muslims and Hindus, Gandhi emphasized time and again that he was strongly opposed to German Nazism and Japanese militarism, and he would not hesitate to counsel the use of radical methods of nonviolent resistance against a Japanese occupying force. In a last-ditch move designed to entice London to quit India by terminating its political control, Gandhi even hinted at the possibility that British troops might be permitted to remain there to carry on the fight against the Japanese.[89]

As far as the specter of civil war was concerned, Gandhi confirmed that he was aware of this threat. But he now openly stated that he preferred the condition of temporary anarchy to the perpetuation of British colonialism. "Give us chaos," he told the British, "and leave India to God." In fact, he expected that such a period of political chaos would give way to eventual concord among the different parties.[90] However much he preferred a nonviolent course of action, Gandhi was determined not to let the likelihood of future incidences of violence on the part of the Indian masses keep him from reaching the ultimate goal of his nationalist cause: "There are people who may call me a visionary but I tell you I am a real bania and my business is to obtain swaraj."[91] As Francis Hutchins points out, by the late spring of 1942,

> Gandhi endorsed violence without advocating it. . . . If the nation chose a violent course, he was prepared to accept it. . . . He was also prepared, as an individual believer in nonviolence, to acquiesce in the use of organized violence by sincere men pursuing good ends, even though he could not approve of such violence or directly associate himself with its use. Whatever might be the consequences, and whatever might the appeal of

Gandhi's personal preferences, Gandhi was determined that India must now act for herself.[92]

In July, Gandhi drafted a resolution for the Congress Working Committee that called on the British to end their rule immediately lest it be prepared to face a massive noncooperation movement:

> Should however the appeal fail, the Congress will be reluctantly compelled to utilize all the non-violent strength it might have gathered since 1920 when it adopted non-violence as part of its policy for the vindication of political rights and liberty. The struggle this time would have to resolve itself into a mass movement on the widest scale possible involving voluntary strikes, voluntary non-cooperation on the part of those who are in Government employ or in departments connected with Government in any shape or form and it may involve also non-payment of land revenue and taxes.[93]

A slightly revised version of his draft was passed by the Working Committee a few days later with the understanding that the All-India Congress Committee would vote on the resolution in early August. Predictably, the raj rejected the resolution, and Leopold Amery, Secretary of State for India, warned the Congress leaders that there would be no compromise in this matter, adding that Britain was determined to act in a decisive manner to put the movement down.

Left with no alternative, Gandhi made the final preparations for an "open rebellion of nonviolent character." On August 4, he drafted instructions for civil resisters reiterating that the goal of the impending *satyagraha* struggle was to secure the withdrawal of British rule and the attainment of independence for the whole of India. Reversing the tendencies of centralization in effect during most of the 1920–22 noncooperation campaign, Gandhi urged every Indian to be his or her own leader, acting in the spirit of "truth and non-violence"—as they conceived it.[94] Four days later, the All-Indian Congress Committee endorsed the Quit India campaign, and Gandhi celebrated their decision with one of the longest speeches in his career. Reaffirming his commitment to nonviolence, the Mahatma was nonetheless in a decidedly militant mood. Imploring all Congress members to imprint on their hearts the mantra, "Do or Die," he told them that he would not be satisfied with any outcome short of complete freedom: "We shall either free India or die in the attempt; we shall not live to see the perpetuation of our slavery. Every true Congressman or [Congress] woman will join the struggle with an inflexible determination not to remain alive to see the country in bondage and slavery."[95] In the morning hours of August 9, he issued his final message to the country: "Everyone is free to go to the fullest length under ahimsa. Complete deadlock by strikes and other nonviolent means. Satyagrahis must go out to die not to live. They must seek and face death. It is only when individuals go out to die that the nation will survive. *Karenge ya marenge* [We will do or die]."[96]

Within an hour of this appeal, the raj moved quickly on a plan of action developed in advance. Gandhi and the entire Working Committee, as well as other Congress leaders were arrested. The raj declared the All-India Congress Committee and provincial Congress committees illegal associations. Gandhi was put under house arrest in the dilapidated palace of Aga Khan in Poona. Here, he received only sparse information on the unfolding events in India. The arrests of the national leaders had resulted in mass demonstrations that the government attempted to suppress rigorously. While Jinnah succeeded in keeping most Muslims on the sidelines, Hindu mass actions against the raj continued simultaneously in widely separated places. Gandhi's disciplined program of nonviolent cooperation was carried out only sporadically. Soon the Quit India Movement turned into a violent rebellion as crowds attacked police stations and other government buildings and set fire to railroad stations and post offices. Within days, a powerful underground movement sprang into existence, coordinating such actions as cutting telephone and telegraph wires, blowing up bridges, and tearing up railway tracks. Jayaprakash "JP" Narayan, one of its principal leaders, was unapologetic in his defense of the armed revolt. Referring to Gandhi's slogan that anarchy was better than slavery, he also used the Congress's unwillingness to consider *ahimsa* an inviolable creed in order to justify violent resistance.[97]

However, the raj was prepared, and within a few weeks the uprising was crushed. Hundreds of demonstrators, police officers, and soldiers had been killed, and over sixty-thousand persons had been arrested.[98] Still, the rebellion had shaken the foundations of British rule in India and the arrival of independence came within a few years. Commenting on the "shocking cases of brutality and violence" committed by Indians during the Quit India campaign, Linlithgow blamed Gandhi and the Congress Committee for the course of events. In a letter to the jailed leader, the Viceroy laid full responsibility for the violence at Gandhi's feet, arguing that, "There is evidence that you and your friends expected this policy [of noncooperation] to lead to violence; and that you were prepared to condone it, and that the violence that ensued formed part of a concerted plan, conceived long before the arrest of Congress leaders."[99]

As Francis Hutchins notes, there is much evidence pointing to the possibility that Gandhi clearly anticipated and implicitly sanctioned—both before and after the fact—the mass outbursts that followed the arrests of August 9. Indeed, his initial comment on the outbreak of hostilities was an expression of surprise that they had not been more severe. Moreover, he argued that such open efforts of "self-defense" were compatible with an adherence to nonviolence.[100] Disputing the notion that Congress was preparing for violent action and registering his disgust with the raj's brutal suppression of the movement, Gandhi expressed his regret for the instances of "mob-violence," but he regarded them as a "flea-bite" in proportion to the vast size of India. Emphasizing that the movement had been "relatively non-violent," Gandhi assigned the blame for the escalation of violence to the government: "The wholesale arrest of the Congress leaders seems to have made the people wild with rage to the point of losing self-control. I feel that the Government, not the Congress, are responsible for the destruction that has taken place."[101]

Gandhi remained in prison until May 1944, eventually agreeing to cooperate with the government in its effort to persuade various underground leaders who had remained in hiding to give themselves up. In the end, his vision of a nonviolent nationalism that would reconcile the dilemma of principles and power had suffered a painful defeat. As Francis Hutchins puts it, Gandhi "disdained violence as a blunt weapon, ill-suited to accomplish the social transformation which alone justified revolution. But he did not shun violence when the [1942] revolution was ready and the regime was not."[102]

CONCLUSION

As has been shown in this chapter, at the height of each crisis, the Mahatma found himself in a position of either having to sacrifice the purity of *ahimsa* or accept political impotence. During the Great War and the Quit India Movement, he countenanced violence in a momentary dilution of his own moral principles, thus infusing *satyagraha* with an instrumental logic. In an effort to keep his theory pure, he was forced to come up with a series of murky rationalizations for his actions that created further contradictions in his nonviolent philosophy. During the final crisis of the 1920–22 noncooperation campaign, however, he opted to keep his means as pure as his desired end, thus accepting the need to pay the ultimate political price for his moral convictions.

The three cases analyzed in his chapter are by no means the only examples that could be used to illustrate the nature of Gandhi's dilemma. The civil disobedience campaigns of 1930–34, the events leading to India's partition in 1947, and the 1947 conflict between India and Pakistan over the Kashmir region would all serve as instructive examples for Gandhi's inability to reconcile nonviolent principles and nationalist power. All these cases represent extremely difficult moments of decision, and one cannot help but be impressed with Gandhi's extraordinary attempts to square the circle. Undoubtedly, most nationalist leaders who have faced similar situations have done much worse than the Mahatma. Still, it is only fair to test Gandhi's vision of nonviolent nationalism according to his own ambitious standards. As the embodiment of the archetypal religious pilgrim yearning for truth, Gandhi himself demanded that his attempts to balance the diverging agendas of his philosophy of nonviolence and national liberation be observed not under laboratory conditions, but in real-life circumstances in which a plethora of obstacles seems to militate against a successful resolution of his dilemma. As he put it in 1936, "[T]he acid test of nonviolence is that one thinks, speaks and acts non-violently, even when there is the gravest provocation to be violent."[103]

The partition of India, the fury of Indian communalism, and the growing instrumentalism of the Indian National Congress led the aging Gandhi to question the wisdom of pursuing his vision of nonviolent nationalism by joining the ranks of the "power politicians"—a choice he had consciously made toward the end of the Great War. Deeply suspicious of the state-centered agenda of political nationalists like Nehru and Jinnah, and, by implication, critical of his own past propensity to listen to their siren calls, Gandhi rejected "modern power politics" as both corrupt and corrupting. In what came to be known as his "last will and testament," written the day before his assassination by the Hindu nationalist Nathuram Godse, he even went so far as to suggest that the venerable institution of the Indian National Congress had outlived its purpose with the achievement of political independence in 1947. Urging his supporters to "keep aloof from power politics and its contagion," he proposed that the Congress and its affiliated organizations be dissolved and replaced by a volunteer service corps of dedicated *satyagrahis* who would work with ordinary people to reform India according to the original vision of nonviolent nationalism he had sketched out in *Hind Swaraj*.[104]

Although he turned his back on conventional politics, Gandhi never gave up on his lifelong dream of "purifying India." Indeed, in the last years of his life, he redoubled his efforts to realize his moral vision of redemptive love and nonviolence through the implementation of his "constructive program," which put forth a rather ambitious agenda: the establishment of communal unity, the removal of untouchability, the reestablishment of rural industries, village sanitation, prohibition, basic education for all, the promotion of a national language, education in health and hygiene, and work toward economic equality. In Gandhi's view, these service-oriented activities constituted a genuine alternative to conventional politics, because the former allowed individuals to activate their "infinite spiritual force" in communal spaces protected from the instrumentalism of power politics and the pressures of modernity. Thus, Gandhi's emphasis on the virtue of constructive work in civil society is part of a larger narrative in political theory that bemoans the degradation of politics and the moral emptiness of modernity. It resonates with what Václav Havel and other Eastern European dissidents would decades later call an "antipolitical politics"—a commitment to ethical responsibility and social initiative that forms an antithesis to politics in the ordinary sense.[105]

Antipolitical politicians like Gandhi and Havel envisioned politics neither as a technology of power and manipulation, nor as the art of the useful, but as a way of seeing and achieving spiritually meaningful lives. As Havel puts it, they favored "politics as practical morality, as service to the truth, as essentially human and humanely measured care for our fellow humans."[106] Supporting a "politics with a spiritual dimension," the proponents of antipolitical politics attacked the instrumental means-ends logic at the center of the modern world view, particularly its tendency to justify violence and oppression in the name of progress and reason. Finding their existential self-affirmation in their moral principles of truth and nonviolence, they stood up to the ridicule and the anger of those political voices who rejected their moralizing form of politics in the name of a sober "realism." Equating "anti-political politics" with "selfless work among the downtrodden," they appeared to be less interested in the tangible goals of political activity than in the modes of action themselves.

At the same time, however, one can find a number of weaknesses and shortcomings in such grand schemes to purify politics. For example, by elevating an imagined pure realm of culture and community over a political arena accused of harboring unprincipled pragmatism, corruption, and greed, Gandhi may have equipped himself with a radical rhetoric of virtue, but it came at the expense of delegitimizing the efforts of the participants in conventional politics. It is therefore hardly surprising that Nehru and many other Congress politicians considered the Mahatma's approach "impractical" and even "incomprehensible" to any anticolonial politician of the mid-twentieth century involved in a sound process of nation-building.[107] By devaluing the conventional political process, Gandhi lifted the idealized mode of antipolitical politics to an unassailable moral high ground.

While justifiably exposing the instrumentalism of power politics, such moralizing forms of politics also tend to aid the formation of an undemocratic, elitist political culture that serves as the fertile soil for much less tolerant social forces. The authoritarian tendencies of antipolitical politics become especially transparent in the intolerant idiom of radical cultural nationalists who inscribe notions of patriotic duty and purity into the construction of the ideal national citizen and the ideal leader. Even Gandhi flirted with such authoritarian notions when he imagined the creation of a nonviolent army of disciplined *satyagrahis* who would acquire political legitimacy through virtuous acts of "terrible self-discipline, self-denial and penance." Exercising their authority "as lightly as a flower," they would help India fulfill its true destiny as the world's first nonviolent nation without engaging in conventional power politics and without recreating the morally corrupt institutions of modern politics. Gandhi's dream of merging moral charisma and political power explicitly drew on the Platonic notion of a dictatorship of the virtuous few who were best equipped to establish a just political order.

Such rare "prophets" or "supermen" would "realize the ideal of ahimsa in its fullness," and ultimately redeem "the whole of society."[108] However, as the violent history of Indian nationalism has shown, this highly idealized construction of a politics of purity spearheaded by leaders of superior moral fiber has also proven itself capable of producing exclusivist sentiments and heinous acts of communal violence.[109]

EPILOGUE

🔖

A Nonviolent Nationalism?

But it should be remembered that virtue in itself is not enough; there must also be the power to translate it into action.

—Aristotle[1]

One can say that the validity of a principle does not depend on its practice, and also that it does. The second statement would be more befitting in the case of a moral principle. What is the use of a principle that nobody puts into practice? What is the test of its validity? What would be the value of ahimsa if nobody observed it?

—M. K. Gandhi[2]

Internationalism presupposes nationalism—not the narrow, selfish, greedy spirit that often passes under the name of nationalism, but the nationalism that, whilst it insists upon its own freedom and growth, will disdain to attain them at the expense of other nations.

—M. K. Gandhi[3]

Frantz Fanon, arguably the developing world's most important theorist of national liberation, advances in his classic study, *The Wretched of the Earth,* the powerful argument that all forms of anticolonial nationalism must, by necessity, contain violence: "National liberation, national renaissance, the restoration of nationhood to people, commonwealth: whatever may be headings used or the new formulas introduced, decolonization is always a violent phenomenon."[4] Fanon arrives at this conclusion after a long and penetrating analysis of how the violence inherent in the colonization process always calls forth an answering violence from the colonized.

Though equally resolved to contribute to ending imperialist oppression, Mahatma Gandhi had a different message for movements of national liberation. He dedicated his life to the creation of a benign nationalism that would propel India into independence without resorting to violent means. The theoretical feasibility of Gandhi's vision required the construction of an inclusive type of nationalism the constitutive elements of which would remain free of all forms of conceptual violence. The practical realization of nonviolent nationalism depended on the resolution of Gandhi's own version of a perennial dilemma in politics involving the tension between moral principles and political power: by remaining faithful to his nonviolent principles, Gandhi jeopardized the political success of India's nationalist movement; yet, by participating in the instrumental process of seizing political power from the British, he risked the dilution of his nonviolent principles. His determined struggle with this dilemma represents unquestionably one of the twentieth century's most admirable and influential experiments with politics as "morality in action." In spite of his many achievements, however, the evidence assembled in this study suggests that Gandhi failed to resolve the dilemma both in theory and in practice.

Looking at India today, one cannot help but be struck by the contrast between the Mahatma's vision of a morally regenerated, nonviolent nation consisting of small, decentralized villages, and the stark reality of large nation-states plagued by communal violence and religious strife. In the decades following Gandhi's death in 1948, the furies of Indian communalism have threatened to tear Indian society apart. In December 1992, for example, extreme Hindu nationalists belonging to organizations like the Rashtriya Swayamsevak Sangh and the National Volunteer Corps engaged in the shameful destruction of the Babri mosque in Ayodhya, which led to months of retaliatory violence throughout the country perpetrated by both Hindus and Muslims. More recently, the systematic terrorization of India's Muslim population through pogroms orchestrated by Hindu nationalists has been complemented by similar acts of violence directed against the country's small Christian minority. In 1997, it appeared that the fiftieth anniversary of India's independence offered a short window of opportunity for collective reflection and national reconciliation. Yet, in spite of the almost ritualistic invocation of Mahatma Gandhi's name and memory, the festivities passed without producing any significant changes in people's communal sentiments.

The lasting popular appeal of Indian political parties committed to Hindu nationalism is especially evident after the decisive 1999 election victory of Prime Minister Atal Bihari Vajpayee's right-wing Bharatiya Janata Party. In addition to the existing intra-Indian communal tensions, the policies of the last few years have produced a further deterioration of the neighborly relations between India and Pakistan to the point where the conflict over disputed territories in Kashmir has raised the specter of nuclear war on the subcontinent. Each year this conflict goes unresolved results in the deaths of hundreds of people on both sides. At the time of this writing, a successful military coup in Pakistan appears to add yet another dangerous ingredient to an already explosive situation. Turning further south to Sri Lanka, one witnesses the perpetuation of the seemingly endless, bloody struggle between Tamil separatists and the Singhalese-dominated government.

Certainly, Gandhi would shudder at these unfortunate developments in contemporary South Asia, wondering what, if anything at all, remained of his efforts to create a unifying framework of a nonviolent, moral Indian nation by balancing governmental needs for national solidarity and social cohesion with the celebration of cultural, religious, and communal differences. How would he explain the stubborn persistence of ethnic and religious violence? Would he view his own nationalist project differently in light of current events? Indeed, this study is premised on the idea that students of Gandhi's life and thought must be prepared to ask tough questions about the extent to which his own theoretical and practical contributions to the phenomenon of nationalism conflicted with his commitment to a philosophy of nonviolence and its implied imperatives of moral universalism. The virtue of raising such questions lies in their ability to yield insightful, albeit often disconcerting, answers to central problems in political and social theory—problems that transcend the narrow framework of my analysis of Gandhi's dilemma. Before turning to at least one such issue regarding the general compatibility of nationalism and nonviolence, I wish to present the reader with a concluding summary of my findings.

As a young man, Gandhi found himself immensely attracted to the empire's rhetoric of liberal nationalism. The latter reflected an ideology of sameness that promised all of Queen Victoria's subjects fair treatment on the basis of universal principles of justice. Contemporary social theorists often refer to such inclusive constructions of national identity as "civic nationalism" or "constitutional patriotism."[5] These terms convey the ideal of a community comprised of equal, rights-bearing citizens who are united in their patriotic attachment to a set of inclusive political practices and values based on the rule of law. The British empire's claim to such a benign type of nationalism, however, was contradicted by its historical practices, which often served the more sinister purposes of political expansion and economic exploitation. In the second half of the nineteenth century, these imperialist impulses found vocal defenders in the liberal camp. Their ideology of difference employed such categories as civilization, race, progress, and culture to justify the unequal treatment of non-European Others.

Exposed to a particularly virulent strain of this degenerated, ethnocentric type of nationalism in South Africa, Gandhi joined the ongoing struggle of the local Indian immigrant community to end the racially discriminatory policies of the colonial administration. Over the years, the young lawyer developed a mixture of constitutional and *satyagrahic* strategies of confronting colonial oppression and exclusion. At this early point in his career, however, Gandhi employed these methods of protest for the sole purpose of appealing to the colonial authorities to rescind their exclusionary laws, which violated the noble spirit of moral universalism. While acknowledging his distinct Indian cultural background, Gandhi saw himself nonetheless first and foremost as a British patriot—a "good" civic nationalist who defended the British liberal tradition and its Enlightenment values of rationality, tolerance, inclusivity, and individual rights.

As the years passed without the Indian community receiving legal justice, Gandhi's British patriotism cooled off significantly. He began to look upon the promise of civic nationalism as an oppressive doctrine of privilege—an impotent universalism that had abandoned its own ideals. As a result of his disappointment in liberalism, his defensive strategy underwent dramatic change. Incessantly attacked in racist terms as an inferior "Indian," Gandhi eventually decided to defend himself as an "Indian." In other words, he increasingly allowed the universalist tone of his defense be eclipsed by an imposed language of particularism the conceptual and rhetorical power of which rested on forms of epistemic violence that resembled the ethnic idiom of the oppressor. This shift in emphasis also explains Gandhi's frequent use of exclusivist ethnic categories in his defense of the right of South African Indians to enjoy the privileges of British citizenship.

As a result of his increasingly particularistic self-understanding, he felt the need to refute European charges of India's civilizational inferiority by engaging in an alternative construction of a virtuous ancient Indian civilization. Yet in spite of its radical rejection of modern civilization, Gandhi's vision of India reverberated with the language of affirmative orientalism and other inverted echoes of European ethnic superiority. His exclusivist response to European policies of racial discrimination may have represented an effective bulwark against racially motivated forms of injustice, but it nonetheless mirrored—albeit to a far lesser degree—the inhumanity, violence, and racism of those who excluded him.[6] Unfortunately, these subtle processes leading to the inversion and reproduction of the oppressor's violence—a phenomenon described so well by Fanon—utterly escaped Gandhi. He failed to notice that his supposedly "nonviolent" construction of an anticolonial nationalism mimicked the exclusionary strategy of the colonial oppressor. Instead, he managed to convince himself that his own brand of nationalism had remained inclusive and tolerant:

> Those who have at all followed my humble career even superficially cannot have failed to observe that not a single act of my life has been done to injure any individual or nation. My nationalism as my religion is not exclusive but inclusive. . . . I claim no infallibility. I am conscious of having made Himalayan blunders but am not conscious of having made them intentionally or having ever harboured enmity towards any person or nation of any life human or subhuman.[7]

Linking his nationalist vision to his political method of *satyagraha* made it easy for Gandhi to believe that he was actually creating the kind of benign nationalism in India that he had originally expected from a reformed British model. Granted, his nationalism served the noble cause of ending colonial oppression, but this does not mean that it remained free of *ahimsa*. A largely derivative enterprise that bore the traces of the rejected paradigm, Gandhi's nationalist vision was, in fact, no longer "nonviolent" according to his own broad definition. Conflicting with his professed moral universalism and inclusivism, these traces of conceptual violence also invaded Gandhi's larger project of self-control as his demands for the cultural regeneration of the nation expressed themselves in rigid, disciplinary schemes for the "purification" of body and soul.

The residual violence lodged in Gandhi's own nationalist vision also impacted his political practice. For example, his early nationalist speeches in India emphasized the "satanic" nature of Western civilization. The use of exclusionary language facilitated the political mobilization of the Indian masses, but it also jeopardized the nonviolent character of Gandhi's *satyagraha* campaigns. Conveying a sense of Indian cultural and spiritual superiority, these speeches contributed to the political potency of his vision, often proving to be more powerful with ordinary Indians than his universalist message of love, more capable of rallying the masses behind the idea of political *swaraj* than his appeals for a selfless service to humanity. Even though Gandhi explicitly disapproved of violent means in the nationalist struggle, the conceptual violence contained in his speeches made it easier for some people to exercise physical violence against those they viewed as "outsiders." Their hostile acts went hand in hand with the employment of condescending stereotypes, invidious comparisons, and the affirmation of the spiritual and moral superiority of their own nation.

Gandhi's difficulties in controlling "undisciplined" crowds exposed how hard it was to suppress the political and social consequences of the conceptually violent formations that clung to his nationalist vision. According to my interpretation, then, Gandhi's admirable attempt to resolve the dilemma of nonviolent principles and nationalist power was already doomed from the moment he conveyed his moral message of nonviolence in the particularistic language of inverted British nationalism. Using Gandhi's own universalist aspirations against his particularist actions, one might say that he failed to realize that his ideal of universal love was ultimately incompatible with the exclusivist tendencies of nationalism, because, unlike the latter, love and nonviolence strive for the abolition of fixed boundaries.[8]

Indeed, all existing forms of nationalism originate in the conceptual creation of limited spaces and collective identities characterized by fixed boundaries. In order to justify the creation of national identity in the first place, nationalists emphasize the "specialness" of the nation and its members. These processes go hand in hand with the proliferation of narratives that attribute exclusionary traits to outsiders, thereby elevating particular symbolic meanings to the only valid constitutive principles of a community. The simultaneous exclusion and suppression of other meanings or symbols results in the hardening of the perceptual boundaries that separate the familiar "us" from the alien "them."[9] Referring to the dangerous potential for violence and aggression contained in the creation of collective identities through the drawing of definite lines of exclusion, Regina Schwartz writes:

> ... [I]magining identity as an act of distinguishing and separating from others, of boundary making and line drawing, is the most fundamental act of violence we commit. . . . Ironically, the Outsider is believed to threaten the boundaries that are drawn to exclude him, the boundaries his very existence maintains. Outside by definition but always threatening to get in, the Other is poised in a delicate balance that is always off balance because fear and aggression continually weight the scales.[10]

This does not mean, however, that all processes of differentiation are equally tainted by conceptual violence. Coming to such an extreme conclusion, Jacques Derrida and other writers in the deconstructivist genre have argued that a primordial "arche-violence" is present in the very act of drawing distinctions between things, persons, and social groups.[11] This implies the existence of some sort of metaphysical "origin" whose pristine nondualism can never be experienced in self-consciousness. Engaged in negative, transcendental deconstruction, Derrida labels as "violent" the transformation of the enabling "thing itself in its absolute proximity" into a system of differentiation or classification that constitutes language and mental representations. In short, he contends that conceptual "arche-violence" is constitutive of all politics and thought.

If this is true, then violence ceases to serve as meaningful concept, for it can no longer be conceptually identified, denounced, and delimited in its spheres of operation.[12] The deficiency of Derrida's deconstructive approach becomes especially apparent when it comes to making normative judgments of political affairs. Given that the very position from which a moral condemnation of violence is articulated is itself only made possible by the primary violence of conceptual differentiation, it is no longer clear how something like a moral critique of violence is possible. In that case, to paraphrase Hegel, we have entered the night in which all cows are black.

Contrary to Derrida, I argue that the act of drawing distinctions between this group and that group amounts to conceptual violence *only* if it is linked to invidious categories of superiority/inferiority and inclusivity/exclusivity which, in turn, contribute to a logic of domination and oppression. Such conceptual violence tends to forestall the possibility of a political accommodation of difference because its exclusivist language and imagery perpetuate hostile attitudes that serve as the necessary precondition for additional acts of violence—whether that violence is exercised by individuals or, alternatively, is implicit within the mundane workings of entrenched institutional structures.

This deconstructivist challenge leads me to raise the final question of this study: can nationalism be purged of its exclusionary tendencies, which encourage acts of intolerance, discrimination, violence, and conquest? After all, Gandhi's failure to fashion a nonviolent nationalism casts doubt on the possibility of constructing a nationalism without relying on *some* forms of conceptual violence. In the wake of the recent resurgence of ethnic hatred and nationalist violence around the world, social and political thinkers have hotly debated the theoretical and practical feasibility of creating benign forms of nationalism.[13]

Michael Ignatieff and other proponents of civic nationalism have argued that it is both possible and desirable to construct and put into practice a benign form of nationalism anchored in the liberal ideals of rationality, accountability, rule of law, procedural fairness, and opportunity for all. At the same time, however, Ignatieff admits that these civic ideals have not been realized in actual practice—not even in the best existing versions of liberal nationalism. According to Ignatieff, the gulf between the ideal and the real remains because many Britons or Americans rely on "thick," or ethnically tinged, definitions of national cohesion and other practices that reinforce hard boundaries of inclusion and exclusion.[14]

As my discussion of Gandhi's dilemma has shown, such patterns of conceptual violence are not merely reflected in obvious, "bad" variants of nationalism, but can also be found in more benign types that serve such noble causes as people's emancipation from colonial oppression. While it would be both foolish and politically dangerous to deny the existence of qualitative differences between various forms of nationalism, the sharp distinction between "civic" and "ethnic" nationalism—a dualism that pervades the literature on the subject—appears to be overdrawn in many cases. Whether one defends nationalism as a regenerative force that seeks to restore the moral purity of an imagined ancient civilization or as a progressive movement of the popular interest against empire, dynasty, and privilege, one can hardly ignore its violent potential. One person may legitimately point to national solidarity and social cohesion as the positive elements of nationalism while another may reasonably choose to emphasize its near-pathological character, its roots in fear and hatred of the Other, and its affinities with racism.[15] In either case, however, it would be a mistake to close one's eyes to the staggering manifestations of violence unleashed by both ethnic and civic nationalist movements over the last two centuries. As Robert Fine notes, "Nationalism is a fickle beast. In its best moods it liberates human beings from colonial oppression and unites people previously fragmented, but it also excludes those deemed not to belong and demands the active assent of its 'own' nationals."[16]

If even the best forms of nationalism contain such structures of conceptual violence, then why continue the doomed quest for a benign, nonviolent nationalism? Rather than engaging in the futile task of purging nationalism of its malign elements, shouldn't the adherents to a philosophy of nonviolence attempt to transcend nationalism altogether? Shouldn't they seek the realization of a nonviolent society according to a cosmopolitan vision that elevates universal human standards over national cultural traditions? Gandhi himself responded to this cosmopolitan challenge with the assertion that his nonviolent nationalism was not only perfectly compatible with the universalist ideals of cosmopolitanism, but that it also constituted a necessary step toward the realization of a global order:

> In my opinion, it is impossible for one to be internationalist without being a nationalist. Internationalism is possible only when nationalism becomes a fact, i. e., when people belonging to different countries have organized themselves and are able to act as one man. It is not nationalism that is evil, it is the narrowness, selfishness, exclusiveness which is the bane of modern nations which is evil. . . . Indian nationalism has, I hope, struck a different path. It wants to organize itself and find full self-expression for the benefit and service of humanity at large. Any way there is no uncertainty about my patriotism or nationalism. God having cast my lot in the midst of the people of India, I should be untrue to my Maker if I failed to serve them.[17]

Gandhi's evolutionary vision of a benign, inclusive nationalism that would ultimately culminate in a genuine cosmopolitanism echoes similar ideas espoused by late-eighteenth-century European thinkers such as C. S. de Montesquieu, Adam Smith, J. G. Herder, and J. G. Fichte. The latter, for example, argued that the altruistic "will to cosmopolitanism" needed to be realized first on the level of the nation before it could spread "to the whole of humankind." Like Gandhi, Fichte predicted that his own country would be the first nation to harmonize universal ethics with nationalist power, because it alone contained the spiritual capacity to "encompass the whole of mankind for the sake of the nation." Thus, both men spoke in glowing terms of the special function of their respective nations—the mission to set a virtuous example for the entire world and thus teach humanity a moral lesson of universal applicability.[18]

There are a number of serious problems with this argument. First, to claim that nationalism is a necessary step toward cosmopolitanism means to presuppose that they are subjected to an inner teleology that makes them two connected points on the same continuum. If this is indeed the case, it is difficult to see how the end product would not be impacted by previous formations. In other words, how can Gandhi's cosmopolitanism remain untainted by the forms of conceptual violence contained in his nationalist vision? Second, assuming the existence of a human desire to be recognized—in this case as the beacon of universalism for the rest of the world—one would expect the emergence of intense rivalries among nations. In the above case, both Germans and Indians might claim the honor of belonging to the most benign nation. Rooted in invidious claims to spiritual and moral superiority, such rivalries would seriously undermine the very spirit of universalism they purport to represent. Third, nationalism always requires the recognition of special ties among the citizens comprising the nation. Cosmopolitanism, on the other hand, seeks to overcome such symbols of particularism, instead promoting the individual's identification with the world as a whole. How is one to reconcile these contradictory impulses? Finally, it is extremely difficult to reroute the emotional fervor of nationalism in a (cosmopolitan) direction without undercutting the citizens' original attachments to the particularist features of their national identity.[19]

Hence, I assert that the realization of nonviolent principles requires a cosmopolitan framework firmly anchored in universal human standards. The construction of a nonviolent, cosmopolitan identity must start by resisting the temptation to fight the violent manifestations of particularism with new forms of particularism that bear the inverted traces of the old paradigm. Oppression and exploitation must be opposed nonviolently through forms of direct action carried out under the universal banner of humanity, not the particularist flags of nation, race, or class. In other words, the universalist tendencies associated with the concept of *ahimsa* demand an ideological vessel that represents an *alternative* to nationalism, not its "purified" end product. Yet, in formulating a cosmopolitan vision that accommodates noninvidious differences, one must be careful not to overvalue one's own model by presenting nationalism as the pernicious Other. Since the exclusivist tendencies of nationalism coexists with its noble longing for harmony and justice, the cosmopolitan thinker is well advised to avoid the trap of devaluing nationalism absolutely. In addition, as Robert Fine observes, cosmopolitans must watch their tendency to pathologize nationalism as the folly of others, thus failing to recognize the existence of exclusionary impulses in themselves.[20]

To be sure, the realization of the cosmopolitan idea also faces many political obstacles. Like it or not, we live in a world of particular solidarities, where international institutions like the United Nations owe their continued existence to the power of nation-states. In fact, even the ability of the individual thinker to publicize her cosmopolitan vision depends largely on her membership in a secure nation-state. Hence, there is some truth to Margaret Canovan's contention that all cosmopolitans find themselves in the predicament of having to advance their principles and projects through the political power provided by national solidarity.[21] At this point, then, the citizen of the world encounters once again the perennial dilemma of moral principles and political power as universal ideals clash with the particularity of collective power. Is it right to use nationalist power to undermine the nation-state? Can it be used at all without compromising one's cosmopolitan principles? How does one reconcile one's commitment to build a nonviolent, cosmopolitan society with the retention of one's passport—in the name of "pragmatism"?

The difficulties raised by these questions are further compounded by a host of other political problems. For example, it is one thing to establish the rational and moral desirability of cosmopolitanism, but quite another to translate it into a viable political program. Any politician or government that is prepared to make a serious attempt to implement cosmopolitan principles would most likely pay the high price of losing the political and emotional support of the masses. The loss of political support would diminish the chance to take any further political action on the same principles.[22]

Thus, it appears that the dilemma of moral principles and political power is insoluble. The marriage of justice and utility—perhaps most eloquently proposed in Jean-Jacques Rousseau's demand to "bring together what right permits with what interest prescribes"—always resists its full political realization. However, the recognition of the dilemma's persistence must not lead to moral despair or political passivity. Quite the contrary. It illuminates the very nature of politics as a contested enterprise that escapes closure, yet beckons its participants to put their ideals into practice. Public action requires both a willingness to compromise and make adjustments and an insistence on transcendent universal values. As the French philosopher Emmanuel Mounier emphasizes, this dual requirement imposes on sound political actors the duty that they do not put off action until they find the perfectly just cause and irreproachable means for pursuing it: "[N]ot only are we never confronted with an ideal situation; we can seldom choose the critical moments at which our intervention is required."[23] Mounier's dual requirement also reminds those practical idealists who are prepared to act not to translate their noble longing for perfection and absolute harmony into a dictatorship of purity.

Although perfect solutions are impossible, lack of progress is inexcusable, because it results in greater human suffering. Applied to Gandhi's dilemma of reconciling nonviolent principles with nationalist power, progress means to advocate forms of collective identity that reduce the human propensity to draw exclusionary boundaries and engage in other manifestations of conceptual violence. Given its historical association with organized violence, the creation of exclusionary identities, and the ideological suppression of transnational interests, nationalism represents a rather poor vehicle for the realization of universal moral principles. Cosmopolitanism, on the other hand, seems to provide a less antagonistic ideological shell for the universal imperatives of *ahimsa*. To engage in politics means the impossibility of finding perfect solutions, hence there will always be a price to pay. Each person who enters the political arena ought to determine in interaction with others how to arrive at an acceptable compromise between the imperatives of power and the voice of conscience. Though still far from political realization, emerging cosmopolitan models of democracy seem to provide the least violent framework for the pursuit of a fair compromise among all citizens of this world.[24]

There were moments when Gandhi not only conceded his inability to solve his dilemma, but even seemed to accept the loss of moral perfection to the moment of uneasy compromise: "I ever compromised my own ideals even in individual conduct not because I wished to but because the compromise was inevitable. And so in social and political matters I have never exacted complete fulfillment of the ideals in which I have believed."[25] Still, one must be extremely careful not to turn the need for compromise into an excuse for unprincipled power politics. Max Weber came dangerously close to the latter position when he categorically rejected the role of a morally pure "ethic of ultimate ends" (*Gesinnungsethik*) in politics. Fearing that this ethic would encourage the vain pursuit of absolute, otherworldly ends, and thereby lead to the frustration and failure of worldly endeavors, the German social thinker insisted that, "Anyone seeking to save his own soul and the souls of others does not take the path of politics in order to reach his goal, for politics has quite different tasks, namely those which can only be achieved by force. The genius—or demon—of politics lives in a state of inner tension with the god of love. . . ."[26] Instead, Weber advocated an "ethic of responsibility" (*Verantwortungsethik*), which represented for him a more appropriate attitude in a realm of politics characterized by irreducible plurality, contingency, and violence. He thought that responsible politicians would do their utmost to serve the interests of their community, but that they would always acknowledge the impossibility of fusing worldly action and spirituality. Faced with the inescapable dilemma of balancing ethics and politics, Weber advised the *Realpolitiker* to engage in the world of violence and discord according to the maxim: "Here I stand; I can do no other."

There exists a genuine concern for the common good in Weber's attempt to draw attention to the political disasters that can befall communities if they allow themselves to be held hostage to the moral purism of unarmed prophets. His realism is, therefore, not bereft of ethical sentiments; in the name of responsibility to the survival of the community, he sought to defend the autonomy of the political realm against the encroachment of spiritual absolutism. At the same time, however, Weber's "realistic" calculation of means led him to go along with the further instrumentalization of the political arena, culminating in his support of the German war effort in the Great War.

In order to avoid the elevation of power above serious ethical concerns, Weber's realism needs to be moderated by a good dose of Gandhian idealism. If the realists of this world have made a convincing argument against the dangers of moral purism in politics, then the representatives of the twentieth-century "Gandhian tradition"—which includes the slain American civil rights leader Martin Luther King; South African Arch-Bishop Desmond Tutu and former President Nelson Mandela; Czech President Vaclav Havel; Petra Kelly, the late founder of the German Greens; the indefatigable Burmese dissident Aung San Suu Kyi; and the Dalai Lama—have shown the world that a moral politics of redemptive love and nonviolence can go much further than the realists ever imagined.

Thus, those who embrace Weber's ethic of responsibility ought to remember the dire consequences of sacrificing to the god of political power the universal norms and values inherent in a commitment to human dignity and social justice. Likewise, those who support Gandhi's moral injunction to remain nonviolent in word and deed ought to be willing to accept that the purity of their moral vision will always be tainted by the inherent frailty of human existence and the vulnerability of the human condition. Therein lies the most valuable lesson to be learned from the dilemma of reconciling moral principles with political power.

ABBREVIATIONS

AB   Mohandas K. Gandhi, *Autobiography: The Story of My Experiments with Truth* (New York: Dover Publications, 1983).

CWMG   *The Collected Works of Mahatma Gandhi.* 100 vols. (New Delhi: Publications Division, Ministry of Information and Broadcasting, Government of India, 1958–1994).

HS   Mohandas K. Gandhi, *Hind Swaraj and Other Writings.* Anthony J. Parel, ed. (Cambridge, U.K.: Cambridge University Press, 1997).

KH   Mohandas K. Gandhi, *Key to Health* (Ahmedabad: Navajivan Publishing House, 1948).

MPWMG   Raghavan Iyer, ed., *The Moral and Political Writings of Mahatma Gandhi.* 3 vols. (Oxford: Clarendon Press, 1986–7).

SRSI   Mohandas K. Gandhi, *Self Restraint versus Self-Indulgence.* 2 vols. (Ahmedabad: Navajivan Publishing House, 1958 [1928]). Please note: The brackets indicate the original date of publication (throughout endnotes).

NOTES

INTRODUCTION

1. Jawaharlal Nehru cited in K. P. Karunakaran, "Gandhi and the Nation-Building in India," *Gandhi Marg* 2.5 (1980), p. 264.
2. Octavio Paz, *In Light of India* (New York: Harcourt Brace & Company, 1997), p. 113.
3. *CWMG* 68: p. 205 [1938]. For an insightful discussion of Gandhi's perspective on nonviolence, see Bhikhu Parekh, *Colonialism, Tradition and Reform: An Analysis of Gandhi's Political Discourse* (New Delhi: Sage, 1989), pp. 107–38.
4. *MPWMG* 2: p. 212 [1916].
5. Ibid., p. 230 [1930].
6. *CWMG* 69: p. 313 [1939]. Dennis Dalton rightfully notes that Gandhi considered anger, contempt, malice, and arrogance as part of the "violence of the spirit." See Dennis Dalton, *Mahatma Gandhi: Nonviolent Power in Action* (New York: Columbia University Press, 1993), p. 42. For a discussion of Gandhi's emphasis on nonviolent speech, see Robert A. Bode, "Gandhi's Theory of Nonviolent Communication," *Gandhi Marg* 16.1 (1994), pp. 5–30.
7. *CWMG* 27: p. 322 [1925].
8. Joan V. Bondurant, *Conquest of Violence. The Gandhian Philosophy of Conflict,* rev. ed. (Princeton: Princeton University Press, 1988), p. 25. See also J. T. F. Jordens, *Gandhi's Religion: A Homespun Shawl* (New York: St. Martin's Press, 1998), pp. 226, 253. Bhikhu Parekh notes that while Gandhi admitted the difficulty of practicing "pure" *ahimsa,* he still postulated the "ideal of a completely non-violent existence" (*Colonialism, Tradition and Reform,* p. 131). After emphasizing Gandhi's "anti-perfectionism" with regard to *ahimsa,* Ronald Terchek, too, ultimately concedes that "Gandhi wants nonviolence to be a way of life and infuse all social relations: familial, political, economic, and educational. There is no room for selective nonviolence in Gandhi's theory. . . ." See Ronald Terchek, *Gandhi: Struggling for Autonomy* (Lanham, MD: Rowman and Little-field, 1998), p. 183.
9. *CWMG* 13: p. 228 [1916].
10. *MPWMG* 2: p. 212 [1916]. According to Johan Galtung, two axioms summarize Gandhism: "*unity-of-life* and *unity-of-means* and end." See Galtung, "Cultural Violence," in Manfred B. Steger and Nancy S. Lind, eds., *Violence and Its*

Alternatives: An Interdisciplinary Reader (New York: St. Martin's Press, 1999), p. 51. For Gandhi's claim that nonviolence was morally right in general, see William Borman, *Gandhi and Non-Violence* (Albany, NY: State University of New York Press, 1986), pp. 120–4.

11. Terchek, *Gandhi,* p. 188.

12. Max Weber, "The Profession and Vocation of Politics," in Peter Lassman and Ronald Speirs, eds., *Max Weber: Political Writings* (Cambridge: Cambridge University Press, 1994), pp. 359–61.

13. See, for example, Peter Gay, *The Dilemma of Democratic Socialism: Eduard Bernstein's Challenge to Marx* (New York: Columbia University Press, 1952); Hannah Arendt, *The Human Condition: A Study on the Central Dilemmas Facing Modern Man.* 2nd ed. (New York: Doubleday, 1959); Michael Walzer, *The Company of Critics: Social Criticism and Political Commitment in the Twentieth-Century* (New York: Basic Books, 1988); Bernard Yack, *The Longing for the Total Revolution: Philosophic Sources of Social Discontent from Rousseau to Marx and Nietzsche* (Berkeley: University of California Press, 1992); John Keane, *Reflections on Violence* (London: Verso, 1996); and Steven Eric Bronner, *Ideas in Action: Political Tradition in the Twentieth Century* (Lanham, MD: Rowman & Littlefield Publishers, 1999).

14. There are several descriptive accounts of Gandhi's statements with regard to nationalism and nonviolence. See, for example, Peter Brock, *The Mahatma and Mother India: Essays on Gandhi's Non-Violence and Nationalism* (Ahmedabad: Navajivan, 1983). However, I found only four studies that offer analytically more rewarding, but still limited, discussions of the relationship between his nationalism and his philosophy of nonviolence: Francis G. Hutchins, *India's Revolution: Gandhi and the Quit India Movement* (Cambridge, MA: Harvard University Press, 1973); Parekh, *Colonialism, Tradition and Reform;* Partha Chatterjee, "The Moment of Manoeuvre: Gandhi and the Critique of Civil Society," in *Nationalist Thought and the Colonial World: A Derivative Discourse?* (Minneapolis, MN: University of Minnesota Press, 1993), pp. 85–130; and Dalton, *Mahatma Gandhi.* Another brief but very useful exploration of the theme can be found in Anthony J. Parel, "Gandhi's Idea of Nation in *Hind Swaraj,*" *Gandhi Marg* 13.3 (October-November 1991), pp. 261–81.

15. See, for example, Yogesh Chadha, *Gandhi: A Life* (New York: John Wiley & Sons, 1997); Martin Green, *Gandhi: Voice of a New Age Revolution* (New York: Continuum, 1993); Judith M. Brown, *Gandhi: Prisoner of Hope* (New Haven: Yale University Press, 1989); Robert Payne, *The Life and Death of Mahatma Gandhi* (New York: E. P. Dutton, 1969); Geoffrey Ashe, *Gandhi* (New York: Stein and Day, 1968); D. G. Tendulkar, *Mahatma* 8 vols. (Delhi: Government of India Publications Division, 1960); B. R. Nanda, *Mahatma Gandhi* (George Allen & Unwin, 1958); Louis Fischer, *The Life of Mahatma Gandhi* (New York: Harper, 1950).

16. *CWMG* 25: p. 369 [1924].

17.   *CWMG* 22: p. 27 [1921].

18.   *MPWMG* 3: p. 310 [1940].

19.   See Bhikhu Parekh, *Gandhi* (Oxford, UK: Oxford University Press, 1997), p. 48; and Raghavan Iyer, *The Moral and Political Thought of Mahatma Gandhi,* 2nd ed. (London: Concord Grove Press, 1983), pp. 40–3.

20.   For various interpretations of Gandhi's "spiritual politics," see Iyer, *The Moral and Political Thought of Mahatma Gandhi;* Bhikhu Parekh, *Gandhi's Political Philosophy: A Critical Examination* (Notre Dame, IN: University of Notre Dame Press, 1989), and *Colonialism, Tradition and Reform;* and Bondurant, *Conquest of Violence.*

21.   C. A. J. Coady, "The Idea of Violence," *Journal of Applied Philosophy* 3.1 (1986), p. 3.

22.   See Hans-Georg Gadamer, *Truth and Method,* ed. Garrett Barden and John Cumming, (New York: Seabury Press, 1975).

23.   Bronner, *Ideas in Action,* pp. 10–11. See also Terence Ball, *Reappraising Political Theory: Revisionist Studies in the History of Political Thought* (Oxford: Clarendon Press, 1995), pp. 31–2.

24.   See Jean Grondin, *Introduction to Philosophical Hermeneutics* (New Haven, CT: Yale University Press, 1994), p. 18.

25.   Bronner, *Ideas in Action,* p. 9. See also Yack, *The Longing for the Total Revolution,* pp. 6–7.

26.   Bruce Haddock, "State and Nation in Mazzini's Political Thought," *History of Political Thought* 20.2 (Summer 1999), p. 313.

27.   This question stands at the center of two recent studies on violence and nationalism: Regina M. Schwartz, *The Curse of Cain: The Violent Legacy of Monotheism* (Chicago: University of Chicago Press, 1997); and Sudhir Kakar, *The Color of Violence* (Chicago: University of Chicago Press, 1996). The arguments of both authors have greatly aided my own interpretation of Gandhi's nonviolent nationalism.

28.   Bhikhu Parekh, "Ethnocentricity of the nationalist discourse," *Nations and Nationalism* 1.1 (1995), pp. 39–41; *Gandhi's Political Philosophy;* and *Colonialism, Tradition and Reform;* Ashis Nandy, *The Illegitimacy of Nationalism: Rabindranath Tagore and the Politics of Self* (Delhi: Oxford University Press, 1994), p. 3; Mool Chand, *Nationalism and Internationalism of Gandhi, Nehru and Tagore* (New Delhi: M. N. Publishers, 1989), pp. 91–124; and Nirmal Kumar Bose, *Lectures on Gandhism* (Ahmedabad: Navajivan, 1971), pp. 86–8.

29.   *MPWMG* 2: p. 296 [1935].

30.   *CWMG* 28: p. 127 [1925]; See also *CWMG* 76: p. 351 [1942].

31.   *CWMG* 21: p. 291 [1921]. For a discussion of the Tagore-Gandhi controversy, see Krishna Dutta and Andrew Robinson, *Rabindranath Tagore. The Myriad-Minded Man* (New York: St. Martin's Press, 1995), pp. 260–65; Dalton, *Mahatma Gandhi,* pp. 67–78; Sibnarayan Ray, "Tagore-Gandhi Controversy," in Sibnarayan Ray, ed., *Gandhi India and the World,* (Philadelphia: Temple University

Press, 1970), pp. 119–141; and Ajai Singh and Shakuntala Singh, "The Tagore-Gandhi Controversy Revisited," *Indian Philosophical Quarterly* 19.4 (October 1992), pp. 265–82.

32. *CWMG* 22: p. 462 [1922].

33. Romain Rolland, *Mahatma Gandhi. A Study in Indian Nationalism* (Madras: S. Ganesan, 1923), p. 98.

34. Ainslee T. Embree, "Gandhi's Role in Shaping an Indian Identity," in Mark Juergensmeyer, ed., *Imagining India: Essays in Indian History* (Delhi: Oxford University Press, 1989), p. 172. For a similar assessment, see Susanne Hoeber Rudolph and Lloyd I. Rudolph, *Gandhi: The Traditional Roots of Charisma* (Chicago: University of Chicago Press, 1983), pp. 64–5; and Terchek, *Gandhi*, p. 1.

35. See Maurice R. O'Connell, *Daniel O'Connell: The Man and His Politics* (Dublin: Irish Academy Press, 1990), pp. 64–88; and Raymond Moley, *Daniel O'Connell. Nationalism Without Violence* (New York: Fordham University Press, 1974), pp. 187–92, 211–36.

CHAPTER 1: THE PROMISE OF BRITISH LIBERALISM

1. From Gandhi's "Farewell Speech" to his fellow students of the Alfred High School in Rajkot. *CWMG* 1: p. 1 [1888].

2. *CWMG* 5: p. 117 [1905].

3. Gadamer cited in Grondin, *Introduction to Philosophical Hermeneutics,* p. 119.

4. Richard G. Fox, *Gandhian Utopia: Experiments with Culture* (Boston: Beacon Press, 1989), p. 16.

5. For the importance of the category of "tradition" in my approach, see my introduction and Bronner, *Ideas in Action.*

6. There are, of course, distinct thematic currents in the British discourse on India. For example, for a discussion of the colonial discourse on labor, see Rajnarayan Chandavarkar, *Imperial Power and Popular Politics: Class, Resistance and the State in India, c. 1850–1950* (Cambridge: Cambridge University Press, 1998).

7. There exists some controversy over the relative impact of "Indian traditions" on Gandhi's political and moral thought. For reasons that will be made clear throughout the book, I argue for the paramount influence of European ideas. This does not mean, however, that Indian traditions played no role at all in the construction of Gandhi's conceptual universe.

8. Richard Bellamy, ed., *Victorian Liberalism: Nineteenth-Century Political Thought and Practice* (London: Routledge, 1990); and *Liberalism and Modern Society: A Historical Argument* (University Park, PA: Penn State University Press, 1992), pp. 9–57. See also Thomas R. Metcalf, *The New Cambridge History of India III.4: Ideologies of the Raj* (Cambridge: Cambridge University Press, 1994), pp. 28–9.

9. See Uday Singh Mehta, *Liberalism and Empire: A Study in Nineteenth-Century British Liberal Thought* (Chicago: University of Chicago Press, 1999), pp. 194–5.

I am aware of important theoretical contrasts between Lockean liberalism and nineteenth-century utilitarianism, but I agree with Mehta's argument that with respect to the "anthropological basis of universalist claims, the two theoretical visions share important and relevant similarities" (p. 48, n. 2).

10. Ibid., p. 194.

11. Metcalf, *Ideologies of the Raj,* pp.33–41.

12. "Queen Victoria's Proclamation, 1 November 1858," in C. H. Philips, H. L. Singh, B. N. Pandey, eds., *The Evolution of India and Pakistan 1858–1947: Select Documents* (London: Oxford University Press, 1962), p. 11.

13. For a concise account of the Anglo-Indian War, see Stanley Wolpert, *A New History of India,* 4th ed. (New York: Oxford University Press, 1993), pp. 233–8.

14. Metcalf, *Ideologies of the Raj;* and Mehta, *Liberalism and Empire.* See also Thomas Pantham, "Post-relativism in Emancipatory Thought: Gandhi's Swaraj and Satyagraha," in D. L. Sheth and Ashis Nandy, eds., *The Multiverse of Democracy: Essays in Honour of Rajni Kothari* (New Delhi: Sage, 1996), p. 212.

15. Megan Vaughan, *Curing their Ills: Colonial Power and African Illness* (Cambridge and Stanford, CA: Polity Press and Stanford University Press, 1991), p. 115.

16. Mehta, *Liberalism and Empire,* pp. 47–64. See also Uday S. Mehta, "Liberal Strategies of Exclusion," in Frederick Cooper and Ann Laura Stoler, eds., *Tensions of Empire: Colonial Cultures in a Bourgeois World* (Berkeley: University of California Press, 1997), pp. 59–86.

17. Mehta, *Liberalism and Empire,* p. 191.

18. For an erudite account of the development of nationalism in England, see Liah Greenfeld, *Nationalism: Five Roads to Modernity* (Cambridge, MA: Harvard University Press, 1992), pp. 27–87.

19. John Stuart Mill, "Representative Government," in *Three Essays* (Oxford: Oxford University Press, 1985), p. 409; and *On Liberty,* ed. Currin Shields (New York: Macmillan, 1987), p. 14.

20. S. M. Burke and Salim Al-Din Quraishi, *The British Raj in India* (Karachi: Oxford University Press), p. 61.

21. Dadabhai Naoroji cited in Elie Kedourie, ed., *Nationalism in Asia and Africa* (New York: The New American Library, 1970), p. 82.

22. Thomas B. Macaulay, "Minute on Indian Education," in J. Clive, ed., *Selected Writings* (Chicago: University of Chicago Press, 1972), p. 249.

23. Ranajit Guha, *Dominance without Hegemony: History and Power in Colonial India* (Cambridge, MA: Harvard University Press, 1997), pp. 33–4.

24. Ashis Nandy, *The Intimate Enemy* (New Delhi: Oxford University Press, 1983), p. xiv.

25. Wolpert, *A New History of India,* p. 257. For a more detailed discussion of the Ilbert Bill debates, see Metcalf, *Ideologies of the Raj,* pp. 203–13; Mehta, *Liberalism and Empire,* pp. 196–201; Burke and Al-Din Quraishi, *The British Raj in India,* pp. 58–61.

26. Hunter cited in Metcalf, *Ideologies of the Raj,* p. 207.

27. Ilbert cited in ibid., p. 205.

28. Wolpert, *A New History of India*, p. 257.

29. Beveridge cited in Metcalf, *Ideologies of the Raj*, p. 212. See also Mrinalini Sinha, "Chathams, Pitts, and Gladstones in Petticoats: The Politics of Race and Gender in the Ilbert Bill Controversy, 1883–84," in Nupur Chaudhuri and Margaret Strobel, eds., *Western Women and Imperialism* (Bloomington, IN: Indiana University Press, 1992), pp. 98–116.

30. Metcalf, *Ideologies of the Raj*, p. 206.

31. "Sir James Fitzjames Stephen on the Principles of British Government in India," (Letter to *The Times*, 1 March 1883), in Philips et al., *The Evolution of India and Pakistan*, p. 57.

32. Alexander Dow cited in Guha, *Dominance without Hegemony*, p. 74; and Dipesh Chakrabarty, "Postcoloniality and the Artifice of History: Who Speaks for 'Indian' Pasts?," *Representations* 37 (Winter 1992), pp. 5–6.

33. See James Fitzjames Stephen, *Liberty, Equality, Fraternity*, ed. Stuart D. Warner (Indianapolis: Liberty Fund, 1993).

34. Editorial article, *The Times*, 26 February 1883, in Philips et al., *The Evolution of India and Pakistan*, pp. 59–60; and Metcalf, *Ideologies of the Raj*, p. 123.

35. Stephen, "Letter to *The Times*," (1 March 1883), in Philips et al., *The Evolution of India and Pakistan*, pp. 59–60; and Metcalf, *Ideologies of the Raj*, p. 209.

36. Metcalf, *Ideologies of the Raj*, p. 211.

37. Ibid.

38. Cited in Burke and Quraishi, *The British Raj in India*, p. 61. S. N. Banerjea, too, emphasizes the importance of the Ilbert Bill controversy in helping to intensify the growing feeling of unity among the Indian people around a rankling sense of humiliation. See Philips et al., *The Evolution of India and Pakistan*, p. 137.

39. Hume cited in Burke and Quraishi, *The British Raj in India*, p. 96.

40. Naoroji cited in Philips et al., *The Evolution of India and Pakistan*, p. 139.

41. Hume cited in ibid., p. 142.

42. Ibid., p. 143.

43. G. K. Gokhale on India and the British Empire, 4 February 1907, in ibid., p. 163.

44. Mehta, *Liberalism and Empire*, p. 77.

45. John Hutchinson, "Moral Innovators and the Politics of Regeneration: the Distinctive Role of Cultural Nationalists in Nation-Building," in Anthony Smith, ed., *Ethnicity and Nationalism: International Studies in Sociology and Social Anthropology* (Leiden: Brill, 1992), p. 103.

46. *CWMG* 1: p. 42 [1891].

47. Dennis Dalton, "Introduction," in *Mahatma Gandhi: Selected Political Writings*, ed. Dennis Dalton (Indianapolis: Hackett, 1996), p. 7.

48. Chadha, *Gandhi*, p. 17.

49. V. S. Naipaul, *India: A Wounded Civilization* (New York: Vintage, 1978), pp. 101–2.

50. *CWMG* 1: p. 3 [1888].

51. Ibid., pp. 57–8 [1891]; *AB*, pp. 33, 36.

52. *CWMG* 1: p. 55 [1891].

53. Brown, *Gandhi*, p. 22.

54. *AB*, pp. 36–7.

55. Ibid., p. 39.

56. Ibid. p. 40.

57. Green, *Gandhi*, p. 88–9.

58. Brown, *Gandhi*, p. 23.

59. S. Sinha cited in Chadha, *Gandhi*, pp. 30–1.

60. Dalton, "Introduction," in *Mahatma Gandhi: Selected Political Writings*, p. 7.

61. James D. Hunt, *Gandhi in London* (New Delhi: Promilla & Co., 1978), p. 38.

62. Tendulkar, *Mahatma*, 1: p. 37.

63. *CWMG* 1: p. 64 [1892].

64. Green, *Gandhi*, pp. 94–112.

65. Thomas K. Trautmann, *Aryans and British India* (Berkeley: University of California Press, 1997), p. 129.

66. Hunt, *Gandhi in London*, pp. 1, 28.

67. *CWMG* 1: p. 30 [1891].

68. Ibid., pp. 32–3 [1891].

69. Ibid., pp. 34–5 [1891].

70. Ibid., p. 52 [1891].

71. Note the stark absence of meat-eating Muslims in Gandhi's conflation of vegetarianism and "India." Although he concedes that not all Indians are vegetarians, Gandhi still claims that "the great majority of the inhabitants of India are Vegetarians" (*CWMG* 1: p. 45 [1891]). In my view, some of the main reasons why many Muslim leaders would later reject Gandhi's discourse on India as "exclusivist" or "limited" are already contained in this early vision.

72. *CWMG* 1: p. 63 [1891].

73. Naipaul, *India: A Wounded Civilization*. p. 104.

74. *AB*, p. 75.

CHAPTER 2: CONFRONTING DIFFERENCE AND EXCLUSION: GANDHI'S STRUGGLE FOR RECOGNITION IN SOUTH AFRICA

1. *CWMG* 23: p. 115 [1922].

2. Judith M. Brown, "The Making of a Critical Outsider," in Judith M. Brown and Martin Prozesky, eds., *Gandhi and South Africa: Principles and Politics* (New York: St. Martin's Press, 1996), p. 22.

3. Iyer, *The Moral and Political Thought of Mahatma Gandhi,* pp. 9–10; and "Introduction," in *MPWMG* 1: p. 2 [1986].

4. Brown, "The Making of a Critical Outsider," in Brown and Prozesky, *Gandhi and South Africa,* p. 22. See also Robert A. Huttenback, *Gandhi in South Africa: British Imperialism and the Indian Question, 1860–1914* (Ithaca, NY: Cornell University Press, 1971); James D. Hunt, "Gandhi in South Africa," in John Hick and Lamont C. Hempel, eds., *Gandhi's Significance for Today* (New York: St. Martin's Press, 1989), pp. 61–81; and Maureen Swan, *Gandhi: The South African Experience* (Johannesburg: Ravan Press, 1985).

5. *AB;* Romain Rolland, *Mahatma Gandhi: The Man Who Became One with the Universal Being* (London: Allen and Unwin, 1924); Fischer, *The Life of Mahatma Gandhi;* B. R. Nanda, *Mahatma Gandhi: A Biography* (London: Allen and Unwin, 1958); Tendulkar, *Mahatma;* Huttenback, *Gandhi in South Africa;* Brown, *Gandhi;* Green, *Gandhi;* Dalton, *Mahatma Gandhi;* and Chadha, *Gandhi.*

6. Brown, "The Making of a Critical Outsider," p. 26.

7. Jane Schneider and Annette B. Weiner, "Introduction," in Annette B. Weiner and Jane Schneider, eds., *Cloth and Human Experience* (Washington, D.C.: Smithsonian Institution Press, 1989), p. 3.

8. Bernard S. Cohn, "Cloth, Clothes, and Colonialism," in ibid., p. 309.

9. Ibid., p. 336.

10. Ibid., p. 341.

11. Queen Victoria cited in Bean, "Gandhi and *Khadi,* the Fabric of Indian Independence," in Weiner and Schneider, eds., *Cloth and Human Experience,* p. 357.

12. Ibid., p. 356.

13. Green, *Gandhi,* p. 121.

14. *AB,* p. 92.

15. Ibid.

16. Nicholas B. Dirks, "Foreword," in Bernard S. Cohn, *Colonialism and Its Forms of Knowledge: The British in India* (Princeton, NJ: Princeton University Press, 1996), p. xv.

17. For such positions stressing the fluidity and hybridity of the colonial order, see, for example, Homi K. Bhabha, *The Location of Culture* (London: Routledge, 1994); and Stuart Murray, ed., *Not On Any Map: Essays on Postcoloniality and Cultural Nationalism* (Exeter: University of Exeter Press, 1997).

18. Ania Loomba, *Colonialism/Postcolonialism* (London: Routledge, 1998), pp. 173, 67–9. See also Mary L. Pratt, *Imperial Eyes: Travel Writing and Transculturation* (London: Routledge, 1992).

19. Cohn, "Cloth, Clothes, and Colonialism in India," pp. 314, 345–6.

20. Bean, "Gandhi and *Khadi,* the Fabric of Independence," pp. 356, 359.

21. Loomba, *Colonialism/Postcolonialism,* p. 173.

22. *AB,* p. 93.

23. Ibid., p. 94.

24. *CWMG* 1: pp. 57–8 [1891].
25. Ibid., p. 58.
26. *AB,* p. 114.
27. Ibid., p. 97.
28. Ibid., p. 122.
29. *CWMG* 1: p. 140 [1894].
30. Erik Erikson, *Gandhi's Truth: On the Origins of Militant Nonviolence* (New York: W. W. Norton, 1969), pp. 165–6.
31. *CWMG* 4: p. 113 [1904].
32. Brown, *Gandhi,* pp. 63–4.
33. *CWMG* 1: p. 159 [1894].
34. *CWMG* 3: p. 354 [1903].
35. *CWMG* 1: pp. 94, 243, 259 [1894/95]; *CWMG* 4: pp. 75, 87, 100 [1903/04].
36. Chadha, *Gandhi,* p. 69.
37. Ibid., p. 81.
38. *CWMG* 2: pp. 47–50 [1896].
39. Hunt, *Gandhi in London,* pp. 41–6.
40. See Brown, "The Making of a Critical Outsider," pp. 21–33.
41. *CWMG* 2: p. 305 [1897].
42. *CWMG* 3: p. 313 [1903]. For Gandhi's journalistic activities, see S. N. Bhattacharyya, *Mahatma Gandhi: The Journalist* (Bombay: Asia Publishing House, 1965).
43. Daleep Singh, "The Socio-Economic Conditions in South Africa 1652–1893," in Shanti Sadiq Ali, ed., *Gandhi in South Africa* (Delhi: Hind Pocket Books, 1994), pp. 82–101.
44. See Swan, *Gandhi,* pp. xv; 1–28; Hunt, *Gandhi in London,* pp. 47–52; and Bill Guest, "Indians in Natal and Southern Africa in the 1890s" in Brown and Prozesky, *Gandhi and South Africa,* pp. 7–20.
45. Swan, *Gandhi,* p. 38. See also Antony Copley, *Gandhi: Against the Tide* (Calcutta: Oxford University Press 1987), p. 21.
46. Paul Dundas, *The Jains* (London: Routledge, 1992), pp. 226–7.
47. Swan, *Gandhi,* p. 49.
48. *AB,* pp. 22–3.
49. *CWMG* 2: p. 163 [1897]. See also Brock, *The Mahatma and Mother India,* p. 90.
50. *CWMG* 9: p. 202 [1909].
51. Swan, *Gandhi,* pp. 243–5, 272–3.
52. *CWMG* 1: pp. 98, 284 [1894/95]; *CWMG* 4: pp. 368, 405 [1905].
53. *CWMG* 1: p. 75 [1894]; *CWMG* 2: p. 12 [1896].
54. Daud Ali, "Recognizing Europe in India: Colonial Master Narratives and the Writing of Indian History," in Jeffrey Cox and Shelton Stromquist, eds., *Contesting the Master Narrative: Essays in Social History* (Iowa City: University of Iowa Press, 1998), p. 108.

55. Ibid., pp. 108–9. Romila Thapar points to the important link between the theory of an Aryan race and the nineteenth-century orientalist construction of Hinduism around an idealized upper caste, Brahmin-dominated identity. Yet early history suggests the existence of multiple Indian communities based on various identities; hence, "The notion of an Aryan race has now been generally discarded in scholarship. . . . There is virtually no evidence of the invasion and conquest of northwestern India by a dominant culture coming across the border" (Romila Thapar, "Imagined Religious Communities? Ancient History and the Modern Search for a Hindu Identity," *Modern Asian Studies* 23.2 (1989), pp. 209–31. See also Ronald Inden, *Imagining India* (Oxford: Basil Blackwell, 1990), pp. 85–130; Wilhelm Halbfass, *India and Europe: An Essay in Understanding* (Albany, NY: State University of New York Press, 1988); and Trautmann, *Aryans and British India*.

56. Daud Ali, "Recognizing Europe in India," p. 109.

57. Indira Chowdhury-Sengupta, "The Effeminate and the Masculine: Nationalism and the Concept of Race in Colonial Bengal," in Peter Robb, ed., *The Concept of Race in South Asia* (Delhi: Oxford University Press, 1997), pp. 282–303. See also Christophe Jaffrelot, *The Hindu Nationalist Movement in India* (New York: Columbia University Press, 1996), pp. 11–64; and Thomas Blom Hansen, *The Saffron Wave: Democracy and Hindu Nationalism in Modern India* (Princeton: Princeton University Press, 1999), pp. 60–90.

58. Susan Bayly, "Caste and 'Race' in the Colonial Ethnography of India," in Robb, *The Concept of Race in South Asia,* pp. 203–4.

59. *CWMG* 1: pp. 149–50 [1894].

60. Beames cited in Susan Bayly, "Caste and 'Race' in the Colonial Ethnography of India," in Robb, *The Concept of Race in South Asia,* p. 188. The idea of a common Indo-Aryan origin was frequently accompanied by a virulent anti-Semitism. Yogesh Chadha reports that during Gandhi's 1906 mission to London, he was promised help by Sir Lepel Griffin, who had been for many years chairman of the East India Association in London. Blaming the behavior of Jewish and Russian traders in the Transvaal—"the very offscourings of the international sewers of Europe"—for causing a xenophobic backlash, Griffin proceeded to assert that Indians were "the most orderly, honourable, industrious, temperate race in the world, people of our own stock and blood" (p. 119).

61. Brown, *Gandhi,* pp. 44, 50.

62. Peter Robb, "South Asia and the Concept of Race," in Robb, ed., *The Concept of Race in South Asia,* pp. 7–8.

63. For Gandhi's relationship to various Chinese communities in South Africa, see Karen L. Harris, "Gandhi, the Chinese, and Passive Resistance," in Brown and Prozesky, *Gandhi in South Africa,* pp. 69–94. In a nutshell, Harris argues that while Gandhi encouraged Chinese participation in the widespread political campaign against racist legislation in South Africa, he also emphasized the principle of differentiation between British Indians and other Asians based on

"the common Indo-Aryan origins of the English and the Indians," which was the cultural mark of the "Natural superior status of the community" he represented (p. 74). Overall, Harris seeks to disprove allegations of Gandhi's complicity in "proto-apartheid" policies; yet her balanced account does not seek to hide the existence of a culturally bound ethnocentrism on both sides as well as Gandhi's sentiments of an implied racial superiority of Indians over Chinese (pp. 85, 89). For assessments of the unsatisfactory relationship between Gandhi and South African blacks, see Ashe, *Gandhi,* p. 125; Les Switzer, "Gandhi in South Africa: The Ambiguities of Satyagraha," *Journal of Ethnic Studies* 14.1 (Spring 1986), pp. 122–8; Copley, *Gandhi,* p. 22; James D. Hunt, "Gandhi and the Black People of South Africa," *Gandhi Marg* (April–June 1989), pp. 7–24; and George M. Fredrikson, *Black Liberation: A Comparative History of Black Ideologies in the United States and South Africa* (Oxford: Oxford University Press, 1995), pp. 226–31; Brian M. du Toit, "The Mahatma in South Africa," *The Journal of Modern African Studies* 34.4 (1996), pp. 643–60; and Anthony Read and David Fisher, *The Proudest Day: India's Long Road to Independence* (New York: W. W. Norton, 1997), pp. 146–7. For a more sympathetic account of Gandhi's attitude toward blacks, see Rajmohan Gandhi, *The Good Boatman: A Portrait of Gandhi* (New Delhi: Viking, 1995), pp. 207–24.

64. *CWMG* 5: p. 243 [1906].

65. For such models, see, for example, Robert Bates, "Modernization, Ethnic Competition and the Rationality of Politics in Contemporary Africa," in Donald Rothchild and Victor Olorunsola, eds., *State Versus Ethnic Claims: African Policy Dilemmas* (Boulder: Westview, 1983), pp. 152–71; and Michael Hechter, "Rational Choice Theory and the Study of Race and Ethnic Relations," in John Rex and David Mason, eds., *Theories of Ethnic and Race Relations* (Cambridge: Cambridge University Press, 1986), pp. 264–79.

66. Hunt, "Gandhi and the Black People of South Africa," p. 20.

67. Ibid., p. 10.

68. *CWMG* 2: pp. 74, 105 [1896]. For more examples of Gandhi's use of exclusionary language with regard to black South Africans, see *CWMG* 1: pp. 184, 200, 220 [1895]; *CWMG* 3: pp. 69 [1899], 234 [1902]; *CWMG* 4: p. 131 [1904]; *CWMG* 5: p. 399 [1906]; and *CWMG* 6: pp. 5, 168–9 [1906], 307 [1907].

69. Gandhi, *Satyagraha in South Africa,* p. 9.

70. Robb, "South Asia and the Concept of Race," p. 7.

71. *CWMG* 9: p. 149 [1909].

72. This is one of the central questions currently debated in the burgeoning field of postcolonial studies. See, for example, Robb, *The Concept of Race in South Asia,* and Loomba, *Colonialism/Postcolonialism.*

73. Robert Ross, ed., *Racism and Colonialism. Essays on Ideology and Social Structure* (The Hague: Nijhoff Publishers, 1982), p. 2.

74. Chatterjee, *Nationalist Thought and the Colonial World,* p. 112.

75. *CWMG* 4: p. 56 [1903].

76. Ibid., p. 125 [1904].

77. Chadha, *Gandhi*, pp. 114–5.

78. M. K. Gandhi, *Satyagraha in South Africa* (Ahmedabad: Navajivan Publishing House, 1928), p. 106.

79. *CWMG* 5: p. 104 [1905]; *CWMG* 6: pp. 359–60 [1907].

80. Hunt, *Gandhi in London,* pp. 58; 60.

81. Chadha, *Gandhi,* p. 121.

82. *CWMG* 10: p. 189 [1909]. See also, P. H. M. van den Dungen, "Gandhi in 1919: Loyalist or Rebel?," in R. Kumar, ed., *Essays in Gandhian Politics: The Rowlatt Satyagraha of 1919* (Oxford: Clarendon Press, 1971), pp. 43–63.

83. Ibid., p. 58.

84. See, for example, Kedourie, *Nationalism in Asia and Africa,* pp. 1–152; Hugh Trevor-Roper, *Jewish and Other Nationalisms* (London: Weidenfeld and Nicolson, 1962); Hans Kohn, *The Idea of Nationalism* 2nd ed. (New York: Collier-Macmillan, 1967); and Greenfeld, *Nationalism.* My wording of Kedourie's arguments owes much to Anthony D. Smith's clear summary in *Nationalism and Modernism: A Critical Survey of Recent Theories of Nations and Nationalism* (London: Routledge, 1998), pp. 99–116.

CHAPTER 3: GANDHI'S CRITIQUE OF LIBERALISM:
EXPOSING THE IMMORTALITY OF MODERN CIVILIZATION

1. *HS,* pp. 30, 33.

2. Tendulkar, *Mahatma* 1: p. 132.

3. Van den Dungen, "Gandhi in 1919: Loyalist or Rebel?," in Kumar, *Essays in Gandhian Politics,* pp. 50–1.

4. *CWMG* 4: p. 374 [1905].

5. Ibid., p. 431 [1905].

6. Ibid., p. 467 [1905]. See also *CWMG* 5: pp. 57–8 [1905].

7. Tendulkar, *Mahatma* 7: p. 18.

8. According to Anthony Parel, Gandhi adopted the slogan "do or die" from Lord Tennyson's "Charge of the Light Brigade," written to commemorate the fate of the English soldiers who perished in the Crimean war (See *HS,* p. 181).

9. Read and Fisher, *The Proudest Day,* p. 89.

10. *CWMG* 5: p. 44 [1905].

11. Ibid.

12. Ibid., p. 132 [1905].

13. Fox, *Gandhian Utopia,* p. 46.

14. *CWMG* 5: p. 156 [1905].

15. I am indebted to Nikhil Aziz's helpful comments on this topic.

16. *CWMG* 9: p. 202 [1909]. See also *CWMG* 5: p. 175 [1906].

17. *CWMG* 5: p. 92 [1905].

18. For a detailed discussion of this mission, see Hunt, *Gandhi in London*, pp. 105–72. For an informative exposition of the genesis of *Hind Swaraj*, see Anthony J. Parel, "The Origins of *Hind Swaraj*," in Brown and Prozesky, *Gandhi and South Africa*, pp. 35–67; and Nageshwar Prasad, ed., *Hind Swaraj: A Fresh Look* (New Delhi: Gandhi Peace Foundation, 1985).

19. Forty years later, Savarkar's name would figure prominently in the secret plot to assassinate the Mahatma For Savarkar's views on Hindu nationalism, see V. D. Savarkar, *Hindutva: Who is a Hindu?* (Bombay: S. S. Savarkar, 1969); and Jaffrelot, *The Hindu Nationalist Movement in India*, pp. 25–33.

20. In 1905, Gokhale had founded the Servants of Indian Society, a moderate nationalist group dedicated to peaceful reforms. Gandhi looked forward to joining the society upon his return to India. Ironically, when he did return ten years later, the Servants rejected his application for membership twice on the grounds that their organization did not share his critique of the modern world, his anarchist beliefs, and his extraconstitutional methods. Indeed, Gokhale had been highly critical of Gandhi's *Hind Swaraj*, which, among other things, had attacked him and the other Congress moderates. See Read and Fisher, *The Proudest Day*, pp. 154–5.

21. Chadha, *Gandhi*, p. 147. For a comprehensive discussion of Gandhi's contacts to Indian revolutionaries, see Rama Hari Shankar, *Gandhi's Encounter with the Indian Revolutionaries* (New Delhi: Siddarth Publications, 1996).

22. See, for example, Parel, "The Origins of *Hind Swaraj*," p. 43; and Chadha, *Gandhi*, p. 148.

23. *CWMG* 9: p. 508 [1909].

24. Ibid., pp. 508–9 [1909].

25. Ibid., p. 389 [1909]. This represents a remarkable change in Gandhi's attitude. Only a few weeks before his arrival, he had felt that "even now, next to India, I would rather live in London than in any other place in the world" (cited in Chadha, *Gandhi*, p. 150). Carpenter must indeed have made quite an impression on him.

26. Chatterjee, *Nationalist Thought and the Colonial World*, p. 85. For an acknowledgment of *Hind Swaraj* as constituting Gandhi's most fundamental work of political thought, see also Parel, "Gandhi's Idea of Nation in *Hind Swaraj*," p. 261; Tendulkar, *Mahatma* 1: p. 132; K. Raghavendra Rao, "The Political Theory in Hind Swaraj: A Preliminary Exploration," *Gandhi Marg* 1.7 (1979), p. 463; Prasad, "Introduction," in *Hind Swaraj: A Fresh Look*, p. 1; Iyer, *The Moral and Political Thought of Mahatma Gandhi*, pp. 24–5; Brown, *Gandhi*, p. 65; Copley, *Gandhi*, p. 25; Huiyun Wang, "Gandhi's Contesting Discourse," *Gandhi Marg* 17.3 (1995), p. 263; Sunil Khilnani, *The Idea of India* (New York: Farrar, Straus, Giroux, 1997), p. 154; Madhuri Santanam Sondhi, *Modernity, Morality and the Mahatma* (New Delhi: Har-Anand Publications, 1997), p. 67; Chatterjee,

Gandhi's Religious Thought, p. 89; Terchek, *Gandhi,* p. 140; and Jordens, *Gandhi's Religion,* p. 41.

27. See, for example, Dalton, *Mahatma Gandhi,* pp. 20–1.

28. M. K. Gandhi, "A Message," in *Hind Swaraj or Home Rule* (Ahmedabad: Navajivan, 1938), p. 17.

29. *CWMG* 81: p. 319 [1945].

30. *HS,* p. 121.

31. Anthony J. Parel, "Introduction," in ibid., p. xiv.

32. *HS,* p. 30. Gandhi later regretted using the metaphor of "prostitute;" in fact, this was the only word he was prepared to drop from the book. I deal with Gandhi's use of gender-specific language in more detail in chapter 5.

33. *HS,* p. 113.

34. Ibid., pp. 31–3. In a footnote to the text (p. 30), Anthony Parel correctly notes that in some of his later writings, Gandhi seems to indicate that he was not entirely against parliamentary systems. Still, in *Hind Swaraj,* the Editor fails to make such a qualification. Moreover, as highlighted in my thesis, Gandhi's wavering views on this subject indicate the extent to which he was wrestling with the dilemma arising from the conflicting demands of instrumental politics and the imperatives of his ethical principles.

35. *Hind Swaraj* contains a wealth of direct and indirect references to Socrates. Indeed, Gandhi lists Plato's *Apology of Socrates* in the appendix. He considered Socrates "a soldier of truth" and a "great *satyagrahi,*" and saw "in the words of a great soul like the Greek philosopher the qualities of an elixir" (*CWMG* 8: p. 173–4 [1908]). As Anthony Parel put it in his Introduction to *Hind Swaraj,* "The Gandhi of *Hind Swaraj* is no doubt the Socrates of modern India" (p. xxxv). Leela Gandhi, too, emphasizes Gandhi's cultural, political, and personal identification with Socrates ("Concerning Violence: The Limits and Circulations of Gandhian *Ahimsa* or Passive Resistance," *Cultural Critique* [Winter 1996–7], pp. 118–20).

36. Parekh, *Gandhi,* p. 43.

37. Ibid., p. 49.

38. *HS,* p. 31. See also Gandhi's Introduction in *AB,* pp. vii–x.

39. Such a reading of Gandhi as emphasizing moral autonomy above all other concerns is reflected in Terchek, *Gandhi.*

40. *MPWMG* 2: p. 55 [1907].

41. *HS,* p. 119. Unfortunately, however, Gandhi made contradictory statements on this subject. For example, when asked what he thought of Christianity, he replied, "Christianity is very good; many Christians are very bad" *MPWMG* 2: p. 167 [1931]. Likewise, in his *Autobiography,* he explicitly blames "individual British officials" for the violence of racial discrimination rather than the entire "British system" *AB,* p. 310.

42. See Parekh, *Gandhi's Political Philosophy,* pp. 124–5.

43. Citing its "open advocacy of passive resistance to subvert British supremacy," British censors in India banned the pamphlet on March 24, 1910. See *HS*, p. 5, n. 2.

44. Parekh, *Gandhi*, pp. 49–50. See also Ashis Nandy, *Traditions, Tyranny and Utopias: Essays in the Politics of Awareness* (Delhi: Oxford University Press, 1987), p. 149.

45. See, for example, *HS*, p. 59.

46. Ibid., pp. 36; 41.

47. Ibid., p. 41.

48. Ibid., p. 40.

49. Ibid., pp. 68–9.

50. Ibid., p. 64.

51. Ibid., pp. 59, 61, 108.

52. Ibid., p. 108.

53. Mark Francis, "The 'Civilizing' of Indigenous People in Nineteenth-Century Canada," *Journal of World History* 9.1 (1998), pp. 51–87. See also, Deepak Shenoy, "Progress to the Rescue: Liberty and Colonialism in the 19th Century." Paper presented at the 1999 Meeting of the Western Political Science Association (March 25, 1999).

54. *HS*, p. 67.

55. Ibid., p. 35.

56. Ibid., p. 38.

57. Ibid., pp. 107, 111, 37, 42, 47.

58. Ibid., p. 108. For the concept of "structural violence," see Johan Galtung, "Violence, Peace, and Peace Research," *Journal of Peace Research* 7.3 (1969), pp. 167–91.

59. *HS*, pp. 84, 90, 95.

60. Ibid., 38.

61. Ibid., pp. 81–2.

62. Ibid., p. 93.

63. Ved Mehta, *Mahatma Gandhi and his Apostles* (New York: Penguin, 1977), p. 123.

64. *HS*, pp. 74, 77, 80.

65. Ibid., p. 28. See also Parekh, *Colonialism, Tradition and Reform*, pp. 154–55.

66. *HS*, p. 113.

67. Ibid., p. 38.

68. Lord Curzon cited in Thomas Pantham, "Gandhi's Intervention in Modern Moral-Political Discourse," in Ramashray Roy, ed., *Gandhi and the Present Global Crisis* (Shimla: Indian Institute of Advanced Studies, 1996), pp. 63–64. For Gandhi's response to Curzon's address, see *CWMG* 4: pp. 333–6 [1905].

69. Nandy, *Traditions, Tyranny and Utopias*, p. 158.

CHAPTER 4: IMAGINING INDIA:
GANDHI'S CONSTRUCTION OF NONVIOLENT NATIONALISM

1. *HS,* p. 7.
2. Paz, *In Light of India,* p. 113.
3. Khilnani, *The Idea of India,* p. 5.
4. Ibid.
5. For a definition of the nation as "imagined political community," see Benedict Anderson, *Imagined Communities,* rev. ed. (London: Verso, 1991), pp. 5–7. However, as Anderson points out, the term "imagined" should not be seen as indicating a instances of "fabrication" or "invention," but rather a creative process drawing on existing cultural resources. Assuming identities that are both invented and inherited, communities like nations or civilizations do represent fictions in some sense, but the processes that go into the creation of these fictions are nonetheless real and open to critical examination.
6. Hansen, *The Saffron Wave,* p. 45.
7. Khilnani, *The Idea of India,* p. 8. For a similar assessment, see Lloyd I. Rudolph, "Contesting Civilizations: Gandhi and the Counter-Culture," *Gandhi Marg* 13.4 (1992), p. 428.
8. For the influence of British and French romanticism on Gandhi, see Krishna Pachegonkar, "Gandhi and the Romantics," *Gandhi Marg* 5.3 (1983), pp. 161–9.
9. Hansen, *The Saffron Wave,* p. 41.
10. Hutchinson, "Moral Innovators and the Politics of Regeneration," in Smith, *Ethnicity and Nationalism,* pp. 103–8. For assessments of Gandhi as a cultural nationalist see also Brock, *The Mahatma and Mother India,* pp. 88–113; John Hutchinson, *The Dynamics of Cultural Nationalism: The Gaelic Revival and the Creation of the Irish Nation State* (London: Allen & Unwin, 1987), p. 43–5; and Franklin Edgerton, *The Bhagavad Gita* (New York: Harper & Row, 1944), p. vii.
11. For a detailed description of these patterns, see Anthony D. Smith, *National Identity* (Reno, NV: University of Nevada Press, 1991); and *Nationalism and Modernism,* pp. 170–99. See also Hutchinson, *The Dynamics of Cultural Nationalism.*
12. *HS,* p. 39.
13. Ibid., p. 41.
14. Chadha, *Gandhi,* p. 156. Gandhi commenced his correspondence with Tolstoy in October 1909. He subsequently received permission to publish and distribute 20,000 copies of Tolstoy's *Letter to a Hindu.* For a detailed account of the intellectual relationship between Tolstoy and Gandhi, see Martin Green, *The Origins of Nonviolence: Tolstoy and Gandhi in their Historical Settings* (University Park, PA: Penn State University Press, 1986), and *The Challenge of the Mahatmas* (New York: Basic Books, 1978).

15. Chatterjee, *Nationalist Thought and the Colonial World,* p. 85.

16. *HS,* pp. 41, 64, 116.

17. Chesterton cited in Chadha, *Gandhi,* pp. 153–4.

18. *CWMG* 9: p. 427 [1910].

19. Fox, *Gandhian Utopia,* p. 89.

20. Hansen, *The Saffron Wave,* pp. 40–2.

21. Fox, *Gandhian Utopia,* pp. 105–28. For an excellent recent study of Annie Besant's orientalism, see Mark Bevir, "In Opposition to the Raj: Annie Besant and the Dialectic of Empire," *History of Political Thought* XIX.1 (1998), pp. 61–77. By now it should be clear that orientalism represents one among several literary influences on the construction of Gandhi's own nationalist project. Much has been written about the eclectic genesis of his political thought by way of ideas taken from Western romantics and critical utopians, such as Plato, Leo Tolstoy, John Ruskin, and Henry David Thoreau; British theosophists and vegetarians, such as Edward Maitland and Henry Salt; and various religious writings, such as the *Upanishads,* the *Bhagavad-Gita,* the Christian Bible, and the Koran.

22. Edward Said, *Orientalism* (New York: Vintage, 1978). See also Ali Behdad, "Orientalism after Orientalism," *L'esprit Createur* 34.2 (Summer 1994), pp. 3–11; Carol A. Breckenridge and Peter van der Veer, "Orientalism and the Postcolonial Predicament," in Carol A. Breckenridge and Peter van der Veer, eds., *Orientalism and the Postcolonial Predicament,* (Philadelphia: University of Pennsylvania Press, 1993), p. 6; and J. J. Clarke, *Oriental Enlightenment: The Encounter between Asian and Western Thought* (London: Routledge, 1997).

23. Fox, *Gandhian Utopia,* pp. 90–103. See also, Hansen, *The Saffron Wave,* pp. 67–71. For the workings of affirmative orientalism in Islamic cultures, see Mohammed Sharafuddin, *Islam and Romantic Orientalism: Literary Encounters with the Orient* (London: I. B. Tauris, 1994).

24. Peter van der Veer, *Religious Nationalism: Hindus and Muslims in India* (Berkeley: University of California Press, 1995), pp. 69–70; and "The Foreign Hand: Orientalist Discourse in Sociology and Communalism," in Beckenridge and van der Veer, *Orientalism and the Postcolonial Predicament,* p. 26. See also Thapar, "Imagined Religious Communities? Ancient History and the Modern Search for a Hindu Identity," pp. 209–31; and Ashutosh Varsney, "Contested Meanings: India's National Identity, Hindu Nationalism, and the Politics of Anxiety," *Daedalus* 122.3 (Summer 1993), pp. 227–61.

25. Partha Chatterjee, *The Nation and Its Fragments: Colonial and Postcolonial Histories* (Princeton: Princeton University Press, 1993), p. 6.

26. *HS,* p. 68.

27. Gandhi's hopes of restoring the *panchayat,* an "ancient" form of governance with a five-member assembly elected by the villagers, owe much to Henry Maine's idealized notion of "village republics" based upon prior writings of German romantics and Victorian liberals. Gandhi cites Maine's and Wilson's

respective studies on the subject as early as the 1890s (*CWMG* 1: pp. 129–30 [1894]; 269–70 [1895]. For a more detailed discussion of the idea of ancient village communities, see Louis Dumont, "The 'Village Community' from Munro to Maine," in *Contributions to Indian Sociology* vol. 9 (1966), pp. 77–89; Inden, *Imagining India,* pp. 137–42; S. K. Ghai, "Gandhi and his Vision of Indian Villages," *Gandhi Marg* 13.3 (1991), pp. 357–361; Birinder Pal Singh, "Gandhi and the Question of National Identity," *Gandhi Marg* 14.4 (1993), pp. 632–42; Wang, "Gandhi's Contesting Discourse," pp. 261–85; Nicholas F. Gier, "Gandhi: Pre-Modern, Modern, or Post-Modern?," *Gandhi Marg* 18.3 (1996), pp. 261–81; Patrick Brantlinger, "A Postindustrial Prelude to Postcolonialism: John Ruskin, William Morris, and Gandhism," *Critical Inquiry* 22 (Spring 1996), pp. 466–85; and Gyan Prakash, *Another Reason: Science and the Imagination of Modern India* (Princeton: Princeton University Press, 1999), pp. 217–8.

28. *HS,* pp. 69; 67; 70.

29. Ibid., p. 84.

30. Ibid., pp. 95–6.

31. Ibid., pp. 89–90.

32. *CWMG* 21: p. 30 [1921]

33. Chatterjee, *Nationalist Thought and the Colonial World,* pp. 92–7. Such an interpretation can also contribute to a better understanding of Gandhi's rather idiosyncratic interpretation of the *Gita* as advocating nonviolence. See M. K. Gandhi, *The Gospel of Selfless Action,* intr. Mahadev Desai (Ahmedabad: Navajivan, 1946). For a discussion of Gandhi's perspective on the *Gita,* see, for example, Kees W. Bolle, "Gandhi's Interpretation of the Bhagavad Gita," in Hick and Hempel, *Gandhi's Significance for Today,* pp. 137–151; S. K. Basu, "The Two Interpretations of the Gita: Tilak's Karmayoga and Gandhi's Anasaktiyoga," in *Gandhi Marg* 5.6 (1983), pp. 315–29; Chatterjee, *Gandhi's Religious Thought;* J. I. Bakker, "Gandhi and the *Gita:* Sanskrit and Satyagraha," *Gandhi Marg* 15.1 (1993), pp. 39–61; and Jordens, *Gandhi's Religion.*

34. Nandy, *The Intimate Enemy,* p. 59; and *Traditions, Tyranny and Utopias,* pp. 147–8.

35. *HS,* p. 70.

36. Hansen, *The Saffron Wave,* pp. 90–1.

37. Henry Tudor, *Political Myth* (New York: Praeger, 1972), p. 139. See also, Anthony D. Smith, "The resurgence of nationalism? Myth and memory in the renewal of nations," *British Journal of Sociology* 47.4 (December 1996), pp. 575–98.

38. Fox, *Gandhian Utopia,* p. 103.

39. Gyan Prakash, "Introduction: After Colonialism," in Gyan Prakash, ed., *After Colonialism: Imperial Histories and Post-Colonial Displacements* (Princeton: Princeton University Press, 1995), p. 7

40. Parel, "Gandhi's Idea of Nation in *Hind Swaraj,*" p. 262.

41. *HS,* p. 48.

42. Ibid., p. 49.

43. Ibid.

44. Ibid., p. 52.

45. Ibid., p. 53.

46. Van der Veer, *Religious Nationalism,* pp. 73, 94–9; and Hansen, *The Saffron Wave,* p. 45. See also Ainslee T. Embree, *Utopias in Conflict: Religion and Nationalism in Modern India* (Berkeley: University of California Press, 1990), p. 45.

47. *HS,* p. 54.

48. Van der Veer, *Religious Nationalism,* pp. 95, 98. See also C. A. Bayly, *Origins of Nationality in South Asia: Patriotism and Ethical Government in the Making of Modern India* (Delhi: Oxford University Press, 1998), p. 120.

49. *HS,* p. 106.

50. Ibid., p. 7. Some authors prefer the term "constructive postmodernism" for Gandhi's position. See, for example, Gier, "Gandhi: Pre-Modern, Modern, or Post-Modern?," pp. 261–81. For the reasons offered above, I would rather emphasize the "pre-modern" quality of his nationalist imagination.

51. *HS,* p. 118.

52. Parel, "Gandhi's Idea of 'Nation' in *Hind Swaraj,*" p. 287.

53. For a review of these arguments, see the introduction of this study. Some scholars might object to my method of criticizing Gandhi's 1909 pamphlet by using definitions of violence he formulated eight to ten years later. However, I think that my method is justifiable for the following reasons: first, as pointed out earlier, Gandhi reaffirmed the content of *Hind Swaraj* as late as the 1940s. Second, as will be discussed in more detail in chapter 6, he continued to employ an even more exclusivist language in later years, particularly during the Non-Cooperation Campaign of 1920–22.

54. Prakash, "Introduction: After Colonialism," in *After Colonialism: Imperial Histories and Post-Colonial Displacements,* p. 6.

55. For a similar assessment, see Hansen, *The Saffron Wave,* pp. 44–6. Even some extremely sympathetic studies of Gandhi's political thought concede that *Hind Swaraj* abounds with instances of exclusivism and a "violence of the spirit." See, for example, Dalton, *Mahatma Gandhi,* pp. 20–1. Yet, Dalton also argues that, "Within ten years, Gandhi's exclusivist attitudes would evolve into an inclusivist approach . . ."(p. 21). I will contest Dalton's interpretation in chapter 6.

56. *HS,* pp. 69–71.

57. Ibid., pp. 7, 72, 114, 116.

58. Ibid., p. 67.

59. Ibid., p. 74.

60. Fox, *Gandhian Utopia,* p. 103.

61. *HS,* p. 115.

62. Ibid., p. 70.

63. Leela Gandhi, "Concerning Violence: The Limits and Circulations of Gandhian *Ahimsa* or Passive Resistance," *Cultural Critique* 35 (Winter 1996–97), p. 124.

64. For a similar argument, see Prasenjit Duara, *Rescuing History from the Nation. Questioning Narratives of Modern China* (Chicago: University of Chicago Press, 1995), p. 227.

65. In his study of Annie Besant's nationalist thought, Mark Bevir comes to a similar conclusion. See "In Opposition to the Raj: Annie Besant and the Dialectic of Empire," p. 77. See also Bayly, *Origins of Nationality in South Asia*, p. 121.

66. On this point, I disagree with Partha Chatterjee's argument in *Nationalist Thought and the Colonial World*, p. 93.

67. L. Gandhi, "Concerning Violence: The Limits and Circulations of Gandhian *Ahimsa* or Passive Resistance," p. 118.

68. See Akhil Gupta, *Postcolonial Developments: Agriculture in the Making of Modern India* (Durham: Duke University Press, 1998), p. 228.

69. Chatterjee, *The Nation and Its Fragments*, p. 5

70. Khilnani, *The Idea of India*, pp. 197–8.

71. L. Gandhi, "Concerning Violence: The Limits and Circulations of Gandhian *Ahimsa* or Passive Resistance," pp. 118, 121.

72. Nandy, *Tradition, Tyranny and Utopias*, pp. 154, 156.

73. *HS*, p. 7.

74. Ibid., pp. 73–4.

75. Fredrickson, *Black Liberation*, p. 227.

76. For the role of "resentment" in the construction of various forms of nationalism, see Greenfeld, *Nationalism*.

77. *HS*, p. 96.

78. Parel, "Gandhi's Idea of Nation in *Hind Swaraj*," p. 261.

CHAPTER 5: PURIFYING SELF AND NATION: GANDHI'S EXPERIMENTS WITH SELF-CONTROL

1. *SRSI* 1: p. 54.

2. Joseph S. Alter, "Gandhi's Body, Gandhi's Truth: Nonviolence and the Biomoral Imperative of Public Health," *The Journal of Asian Studies* 55.2 (May 1996), pp. 301–22.

3. Aristotle, *The Politics,* Book V, trans. T. A. Sinclair (New York: Penguin Books, 1957), p. 330.

4. Hansen, *The Saffron Wave,* p. 90.

5. For various theories advancing a performative construction of identity with regard to gender, see Judith Butler, *Gender Trouble: Feminism and the Subversion of Identity* (New York: Routledge, 1990); Seyla Benhabib, Judith Butler, Drucilla Cornell, and Nancy Fraser, eds., *Feminist Contentions: A Philosophical Exchange* (New York: Routledge, 1995); and R. Claire Snyder, *Citizen-Soldiers and Manly Warriors: Military Service and Gender in the Civic Republican Tradition* (Lanham, MD: Rowman & Littlefield, 1999).

6. L. Gandhi, "Concerning Violence: The Limits and Circulations of Gandhian *Ahimsa* or Passive Resistance," p. 118.

7. *MPWMG* 3: p. 46 [1917]; See also *CWMG* 21: pp. 112–113 [1921].

8. *CWMG* 10: p. 207 [1910].

9. *SRSI* 2: p. 83.

10. Hutchinson, "Moral Innovators and the Politics of Regeneration," p. 104.

11. Parekh, *Colonialism, Tradition and Reform,* p. 181.

12. See Alter, "Gandhi's Body, Gandhi's Truth," p. 307. For an alternative reading of Gandhi as addressing mostly an "indigenous bourgeoisie" even after 1909, see Guha, *Dominance Without Hegemony,* pp. 126–51.

13. *HS,* p. 96. Italics are mine.

14. See, for example, Erikson, *Gandhi's Truth;* E. V. Wolfenstein, *The Revolutionary Personality* (Princeton: Princeton University Press, 1967); Rowland Lorimer, "A Reconstruction of the Psychological Roots of Gandhi's Truth," *Psychoanalytic Review* 63 (1976), pp. 191–207; Howard Adelman, "Hitler and Gandhi: The Will as Spirit and as Flesh," *Psychoanalytic Review* 67 (1981), pp. 543–61; Rudolph and Rudolph, *Gandhi: The Traditional Roots of Charisma;* Sudhir Kakar, *Intimate Relations: Exploring Indian Sexuality* (Chicago: University of Chicago Press, 1990); and Nandy, *The Intimate Enemy.*

15. On this point, I follow Joseph Alter's recommendations. See "Gandhi's Body, Gandhi's Truth," pp. 301–4.

16. *AB,* p. ix; *MPWMG* 2: p. 177 [1946]; pp. 165–6 [1931]; p. 172 [1932]. See also Glyn Richards, *The Philosophy of Gandhi: A Study of His Basic Ideas* (Atlantic Highlands: Humanities Press, 1991), p. 8.

17. *MPWMG* 2, p. 176 [1945]. For an enlightening discussion of Gandhi's conception of "absolute" and "relative" truth, see Iyer, *The Moral and Political Thought of Mahatma Gandhi,* pp. 158–64. As William Borman points out, this distinction left Gandhi with yet another philosophical dilemma: without absolute truth, life was incomplete, and with absolute truth, life was unnecessary (*Gandhi and Non-Violence,* pp. 9–10).

18. *MPWMG* 2, pp. 162–3 [1930].

19. *AB,* p. ix; See also *CWMG* 21: p. 469 [1921].

20. *AB,* p. viii.

21. *SRSI* 1: p. 31. See also my discussion in chapter 3.

22. Gandhi's views on moral perfection are notoriously ambiguous, if not contradictory. In 1918, he wrote that, "To say that perfection is not attainable on this earth is to deny God." While he maintained this view throughout his life, he later qualified it by insisting that, "Not one of us is able to realize the whole of our spiritual ambition" (*MPWMG* 2: pp. 36–40 [1918, 1926, 1927]. Hence, some Gandhi scholars read Gandhi as emphasizing perfection while others argue that he denied perfection.

23. See Chatterjee, *Nationalist Thought and the Colonial World,* p. 102.

24. *AB,* p. ix; *MPWMG* 2: p. 166 [1931].

25. Iyer, *The Moral and Political Thought of Mahatma Gandhi,* p. 125.

26. Ibid., p. 128. See also *MPWMG* 2: p. 166 [1931].

27. Ibid., p. 167 [1931].

28. Pyarelal, *Mahatma Gandhi: The Last Phase* (Ahmedabad: Navajivan Publishing House, 1958), p. 460.

29. Iyer, *The Moral and Political Thought of Mahatma Gandhi,* p. 238.

30. *MPWMG* 1: p. 374 [1915]. See also *CWMG* 13: pp. 66, 79 [1915]; 221, 234 [1916].

31. "Economic Development and Moral Development," in *HS,* p. 162 [1916]; See also *CWMG* 10: p. 5 [1909].

32. Gandhi cited in Judith M. Brown, *Gandhi's Rise to Power: Indian Politics 1915–1922* (Cambridge: Cambridge University Press, 1972), p. 13. In 1914, Gandhi argued that "it now appears that there is no institution today in the world to excel Phoenix [Gandhi's South African ashram] in its ideals or its way of life" (*CWMG* 12: p. 560 [1914]).

33. *SRSI* 1: pp. 89–90.

34. *HS,* p. 97.

35. For the influence of Thoreau's political thought on Gandhi, see my article, "Mahatma Gandhi and the Anarchist Legacy of Henry David Thoreau," *Southern Humanities Review* XXVII.3 (Summer 1993), pp. 201–15.

36. *SRSI* 1: pp. 2, 6, 15, 63.

37. For a discussion of Gandhi's views on science, see, for example, Terchek, *Gandhi,* pp. 88–92; and Nandy, *Traditions, Tyranny, and Utopia,* pp. 129–62.

38. *SRSI* 1: pp. 118–20; *SRSI* 2, pp. 13–5.

39. See Nirmal Kumar Bose, *My Days with Gandhi* (Bombay: Orient Longman, 1974), pp. 151–1.

40. *SRSI* 2: pp. 8–13; *SRSI* 1: pp. 19–20. Much has been written about Gandhi's assumption that sexual self-control and the conservation of "vital fluids" would lead to the accumulation of great powers to be used in the political arena. See, for example, Mehta, *Mahatma Gandhi and his Apostles,* pp. 179–213; Rudolph and Rudolph, *Gandhi: The Traditional Roots of Charisma,* pp. 38–62; Kakar, *Intimate Relations,* pp. 85–128; and Arvind Sharma, "Gandhi and Celibacy," in Hick and Hempel, *Gandhi's Significance for Today,* pp. 59–60.

41. *SRSI* 1: p. 38.

42. Ibid., p. 80; *SRSI* 2: p. 79. Gandhi's view on *brahmacharya* for married couples was also strongly influenced by Leo Tolstoy's ideas on chastity in marriage.

43. Ibid.

44. *HS,* p. 97.

45. *SRSI* 1: p. 49.

46. *CWMG* 72: p. 239 [1940].

47. *SRSI* 1: p. 88; *SRSI* 2: p. 84.

48. Ibid., p. 85.

49. *SRSI* 1: pp. 53, 79; *SRSI* 2, p. 84.

50. *KH,* pp. 37, 39.

51. Ibid., pp. 32–33.

52. Manu Gandhi cited in Bose, *My Days with Gandhi,* p. 176.

53. Ibid., p. 174.

54. Ibid., p. 133. See also Kakar, *Intimate Relations,* p. 97; Mehta, *Mahatma Gandhi and His Apostles,* p. 191; and Chadha, *Gandhi,* p. 425.

55. Brown, *Gandhi,* p. 209.

56. See, for example, Avind Sharma, "Gandhi as Feminist Emancipator and Kasturba as a Martyr," *Gandhi Marg* 3.4 (1981), pp. 214–20; Madhu Kishwar, "Gandhi on Women," *Economic and Political Weekly* (October 5, 1985), pp. 1691–1702, and *Economic and Political Weekly* (October 12,1985), pp. 1753–8; Sujuta Patel, "Construction and Reconstruction of Woman in Gandhi," *Economic and Political Weekly* (February 20, 1988), pp. 377–87; Barbara Southard, "The Feminism of Mahatma Gandhi," in V.T. Patil, ed., *New Dimensions and Perspectives on Gandhism* (New Delhi: Inter-India Publications, 1989), pp. 387–410; Sushila Gidwani, "Gandhian Feminism," in Hick and Hempel, *Gandhi's Significance for Today,* pp. 226–35; Ketu H. Katrak, "Indian Nationalism, Gandhian 'Satyagraha,' and Representations of Female Sexuality," in Andrew Parker, Doris Summer, and Patricia Yaeger, eds., *Nationalisms & Sexualities* (New York: Routledge, 1992), pp. 395–406; L. Gandhi, "Concerning Violence: the Limits and Circulations of Gandhian *Ahimsa* or Passive Resistance," pp. 105–47; Aparna Mahanta, "The Indian State and Patriarchy," in T.V. Satyamurthy, ed., *State and Nation in the Context of Social Change* (Delhi: Oxford University Press, 1997), pp. 87–131; and Arun and Sunanda Gandhi, *The Forgotten Woman: The Untold Story of Kastur, Wife of Mahatma Gandhi* (Huntsville, AR: Ozark Mountain Publishers, 1998).

57. Patel, "Construction and Reconstruction of Woman in Gandhi," p. 378.

58. *CWMG* 14: pp. 207–8 [1918].

59. Katrak, "Indian Nationalism, Gandhian 'Satyagraha,' and Representations of Female Sexuality," p. 398.

60. Patel, "Construction and Reconstruction of Woman in Gandhi," p. 379.

61. Ibid., p. 386.

62. *CWMG* 27: p. 220 [1925].

63. See, for example, Southard, "The Feminism of Mahatma Gandhi," p. 387; and Katrak, "Indian Nationalism, Gandhian 'Satyagraha,' and Representations of Female Sexuality," pp. 395–6.

64. Patel, "Construction and Reconstruction of Woman in Gandhi," p. 379.

65. *CWMG* 70: p. 381 [1931]. See also Nandy, *The Intimate Enemy,* p. 54; and Katrak, "Indian Nationalism, Gandhian 'Satyagraha,' and Representations of Female Sexuality," p. 397.

66. *CWMG* 68: p. 53 [1938].

67. *CWMG* 21: p. 123 [1921].

68. *CWMG* 17: p. 326 [1920].

69. M. K. Gandhi, *Birth Control: The Right Way and The Wrong Way* (Ahmedabad: Navijivan Publishing House, 1959 [1935]), p. 28.

70. *CWMG* 22: p. 524 [1924]. See also Patel, "Construction and Reconstruction of Women in Gandhi," p. 385. The abiding force of this ascetic female ideal in Indian politics is clearly evident in Indira Gandhi's attempts to justify her "benevolent" dictatorship by presenting herself as India's "widowed mother." See L. Gandhi, "Concerning Violence: The Limits and Circulations of Gandhian *Ahimsa* or Passive Resistance," p. 110.

71. *CWMG* 46: p. 75 [1931].

72. *CWMG* 87: p. 293 [1947].

73. *SRSI* 2: pp. 106; 110.

74. Ibid., p. 112. See also *CWMG* 83: p. 398 [1946]. For Gandhi's notion that women's lives were fuller and less restricted in "ancient India," see Southard, "The Feminism of Mahatma Gandhi," pp. 392–3.

75. See Patel, "Construction and Reconstruction of Woman in Gandhi," p. 382.

76. *CWMG* 21: p. 106 [1921]. See also *CWMG* 27: pp. 290–1 [1925]; and Patel, "Construction and Reconstruction of Woman in Gandhi," p. 384.

77. *SRSI* 1: p. 115.

78. Alter, "Gandhi's Body, Gandhi's Truth," p. 312.

79. *KH*, pp. 4–5.

80. *CWMG* 12: p. 166 [1913]; *CWMG* 78: p. 321 [1944].

81. *KH*, p. 6.

82. *CWMG* 33: p. 142 [1927]; See also *CWMG* 15: p. 55 [1918]; *CWMG* 12: p. 24 [1913]. See also Alter, "Gandhi's Body, Gandhi's Truth," p. 312.

83. Ibid., p. 314.

84. *KH*, p. 37. During his confinement in the Aga Khan Palace at Poona in the years 1942–44, Gandhi wrote a new edition of *Guide to Health* that bears the new title, *Key to Health*. The relevant citations are taken from this updated version.

85. *AB*, p. 286.

86. Gandhi, *Prohibition At Any Cost* (Ahmedabad: Navajivan, 1960), pp. 9, 3–5.

87. *CWMG* 65: p. 144 [1937].

88. *CWMG* 66: p. 81 [1937].

89. *CWMG* 34: p. 185 [1927]

90. David Arnold, *Colonizing the Body: State Medicine and Epidemic Disease in Nineteenth-Century India* (Berkeley: University of California Press, 1993), p. 288. See also Prakash, *Another Reason,* pp. 155–6.

91. Alter, "Gandhi's Body, Gandhi's Truth," p. 316.

92. Kakar, *Intimate Relations,* p. 99. See also Prakash, *Another Reason,* pp. 123–4.

93. Martha Nussbaum, *The Fragility of Goodness: Luck and Ethics in Greek Tragedy and Philosophy* (Cambridge: Cambridge University Press, 1993), p. 2; and L. Gandhi, "Concerning Violence: the Limits and Circulations of Gandhian *Ahimsa* or Passive Resistance," p. 106–8.

94. L. Gandhi, "Concerning Violence: the Limits and Circulations of Gandhian *Ahimsa* or Passive Resistance," p. 109.

95. See Michel Foucault, *The Archeology of Knowledge* (New York: Harper Torch-books, 1972), p. 220; *Discipline and Punish: The Birth of Prison* (New York: Vintage, 1979); and *The History of Sexuality* (New York: Vintage, 1980).

96. John Neville Figgis, *The Political Aspects of St. Augustine's* 'City of God' (London: Longmans, Green, and Co., 1921), p. 56.

97. Jawaharlal Nehru, *An Autobiography* (London: Bodley Head, 1936), pp. 72–3. For the differences between Gandhi's and Nehru's nationalist imagination, see, for example, Prakash, *Another Reason,* pp. 201–26.

98. L. Gandhi, "Concerning Violence: the Limits and Circulations of Gandhian *Ahimsa* or Passive Resistance," p. 137.

99. *HS,* p. 132.

100. See Mark Juergensmeyer, "Saint Gandhi," in John Stratton Hawley, ed., *Saints and Virtues,* (Berkeley: University of California Press, 1987), pp. 187–203.

101. Prakash, *Another Reason,* pp. 226, 220–1.

CHAPTER 6: RECONCILING NONVIOLENT PRINCIPLES WITH NATIONALIST POWER? THREE CASES

1. Niccolo Machiavelli, *The Prince,* 2nd ed., trans. and ed. Robert M. Adams (New York: W. W. Norton, 1992), p. 42.

2. G. Aloysius, *Nationalism without a Nation in India* (Delhi: Oxford University Press, 1998), p. 176.

3. *CWMG* 17: p. 406 [1920].

4. Gandhi, *Satyagraha in South Africa,* p. 72.

5. *CWMG* 3: pp. 113–14 [1899].

6. Ibid., p. 222 [1902].

7. *CWMG* 2: p. 43 [1896].

8. *CWMG* 3: p. 223 [1902]; *AB,* p. 188.

9. See Peter Brock, "Gandhi's Nonviolence and His War Service," *Gandhi Marg* 2.11 (1981), p. 604.

10. Gandhi, *Satyagraha in South Africa,* p. 72.

11. In 1921, Gandhi published a lengthy explanation of why he offered his assistance to the British in the South African wars and the Great War. See *CWMG* 21: pp. 438–9 [1921].

12. Gandhi, *Satyagraha in South Africa,* p. 73.

13. *CWMG* 5: p. 353 [1906].

14. Ibid., p. 366 [1906].

15. Chadha, *Gandhi,* p. 111.

16. *AB,* p. 281.

17. *CWMG* 12: p. 527 [1914]. See also *AB,* p. 314.

18. Brock, "Gandhi's Nonviolence and His War Service," p. 605.

19. Hunt, *Gandhi in London,* p. 164.

20. *CWMG* 12: pp. 531–32, 554–5 [1914].
21. Ibid., p. 555 [1914].
22. *AB,* p. 313.
23. *CWMG* 13: p. 80 [1915].
24. *AB,* p. 313.
25. *CWMG* 14: pp. 299, 377–8 [1918].
26. Ibid., p. 378 [1918].
27. Brown, *Gandhi's Rise to Power,* p. 147. See also Brock, "Gandhi's Nonviolence and His War Service," p. 607.
28. *CWMG* 14: pp. 407–8 [1918].
29. Brock, "Gandhi's Nonviolence and His War Service," p. 608.
30. *CWMG* 14: p. 379 [1914]; and *CWMG* 12: p. 52–3 [1913]. For a comprehensive idea of Gandhi's idea of a nonviolent peace army (*shanti sena*), see Thomas Weber, *Gandhi's Peace Army: The Shanti Sena and Unarmed Peacekeeping* (Syracuse, NY: Syracuse University Press, 1996).
31. *CWMG* 14: pp. 510, 477 [1918].
32. Ibid., p. 520 [1918]. See also *CWMG* 15: p. 2 [1918].
33. *CWMG* 14: pp. 463, 485 [1918].
34. Ibid., pp. 444, 454 [1918].
35. Ibid., p. 505 [1918]; See also Brock, "Gandhi's Nonviolence and his War Service," p. 611.
36. *CWMG* 18: p. 132 [1920].
37. *CWMG* 14: p. 438 [1918].
38. Brown, *Gandhi's Rise to Power,* p. 148.
39. *CWMG* 15: p. 52 [1918].
40. See, for example, Paul F. Power, *Gandhi on World Affairs* (Washington, D. C.: Public Affairs Press, 1960), p. 35.
41. See, for example, Rashmi-Sudha Puri, *Gandhi in War and Peace* (New York: Praeger, 1987), especially chapter 3.
42. See David Carroll Cochran, "War-Pacifism," *Social Theory and Practice* 22.2 (Summer 1996), pp. 161–80.
43. See, for example, Weber, *Gandhi's Peace Army,* p. 49.
44. Puri, *Gandhi On War and Peace,* p. 81; and Brock, "Gandhi's Nonviolénce and His War Service," p. 616.
45. Brown, *Gandhi's Rise to Power,* p. 354.
46. Ibid., p. 229. See also B. R. Nanda, *Gandhi: Pan-Islamism, Imperialism and Nationalism in India* (Bombay: Oxford University Press, 1989).
47. *CWMG* 15: pp. 110, 121 [1919].
48. Chadha, *Gandhi,* p. 240.
49. Brown, *Gandhi's Rise to Power,* p. 239.
50. *CWMG* 17: p. 483 [1920]. See also Brown, *Gandhi's Rise to Power,* p. 245.
51. Chadha, *Gandhi,* p. 250.
52. *CWMG* 18: p. 316 [1920].

53. Ibid., p. 350 [1920]. For an excellent summary of Gandhi's use of the term "satanic" throughout the noncooperation campaign of 1920–22, see William W. Emilsen, "Wrestling the Serpent: Gandhi, Amritsar and the British Empire," *Religion* 24 (1994), pp. 143–53.

54. *CWMG* 22: p. 389 [1922].

55. Dalton, *Mahatma Gandhi,* p. 21.

56. Narhari Parikh, "Preface," in M. H. Desai, *Day-To-Day with Gandhi* (Varanasi: Savu Seva Prakashan, 1968), p. 5.

57. *CWMG* 18: p. 448 [1920].

58. Ibid., pp. 373–75 [1920]; *CWMG* 20: pp. 366–68 [1921].

59. Emilsen, "Wrestling the Serpent," p. 146.

60. See Hugh Owens, *The Indian Nationalist Movement, c. 1912–22: Leadership, Organization and Philosophy* (New Delhi: Sterling Publishers Private Ltd., 1990), pp. 206–29.

61. *CWMG* 20: pp. 336, 331–2 [1921].

62. Ibid., p. 486 [1921].

63. Ibid., p. 54 [1921].

64. Chadha, *Gandhi,* p. 255.

65. *CWMG* 21: p. 465 [1921].

66. See Paul Mundschenk, "The Heart of Satyagraha: A Quest for Inner Dignity, not Political Power," in Hick and Hempel, *Gandhi's Significance for Today,* p. 31.

67. Jawaharlal Nehru cited in Rajani Palme Dutt, "Gandhi and the Nationalist Movement: A Marxist View," in Martin Deming Lewis, ed., *Gandhi: Maker of Modern India* (Boston: D. C. Heath and Company. 1965), p. 31.

68. Ibid., pp. 31–2.

69. Jawaharlal Nehru, *Nehru on Gandhi: A Selection, Arranged in the Order of Events, from the Writings and Speeches of Jawaharlal Nehru* (New York: The John Day Company, 1948), pp. 38–9.

70. *CWMG* 22: pp. 351, 462–3. [1922].

71. Ibid., pp. 377, 379, 387 [1922].

72. *CWMG* 18: p. 133 [1920].

73. Mundschenk, "The Heart of Satyagraha: A Quest for Inner Dignity, not Political Power," p. 29.

74. *CWMG* 18: pp. 240–4, 274 [1920]. For an enlightening discussion of Gandhi's interactions with crowds during the noncooperation campaign, see Guha, *Dominance without Hegemony,* pp. 135–51; and Shahid Amin, *Event, Metaphor, Memory: Chauri Chaura 1922–1992* (Berkeley: University of California Press, 1995); and "Gandhi as Mahatma: Gorakhpur District, Eastern UP, 1921–1," in Ranajit Guha and Gayatri Spivak, eds., *Selected Subaltern Studies* (New York: Oxford University Press, 1988), pp. 288–342. For an insightful critique of Gandhi's methods of political mobilization, see Aloysius, *Nationalism without a Nation,* pp. 201–6.

75. John D. Kelly, *A Politics of Virtue: Hinduism, Sexuality, and Counter-Colonial Discourse in Fiji* (Chicago: University of Chicago Press, 1991), p. 195.

76. *CWMG* 23: p. 114 [1922].

77. Lord Lloyd cited in Dutt, "Gandhi and the Nationalist Movement: A Marxist View," in Lewis, *Gandhi: Maker of Modern India,* p. 33.

78. Chadha, *Gandhi,* pp. 362–7.

79. *CWMG* 70: p. 203 [1939].

80. Stanley Maron, "The Non-Universality of Satyagraha," in Sibnarayan Ray, ed., *Gandhi India and the World: An International Symposium* (Philadelphia: Temple University Press, 1970), p. 276.

81. Jinnah cited in Chadha, *Gandhi,* p. 368. For a recent interpretation of Jinnah's role in nationalist politics, see Akbar S. Ahmed, *Jinnah, Pakistan and Islamic Identity: The Search for Saladin* (London: Routledge, 1997).

82. Hutchins, *India's Revolution,* pp. 185–6.

83. Chadha, *Gandhi,* pp. 370–1.

84. Hutchins, *India's Revolution,* p. 187.

85. For the full text of the Cripps Plan, see *CWMG* 76: pp. 422–4 [1942].

86. *CWMG* 76: pp. 114–5 [1942]. See also Tendulkar, *Mahatma* 6: pp. 76, 94, 100, 106.

87. *CWMG* 76: pp. 159–60 [1942].

88. Ibid., p. 302 [1942].

89. Hutchins, *India's Revolution,* p. 203.

90. *CWMG* 76: pp. 109, 184, 197, 220, 284, 296 [1942].

91. Ibid., p. 381 [1942].

92. Hutchins, *India's Revolution,* pp. 199, 205.

93. *CWMG* 76: p. 284 [1942].

94. Ibid., pp. 364–7 [1942].

95. Ibid., p. 392 [1942].

96. Ibid., p. 403 [1942].

97. See Hutchins, *India's Revolution,* pp. 246–7.

98. For exact casualty figures, see ibid., pp. 230–2. For a detailed description of the Quit India Movement in various parts of India, see Gyanendra Pandey, ed., *The Indian Nation in 1942* (Calcutta: Centre for Studies in Social Sciences, 1988).

99. Linlithgow cited in Hutchins, *India's Revolution,* p. 265.

100. Ibid., pp. 266, 279–80. See also Gail Omvedt, "The Satara Prati Sarkar," in Pandey, *The Indian Nation in 1942,* p. 237; and V. T. Patil, "Gandhi and the Strategy and Tactics of the Quit India Movement," in Patil, *New Dimensions and Perspectives in Gandhism,* pp. 325–9.

101. *CWMG* 76: pp. 406–10, 414 [1942]; *CWMG* 77: pp. 105–99 [1943].

102. Hutchins, *India's Revolution,* p. 138.

103. *MPWMG* 2: p. 357 [1936].

104. *CWMG* 90: pp. 526–8 [1948]; Tendulkar, *Mahatma* 8: pp. 278–80; Weber, *Gandhi's Peace Army,* pp. 66–8.

105. For a discussion of Havel's antipolitical politics, see my article, "Of Means and Ends: 1989 as Ethico-Political Imperative," *New Political Science* 21.4 (1999), pp. 501–16. See also Jeffrey C. Isaac, "The Meanings of 1989," *Social Research* 63.2 (1996), pp. 291–344.

106. Vaclav Havel, "Politics and Conscience," in Jan Vladislav, ed., *Living in Truth* (London: Farber and Farber, 1986), p. 155.

107. Nehru, *An Autobiography,* pp. 72–3.

108. *CWMG* 76: p. 421–22 [1942]; and *CWMG* 72: p. 105 [1940]. For a similar assessment of Gandhi's Platonic elitism, see Parel, "Gandhi's Idea of Nation in *Hind Swaraj,*" p. 279.

109. See Hansen, *The Saffron Wave,* pp. 3–13, 50–9.

EPILOGUE: A NONVIOLENT NATIONALISM?

1. Aristotle, *The Politics,* Book VII, p. 400.

2. *CWMG* 76: pp. 57–8 [1942].

3. *CWMG* 31: p. 181 [1926].

4. Frantz Fanon, *The Wretched of the Earth* (New York: Grove Press, 1966), p. 29.

5. See, for example, Robert Fine, "Benign Nationalism? The Limits of the Civic Ideal," in Edward Mortimer, ed., *People, Nation & State* (London: I. B. Tauris, 1999), p. 149; Nicholas Xenos, "Civic Nationalism: Oxymoron?," *Critical Review* 10.2 (Spring 1996), pp. 213–31; Bernard Yack, "The Myth of the Civic Nation," in ibid., pp. 193–211; Yael Tamir, *Liberal Nationalism* (Princeton: Princeton University Press, 1993); Michael Ignatieff, *Blood and Belonging: Journeys into the New Nationalism* (New York: Farrar, Straus and Giroux, 1993); and Jürgen Habermas, *Faktizität und Geltung* (Frankfurt: Suhrkamp, 1992).

6. See also Fine, "Benign Nationalism? The Limits of the Civic Ideal," p. 152.

7. *CWMG* 51: p. 129 [1932].

8. *MPWMG* 2: p. 296 [1935].

9. For an excellent discussion of the creation of "hard boundaries" and national identity, see Prasenjit Duara, "Historicizing National Identity, or Who Imagines What and When?," in Geoff Eley and Ronald Grigor Suny, eds., *Becoming National: A Reader* (New York: Oxford University Press, 1996), pp. 151–77. See also Frederik Barth, *Ethnic Groups and Boundaries* (Bergen: Universitats-fur Paget, 1969); Martin Tyrrell, "Nation-States and States of Mind: Nationalism as Psychology," *Critical Review* 10.2 (Spring 1996), pp. 233–50; Michael J. Shapiro and Hayward R. Alker, *Challenging Boundaries: Global Flows, Territorial Identities* (Minneapolis: University of Minnesota Press, 1996); and Michael J. Shapiro, *Violent Cartographies: Mapping Cultures of War* (Minneapolis: University of Minnesota Press, 1997).

10. Schwartz, *The Curse of Cain,* p. 5. See also Kakar, *The Color of Violence,* p. 189; and Slavoj Zizek, "Eastern Europe's Republics of Gilead," in Chantal Mouffe,

ed., *The Dimensions of Radical Democracy* (London: Verso, 1992), p. 196. For a useful treatment of the interrelationship between (non)violence and rhetoric, see Ellen W. Gorsevski, "Nonviolent Theory on Communication: The Implications for Theorizing a Nonviolent Rhetoric," *Peace & Change* 24.4 (October 1999), pp. 445–75.

11. Jacques Derrida, *Of Grammatology* (Baltimore: Johns Hopkins University Press, 1976); and *Writing and Difference* (London: Routledge, 1978).

12. See Elizabeth Grosz, "The Time of Violence: Deconstruction and Value," *Cultural Values* 2.2/3 (June 1998), p. 192.

13. Michael Ignatieff, "Benign Nationalism? The Possibilities of the Civic Ideal," in Mortimer, *People, Nation & State,* p. 141–7; Fine, "Benign Nationalism? The Limits of the Civic Ideal," in ibid., pp. 149–61; David Brown, "Are there good and bad nationalisms?," *Nations and Nationalism* 5.2 (1999), pp. 281–302; Sasja Tempelman, "Constructions of Cultural Identity: Multiculturalism and Exclusion," *Political Studies* XLVII (1999), pp. 17–31; and Nicholas Buttle, "Critical nationalism: a liberal prescription?," *Nations and Nationalism* 6.1 (2000), pp. 111–27.

14. Ignatieff, "Benign Nationalism? The Possibilities of the Civic Ideal," pp. 146–7.

15. See Anderson, *Imagined Communities,* p. 141. Some of the most seminal, recent studies of nationalism include, in addition to the ones cited above, Ernest Gellner, *Nations and Nationalism* (Ithaca, NY: Cornell University Press, 1983); Elie Kedourie, *Nationalism* 2nd ed. (London: Blackwell, 1990); Eric J. Hobsbawm, *Nations and Nationalism since 1780: Programme, Myth and Reality* (Cambridge: Cambridge University Press, 1990); Homi K. Bhabha, ed., *Nation and Narration* (London: Routledge, 1990); Greenfeld, *Nationalism;* Tom Nairn, *Faces of Nationalism: Janus Revisited* (London: Verso, 1997); and Smith, *Nationalism and Modernism.*

16. Fine, "Benign Nationalism? The Limits of the Civic Ideal," p. 154.

17. *CWMG* 27: pp. 255–6 [1925]. See also *MPWMG* 1: p. 45 [1920].

18. Johann Gottlieb Fichte, *Fichtes Werke* (Reprint), 11 vols., ed. Immanuel Fichte (Berlin: de Gruyter, 1971), 11: p. 229 [1806]; *CWMG* 28: p. 127 [1925]. Criticizing the German philosopher, Reinhold Niebuhr notes that the Fichte's expression of national pride was riddled with invidious comparisons and other forms of conceptual violence: "The pride took the form of the complacent assumption that German philosophy enabled the German nation to achieve a more perfect relation to the community of mankind than any other nation." Niebuhr's observation applies to Gandhi's Indian nationalism as well. See Reinhold Niebuhr, "The Children of Light and the Children of Darkness," in Robert McAfee Brown, ed., *The Essential Reinhold Niebuhr: Selected Essays and Addresses* (New Haven, CT: Yale University Press, 1986), p. 180. For excellent treatments of Fichte's argument in favor of the compatibility of nationalism and cosmopolitanism, see Hans Kohn, "The Paradox of Fichte's Nationalism,"

Journal of the History of Ideas 10.3 (1949), pp. 319–343; and Friedrich Meinecke, *Cosmopolitanism and the National State* (Princeton: Princeton University Press, 1970).

19. For a comprehensive discussion on the pros and cons of cosmopolitanism that includes contributions from some of the most prominent Anglo-American thinkers on this subject, see the Special Issue of *Boston Review* 19.5 (October/November 1994), titled "Patriotism or Cosmopolitanism?"

20. Fine, "Benign Nationalism? The Limits of the Civic Ideal," p. 159.

21. Margaret Canovan, *Nationhood and Political Theory* (Cheltenham, U.K.: Edward Elgar, 1996), p. 134.

22. Ibid., p. 137.

23. Emmanuel Mounier cited in Bernhard P. Dauenhauer, *Paul Ricoeur: The Promise and Risk of Politics* (Lanham, MD: Rowman & Littlefield Publishers, 1998), p. 12.

24. For two particularly thoughtful and sophisticated formulations of a cosmopolitan model of democracy, see David Held, *Democracy and the Global Order: From The Modern State to Cosmopolitan Governance* (Stanford: Stanford University Press, 1995); and Richard Falk, *On Human Governance: Toward a New Global Politics* (Cambridge, U.K.: Polity Press, 1995). For a concise cosmopolitan political agenda, see Ulrich Beck, "Democracy Beyond the Nation-State: A Cosmopolitan Manifesto," *Dissent* (Winter 1999), pp. 53–5.

25. *CWMG* 36: p. 102 [1928].

26. Weber, "The Profession and Vocation of Politics," in *Political Writings*, p. 366.

INDEX